Patient Safety
Investigating and Reporting
Serious Clinical Incidents

Patient Safety
Investigating and Reporting Serious Clinical Incidents

Russell Kelsey MB.BS MRCGP

General Practitioner. Worcestershire, UK

CRC Press
Taylor & Francis Group
Boca Raton London New York

CRC Press is an imprint of the
Taylor & Francis Group, an **informa** business

CRC Press
Taylor & Francis Group
6000 Broken Sound Parkway NW, Suite 300
Boca Raton, FL 33487-2742

© 2017 by Taylor & Francis Group, LLC
CRC Press is an imprint of Taylor & Francis Group, an Informa business

No claim to original U.S. Government works

Printed on acid-free paper
Version Date: 20161024

International Standard Book Number-13: 978-1-4987-8116-9 (Paperback)

Visit the Taylor & Francis Web site at
http://www.taylorandfrancis.com

and the CRC Press Web site at
http://www.crcpress.com

To Susan, for your love and your faith in me and for keeping me on track. I could not have done this without you. xx

About the author

Dr Russell Kelsey is a GP who has extensive experience in senior medical director roles in primary care both in the UK and in his native New Zealand. His experience in clinical governance led to him becoming a subject matter expert in serious clinical incident investigation and to undertake advanced training in root cause analysis and incident investigation. Based upon many years of experience of investigation, Dr Kelsey developed a highly popular continuing professional development (CPD) accredited training course on serious incident recognition and root cause analysis investigations specifically targeted at services outside acute hospital settings. He has developed a number of techniques and tools to make the investigatory process easier and he shares these in this book as well as in his training courses and on his website.

Dr Kelsey has a keen interest in 'human factors' and how these impact upon clinical practice in primary care as well as in how service design impacts upon clinical risk in healthcare settings. He provides serious incident and root cause analysis training to a number of organisations and also undertakes independent investigations as well as maintaining clinical practice.

Via his website – www.PatientSafetyInvestigations.com – Dr Kelsey provides ongoing support and information for those undertaking incident investigations as well as engaging in patient advocacy and support.

Contents

Introduction: Why do we still miss appendicitis?

'No matter what measures are taken, doctors will sometimes falter, and it isn't reasonable to ask that we achieve perfection. What is reasonable is to ask that we never cease to aim for it.'

Atul Gawande, *Complications: A surgeon's notes on an imperfect science*
(London: Profile Books, p. 70)

CASE SUMMARY

Lauren's parents brought her to see a doctor three times over a 26-hour period.

- First contact – diagnosis gastroenteritis
- Second contact – diagnosis urinary tract infection
- Third contact – diagnosis appendicitis – referred to surgeons

At theatre, Lauren was found to have a ruptured appendix with peritonitis. Lauren recovered but has had a number of further presentations of severe abdominal pain with symptoms suggestive of adhesions.

We still miss appendicitis. While this is not surprising in itself – after all, appendicitis is known to be a condition that may be elusive and may masquerade as other pathologies – what is surprising to me in my work as an investigator of serious clinical incidents is the number of occasions when appendicitis does not appear to have occurred to a clinician as a possible diagnosis. If it features at all within the clinical notes it appears almost by proxy in the form of single comments in the examination notes, such as 'no guarding, no rebound' from which clinical colleagues may infer that the clinician had excluded the presence of appendicitis.

Where appendicitis is missed the notes may not only fail to mention the condition but the patient, or relatives of the patient may also struggle to recall the clinician whom they saw mentioning appendicitis as a possibility. If they do recall the name, they often report that the clinician confidently dismissed appendicitis as a possibility and reassured that all would be well again soon – a situation that leads to two questions in my mind. Firstly, why do we still miss appendicitis? And, secondly, how can we learn from those occasions when we do miss appendicitis to try to help us avoid doing it again?

These two questions are at the heart of this book:

- Why did something go wrong?
- What can we learn to help us stop it from happening again?

Medicine is a discipline that is practised by humans and humans will make mistakes. Quite rightly there is an increasing emphasis in healthcare worldwide on understanding the origins of clinical error and reducing its incidences. This is not just because of the human suffering that clinical errors may cause but also the considerable economic impact of missed diagnoses or clinical errors in healthcare economies. The National Health Service (NHS) in England paid more than one billion pounds in legal claims in 2014 alone.

Serious attempts to address the impact of clinical errors in medicine have been made in the past years and one of the biggest advances has been the introduction of formalised procedures for investigation. Specifically, there has been the use of a technique called root cause analysis (RCA) to investigate serious clinical incidents. Root cause analysis is an investigative tool designed to answer the questions 'What went wrong?' and 'What can we do to fix it?' While there have been some very striking successes arising out of RCA investigations and other patient-safety initiatives, there is a depressing stubbornness about the persistence of clinical errors. From 2006 to 2014 there was a 112 per cent increase in the number of adverse patient-safety incidents reported in the NHS. Of more than one and a half million patient-safety incidents reported in 2014, some ten thousand were serious incidents.

This begs a further question – why do patient-safety initiatives fail? Many clinicians, clinical governance leads and service managers are trying hard every day to make services safer – investigating incidents, identifying any learning that may arise and trying to implement improvements. So why are healthcare systems not in turn getting safer and safer every day?

In eight years spent as a regional medical director for a large healthcare provider I was involved in the investigation of many serious clinical incidents. I underwent advanced training in incident investigation and spent considerable time refining and revising investigation techniques and processes. It is perhaps no surprise to find out that the more cases I investigated, the more I learned about the challenges of the process of investigation itself. The more initiatives I tried to implement to improve safety, the more I learnt about the challenges of implementing safety initiatives. I came to see that root cause analysis – a process that appears to be simple and logical in training manuals and courses – is actually quite a complex and nuanced tool that takes a lot of time and effort to understand and apply appropriately. I also came to understand that one of the key elements of the RCA process, that is, learning how to prevent the same mistake occurring again, is a seriously underestimated and frequently poorly performed skill. The principles of RCA are easy to understand but are actually very difficult to apply consistently across a range of different incident types. Being able to identify useful and meaningful learning from an incident is a skill in itself that is fundamental to ensuring that risks in healthcare systems are identified and addressed. And as if these challenges are not enough for the incident investigator, there is a further potentially massive issue to face when an investigation is complete and learning and recommendations are formulated. How do you tackle the immense inertia of most healthcare systems to implement changes in custom or practice that you believe will improve patient safety?

Whichever field you practise in, whichever country you work in, these issues are pertinent. The process of recognition of incidents and investigation via root cause analysis is universal. This book is intended to serve as a manual of technical information as well as guidance for best practice to help colleagues undertake serious clinical incident investigations. Over the years I have taught investigation and safety implementation skills to many colleagues, both clinical colleagues and service managers, and, while training courses are highly appreciated and valuable, the following represents the universal experience:

> 'The course was great and I thought I understood what to do . . . but now I am faced with a real case and I am not quite sure I have got things right.'

This is entirely understandable – it takes a lot of practice to become good at any skill and incident investigation is no different. I have written this book to try to provide guidance and answers to many of the questions that arise after the training course and when you begin to investigate actual cases. Real case examples are used throughout to illustrate learning points and I have endeavoured to provide sufficient detail to enable readers to 'get inside the head' of an experienced investigator in order to get a real sense of not just how to perform an investigation but also how to think it through; that is, how to approach the different areas of challenge and how to tackle and solve the many different problems and dilemmas that may arise within an investigation. There are some new tools that I have introduced to try to help with some of the more difficult judgements that arise and in addition to the resources contained within this book there are further case examples and resources available on my website: www.PatientSafetyInvestigations.com

Clinical leaders and service managers who have a clinical governance role will be required to conduct investigations into clinical incidents and it is essential that they understand the technical aspects of the investigatory process. However, in a world in which clinicians and services are under increasing scrutiny from external and professional regulators, it is possible and even likely that over a career any clinician may find themself on the receiving end of an investigatory process as well. Understanding how investigatory processes work and, importantly, how investigators think through an incident and put together a report should become part of the basic training of all clinicians and service managers. Indeed, it is possible that just understanding the process for investigating and learning from incidents in general, and particularly understanding how 'human factors' feature in clinical incidents, will in itself lead to safer practice on the part of the clinician involved.

Root cause analysis is a universal tool. In this book most of the case examples discussed occur in a primary care setting, be that general practice (GP), out-of-hours services, NHS 111 services or Urgent Care Services (UCCs). The book has a particular value for primary care practitioners as the nature of incidents in primary care tends to be more complex and the traditional training and resources available for use in RCA training tend to focus on secondary care. Nonetheless, the principles outlined in the book and the methodologies used for exploring cases are universal to all clinical incidents and so I would hope that the book is of value to clinicians or service managers in any clinical field. While much of the reference to regulatory bodies refers to bodies operational in England, the principles of recognition of serious clinical incidents and the need for reporting mechanisms and formal investigation using root cause analysis are much the same worldwide. Thus, I would also hope that the practical principles and techniques that I am sharing are of value wherever you may be working in the world.

Root cause analysis: Background and context

Two phenomena intersected in the 1950s and 1960s that were to have a profound influence upon patient safety in the healthcare sector – the emergence of the Japanese motor industry and the massive expansion of the aviation industry. It is within these two industries that the concept of root cause analysis as a means of identifying and solving problems arose.

The origin of root cause analysis is important. It explains both why it is so potentially useful but also why it often fails to work well in healthcare. It is salutary for clinicians and service managers to realise that while the processes and techniques we use to manage clinical encounters are vested in many years of professional clinical experience and scientific development, most of the processes and techniques that are used to manage the logistics and in particular the governance of healthcare have been adopted from other industries.

Sakichi Toyada, the founder of Toyota Motor Corporation, is credited with developing formal techniques for improving production quality, including the '5 Whys' technique that was used to analyse production failings to find the ultimate root cause of failure. Researchers in the emerging Japanese industrial giants, including Kaoru Ishikawa working for the Kawasaki company – famous for his 'fishbone' diagram – developed the concept of total quality management (TQM). Arising from these concepts and processes come other industrial quality-improvement processes increasingly familiar in healthcare such as Six Sigma and lean management. At the same time, in the United States the responsibility for investigating aviation safety was delegated to National Aeronautics and Space Administration (NASA) and scientists there started to develop formalised techniques for incident investigations. The results of the use of formalised investigation aimed at learning from identified errors was striking:

- Using 'quality-management' techniques Japanese industry reduced errors in component production to a fraction of 1 per cent.
- Using the Aviation Safety Reporting System (ASRS) (an original form of root cause analysis), the Federal Aviation Administration (FAA) and NASA reduced the number of aviation accidents by 80 per cent. (See www.brighthubpm.com for a succinct overview of the evolution of RCA.)

In 1999 the US Institute of Medicine published a report titled *To Err is Human: Building a safer health system* (Linda T. Kohn, Janet M. Corrigan and Molla S. Donaldson, eds, *To Err is Human: Building a safer health system*, Washington, D.C.: National Academy Press, 1999). This document acknowledged the lack of formal engagement in recognising safety issues in healthcare and called for a range of reforms, including the introduction of formalised systems for reporting and learning, citing experience from other industries. At the same time in the UK, two Parliamentary White Papers appeared in 1997 and 1998, *A First Class Service: Quality in the new NHS* (Department of Health, *A First Class Service: Quality in the new NHS*, 1998, HMSO, London) and *The New NHS: Modern, dependable* (Department of Health, *The New NHS: Modern, dependable*, 1997, HMSO, London). These papers introduced the concept and practice of clinical governance to the National Health Service, adopting principles derived from industry including use of RCA tools to investigate serious incidents. The National Patient Safety Agency (NPSA) was established in the UK to become the guardian of the drive to improve safety and to champion the use of formalised structured reporting and learning systems. Although it was disbanded in 2012 much useful information about patient safety and the RCA process remains available via its former website, now hosted by NHS England (www.npsa.nhs.uk). The issue concerning both the Institute of Medicine in the US and the NHS in the UK was the alarming number of patient-safety incidents occurring in hospitals, particularly incidents involving errors relating to medication use and incidents involving errors during surgical procedures. For the most part, patient-safety initiatives and processes and procedures for undertaking root cause analysis in healthcare have been driven by clinicians and managers working in hospitals or secondary care. Little resource, time or expertise has been directed at incidents in primary care and, in my own personal experience, when primary care clinicians and managers do utilise RCA to investigate incidents there are some particular problems to overcome in order to make the process work.

The issue of resources and training for investigation are addressed further below but a key conceptual issue that is particularly relevant in primary care is the need to be aware of a specific weakness in the RCA tool. As we have seen, RCA is a process that was adopted into healthcare but with its origins in industry. RCA arose as a method of studying what may have gone wrong with industrial process lines or, in the slightly more complex field of aviation, when an accident occurred. The point is that a process line and even an aircraft flight is a linear process that is designed to work correctly each time, all things being equal. In simplistic terms, giving a patient an insulin injection on a hospital ward or operating to remove an ischaemic lower limb are also processes that are linear and designed to work correctly each time. That is to say, in all of the above cases nothing should go wrong: a widget should come off a production line, a plane should arrive at its destination, a patient should receive the right dose of insulin and another patient should have the right leg removed (or the left leg!). When something goes wrong it is highly likely that an investigation will identify one or more errors – often called 'acts or omissions' – that, in turn, will have been caused by human or systems errors that may be identified by the RCA process and, it is hoped, fixed. The problem for healthcare arises when we use RCA to look at more complex healthcare incidents – that is, events in which there is not a simple procedural-type patient contact but one which involves a patient who may not only have a complex underlying medical condition but also a complex underlying personality.

The natural pathology of an illness is a contributory factor in many healthcare-related adverse events. While we may know a lot about natural pathology, it can become very difficult to know whether an eventual outcome may have been significantly altered had a medical intervention either occurred earlier or occurred differently. As an example, I once spent time in a coroner's court discussing treatment for a deep vein thrombosis (DVT) with the coroner and a family's legal adviser. One of the doctors in my urgent care service had seen a patient in the community and diagnosed a probable deep vein thrombosis. He had prescribed injection of low molecular weight heparin pending a Doppler ultrasound. He arranged for a community nurse to give the injection that afternoon. For reasons beyond his control the injection was delayed by 24 hours. Two days later the patient was admitted with an associated lower respiratory infection and a day after this he died of a massive pulmonary embolism. The RCA that I conducted was very useful in enabling us to learn how to improve our liaison with community nursing staff to ensure timely injections of medication but I was left with a dilemma in determining the significance of a delay in receipt of low molecular weight heparin of 24 hours for a patient who died more than 72 hours later. This was probably of some significance to the final outcome but in reality that significance is likely to be quite small. While the RCA investigation reveals useful learning in this case, the root cause of the final outcome was in fact the patient's underlying pathology.

TOP TIP

RCA is designed to uncover learning from simple linear processes and works very well for incidents such as medication dispensing errors and elective surgical procedures. Incidents involving errors in diagnosis or choice of treatment regime and any error in which the patient is unwell with a complex and progressive underlying pathology are difficult to investigate. Later chapters deal with considering 'patient factors' within the RCA.

RCA AND REGULATORY BODIES

In March 2015 NHS England, the body commissioned by the UK government to oversee health services in England, published revised framework guidance on the recognition, investigation and reporting of serious incidents. The document updated previous guidance published in 2010. In short, the guidance suggests which types of incidents may be regarded as 'serious incidents' that require reporting via the formal reporting process that exists in the UK. It also suggests that incidents should be investigated using a structured in-depth investigation technique such as root cause analysis and that staff undertaking investigations, or at least those leading them, should have received training in how to perform them. Similar guidance may be found in any advanced healthcare economy the world over and regardless of which country you practise in there is a recognition of the need to identify serious clinical incidents, to investigate them formally and to have a process to ensure that health services learn from them. While there will be some differences in processes for recognition and recording, the basic principles are the same and the final goal is definitely the same – we must learn from our mistakes.

Despite the very useful guidance of the 2015 document, recognising when a serious incident has occurred remains a challenge and this is addressed in the next two chapters. Learning from incidents is the primary objective and apart from the learning obtained from the incident under investigation, regulatory bodies recognised the need to collate information centrally in order to increase the capacity to spot trends and to ensure that key learning is shared as widely as possible. In the UK the NHS established the National Reporting and Learning System (NRLS), as a national database of learning from serious incidents. In order to enter data about an incident onto the NRLS, it must first be recorded on a separate database that houses all newly declared incidents pending investigation and closes off incidents when the investigation is completed. The database is called the Strategic Executive Information System (STEIS). While the principles discussed in this book may be applied to any type of clinical incident, they are particularly useful for the recognition and investigation of incidents that reach the threshold to be declared on STEIS or similar national reporting and recording systems.

NEVER EVENTS

A final note on regulatory bodies concerns the concept of 'never events'. The title is aspirational rather than factual. Never events are occurrences that should never occur within a well-*organised* and well-*managed* health service. I have emphasised the words 'organised' and 'managed' for a reason. As we will explore throughout this book, most serious clinical incidents are a result of a combination of pathology mixed with individual human errors on the part of clinicians or clinical teams and the design or function of the systems within which they work. Notionally, however, a never event should remove the human element. Never events are occurrences wherein there should be sufficient fail-safe mechanisms built into a system of delivery of healthcare that the event should never occur. Never events represent catastrophic or major incidents that have been of such significance that they have prompted major system redesign with the aim of preventing just such an event from ever happening again. Individual human error may play a part in why a never event occurs but this is usually in the context of multiple deviations from a well-established and theoretically safe protocol of care. Examples of never events within the NHS include:

- Wrong site surgery – removing the wrong limb, tooth, organ and so forth
- Wrong implants/prosthesis
- Retained foreign object post-procedure
- Wrong route of administration of medication – the infamous intravenous chemotherapy administered via the intrathecal route (NPSA training case)
- Failure to install functional collapsible shower or curtain rails – mental health institutes where suicide has occurred by hanging from rail
- Falls from poorly restricted windows
  (NHS Never Events List 2015/16, www.england.nhs.uk/wp-content/uploads/2015/03/never-evnts-list-15-16.pdf, accessed 1 July 2016)

This list is approximately only a quarter of the full list but it gives a indication of the complete list. Never events primarily involve surgical procedures, hospital-based medication errors and hospital-based safety incidents involving patient self-harm where safety equipment has not been installed or is not working. There is very little on the list that applies in primary care and this reflects the origins of the notion of improving patient safety within healthcare arising primarily within hospital settings. As evidence accumulates, this situation may change and it is always worth reviewing never event lists to identify new issues.

THE SEVEN PRINCIPLES OF INVESTIGATION

In its 2015–16 guidance to serious incident investigation, NHS England identified seven key principles that should underpin the investigation of a serious clinical incident within the NHS. The principles are essentially just good practice guidance that may apply to an investigation of any incident but there are some aspects that do benefit from elaboration. I address them as imperatives in a loose order of merit based upon those principles that I think are most fundamental to the investigatory process.

1. Be preventative
2. Be objective
3. Be proportionate
4. Be open and transparent
5. Be systems based
6. Be collaborative
7. Be timely and responsive

1. BE PREVENTATIVE

Try to remember that being preventative is the main principle that should underpin your efforts. It is very easy to lose focus in a serious incident investigation and to become overwhelmed with the questions What? How? and Why? Understanding what has happened in a clinical incident and exploring the deeper contributory factors can be a fascinating exercise but it is vital to realise that this process is merely a means to an end and that end is to understand what happened in a way that enables us to prevent such an incident from occurring again. Common failings of RCA investigations arise in the learning and recommendation section of the report with either weak learning or learning that bears little direct relationship to the event or the contributory factors identified in the report. It behoves investigators to remember that sufficient time and effort should go into the second phase of the report – what have we learnt from this incident and what can be done to prevent a repetition? If you are new to RCA investigations this is a key area where you are likely to make errors. Chapters 13 and 14 explore how these errors can be reduced and how meaningful learning can be derived from clinical incidents.

2. BE OBJECTIVE

You will not be objective. Neither will the patient nor their relatives. Neither will the commissioners of your service nor the staff involved nor anyone else who gets to hear of the incident. As a lead or principle investigator, you must be aware of the two key human biases that will affect everyone involved in the incident and how these biases need to be managed: outcome bias and hindsight bias.

OUTCOME BIAS

Outcome bias is the tendency to judge the merits of a decision or action based upon its outcome.

> A two-year-old child with a fever was seen by a GP who diagnosed tonsillitis and prescribed antibiotics. Twenty-four hours later the child was found dead.

What did the GP miss? Why did he not admit the child for further tests or management in hospital?

Everyone involved with the case will be asking the same question – what went wrong? Unfortunately, from an investigatory point of view, this is the wrong question and through asking it they will be demonstrating a bias that exists almost universally. If a patient suffers then it is typically presumed that something must have gone wrong. Even after many years of investigations I have to fight my first instinct and instead of asking what went wrong, ask instead, what happened?

If you start an investigation with a view that you are there to uncover something that has gone wrong it will taint your investigation. It will make you more likely to commit errors in interpretation of evidence, you will not produce a fair investigation and, most importantly, what you learn may not be relevant or true. So do not ask what went wrong – ask simply, 'What happened?'

HINDSIGHT BIAS

Hindsight bias is the tendency to judge the merits of decisions or actions within an incident based upon information not available at the time of the incident.

Once you have overcome outcome bias and commenced an investigation a lot of information will come to hand and you will have to make interpretations and judgements. The value of any given piece of information may be greatly distorted by knowing a final outcome. An elevated pulse rate is frequently dismissed in primary care as a physiological response to a fever. A patient would not be admitted nor investigated further simply because they had an elevated pulse rate. In a patient who dies of overwhelming sepsis, however, an elevated pulse rate 24 hours prior to death may be seen as an early warning sign of incipient sepsis. The value of this clue, however, is only apparent in retrospect, with the benefit of hindsight. This is because in the absence of other significant clues an isolated clinical sign would not prompt a different action from any other clinician. It is very easy to notice 'clues' when investigating serious incidents and to over-interpret their value. It is vital that investigators do not confound a clue that has 'foresight' value with one that only has value in hindsight. For example, if, when investigating a patient who died of overwhelming sepsis, one discovers in the clinical notes that the clinician identified that the patient had a fever and a non-blanching petechial rash, one now has a clue that has much more relevance. A petechial rash alone is a cause of great concern and one can foresee a problem if this is not explored fully. This clue enables one to foresee that a problem may occur in this case – even without knowing the final outcome – in a way that the finding of an elevated pulse does not.

The final investigation may be read by clinical colleagues (or lawyers) who may well misinterpret the value of data and try to second-guess your report based upon clues only evident in hindsight. Being aware of hindsight bias will enable you to factor this into both your investigation and in the way you structure and phrase your report.

OBJECTIVE EVIDENCE

Apart from ridding yourself of outcome and hindsight biases, you will also need to demonstrate objectivity in your analysis and interpretation of what happened. At the heart of an RCA investigation lies a series of tests and comparisons of what actually happened during the incident in question against what 'should' have happened. At all times it is helpful to be as objective as possible when assessing what happened by using recognised and objective sources to make comparisons against. This is explored further in Chapter 7 where we look at the use of standardised templates to assist in the process of change analysis when you try to identify what happened within an incident. We also look at other reliable sources of evidence that may be used to support notions of best or common practice. Use of standardised evidence sources or templates moves the spotlight away from the opinions or intuitions of individual investigators or 'experts' in the field and enables an investigation to be more objective.

3. BE PROPORTIONATE

Many factors may influence the proportionality of an investigation into a clinical incident. From a patient-safety perspective, the key driver of the proportionality of a response should be the potential for learning from the incident. The greater the potential degree of learning, the greater the degree of effort that should be made with regard to the investigation. At the outset, however, it is not always clear whether there will be a great degree of learning or not. As important as the proportionality of the initial response is the need to recognise that the degree of response required to an incident may change as new information comes to hand. Investigators need to know how and when to escalate concerns to the highest level within their organisation if they feel that the risks identified are significant. This is why the ability to assess risk in clinical incidents is so important. As discussed in greater length in Chapter 4, risk assessment is primarily a matter of understanding probability or likelihood of recurrence. If you understand this and are able to accurately interpret consequences – real or potential – your risk score should help you to determine the proportionality of your investigatory response. Services, such as ambulance or emergency department services or prison health services, may have unique aspects to the nature of their service or the nature of their patients that makes determining the risk of an event particularly difficult. Particular care is needed to explore the nature of causality when dealing with emergency care where, by virtue of the nature of the service, most cases represent unexpected and severe outcomes and the impact of the actions of the service may be difficult to determine. On the other hand, in the UK, prison healthcare services are required to record and investigate all deaths in custody as serious incidents regardless of their circumstances.

Given that investigations are both labour and resource intensive it is important that senior clinical and operational management in the service are aware of the risks identified and are in agreement with the scale and scope of the proposed investigation. In general, secondary care or larger institutions tend to have greater resources in terms of trained staff and flexibility of cover with which to mount an in-depth investigation. In primary care, larger service organisations such as out-of-hours care providers or the new NHS 111 call centres tend to have resources but often lack trained staff. In community general practice there may be a scarcity both of staff and training with which to conduct in-depth investigations.

A further aspect of risk that may impact upon the proportionality of an investigatory response is the political, with a small 'p', implications of an incident. It is important to understand that organisations or commissioners may choose to target certain types of incident for in-depth RCA investigation regardless of whether they fit 'true' criteria for a serious incident requiring investigation outlined in regulatory guidance. This issue is explored further in the next chapter but it is important to note that an organisation or commissioner may decide to conduct an in-depth investigation into an individual case or range of a certain type of case if they think that a service may have a vulnerability in a particular area. This may simply be because a service is new. When the new NHS 111 telephone call service was launched in 2013 I was a medical director responsible for one of the largest service providers in the UK. We reported and investigated a large number of incidents simply because we were dealing with a brand new type of service in which norms of practice were unknown. Sometimes it is helpful to investigate in depth simply to learn what is normal, even if significant preventative action does not arise.

4. BE OPEN AND TRANSPARENT

It is important to draw a distinction between openness and candour. This is because in England there is now a statutory duty placed upon registered providers of NHS care. This statutory duty is called the 'duty of candour' and it has a specific meaning with respect to patient-safety incidents and in particular serious clinical incidents. The existence of this statutory duty does create confusion among many as it overlaps with what may be considered a professional obligation to be open and transparent with regard to investigating an incident. While other countries do not make 'candour' a statutory requirement it is usually the subject of professional guidance in most countries. Chapter 5 addresses the issue of openness and the duty of candour.

5. BE SYSTEMS BASED

Theoretical constructs, research findings and incident-based evidence all point to the need to understand clinical incidents within a wider systems context. Even the single-handed general practitioner (GP) works within wider systems of care, be they local treatment or referral protocols or be they national guidance on the management of a particular condition. When you investigate what happened in an incident it is important to identify what wider systems individuals were working within at the time. When analysing why something happened it is important to identify how a given system interacts with the individual within the context of that particular event. Did the system help? Did it hinder? Or was it neutral? I learnt the value of this approach when investigating incidents within the new NHS 111 telephone service. This service involves both clinical and non-clinical staff using a series of question sets to assess symptoms presented by patients.

The question sets are very cleverly designed and when used effectively they are capable of enabling trained staff to quickly and accurately risk-assess symptoms and direct patients to appropriate services. When we investigated clinical incidents involving the new service we repeatedly identified errors by staff who had misinterpreted the responses to questions and ticked an inappropriate answer box on the electronic questionnaire that in turn results in an inappropriate outcome for the patient. A critical learning point became the understanding that staff working in such an environment were subject to a new set of systemic risks. Question sets work well with standard presentations but if the symptom pattern is unusual or if a patient expresses their symptoms in an unusual way, it is easy for staff to get the answer wrong. Is this the fault of the human operator or the system we are asking them to operate? Using an analogy with motor vehicle safety works well to help us understand this risk. In most serious clinical incidents one can place the clinician involved as the driver of a car involved in a motor vehicle accident. While driver error is easy to identify in the vast majority of motor vehicle accidents improved road safety has only really come about as a result of improvements in the design of both vehicles and the roads that they drive upon. It is important to understand driver error but if you do not think about the car they were driving or the road they were driving on you are likely to miss a much bigger opportunity for learning. These issues are addressed in Chapters 8 to 10 where we look at contributory factors in serious incidents.

6. BE COLLABORATIVE

When you investigate an incident it is important to think about the scope of what you will be investigating. You may also need to be flexible about the scope and amend this if new evidence comes to light. Most simple investigations are single-service investigations in which the scope of the investigation is limited to the circumstances of a patient journey within a single service. In practice a patient will often have made contact with several services before an adverse outcome occurs. While the guidance from NHS England is to be 'collaborative', most investigators will come up against the rallying of the troops and the circling of the wagons when they try to explore events outside their organisation. It is important to know that there is, at least in principle, a formal model for collaborative investigation of a serious incident. It is up to the lead commissioning body to implement the RASCI (responsible, accountable, supporting, consulted, informed) model and in my experience this is seldom done, but do not be afraid to seek RASCI collaboration. Even if it is declined, your request will be evidence of good practice on your part.

RASCI is an acronym for an approach advocated by NHS England to the investigation of incidents involving multiple agencies. In an ideal world the RASCI model would work like this:

RASCI – Incident investigation collaboration model

Responsible: The commissioner would appoint a responsible provider to lead the investigation and would vest in this provider the ability to mobilise resources needed to support the investigation. This would usually be the organisation that appears to hold most responsibility for the incident.

Accountable: Commissioners would determine which providers may be accountable to the responsible organisation – they are required to cooperate in providing resources to support an investigation that may include conducting investigations within their own organisation as well as participating in meetings to explore issues that may be outside their organisation.

Supporting: Commissioners and the lead investigator would determine which provider may have some useful information or guidance to support the investigation but that may not warrant investigation themselves. This may include being able to access records or staff for data retrieval.

Consulted: Commissioners and the lead investigator would determine which organisations or individuals may need to be consulted for information either in confirmation of events or to provide expert evidence.

Informed: Commissioners and the lead investigator would determine which individuals and organisations need to be informed of the investigatory process or outcome of investigation but that may play no part in the investigation itself.

In practice a multi-agency incident may result in the commissioner of services collating several individual incident reports into a single narrative – usually a cut-and-paste job. This is understandable, as in the current NHS different providers have different resources available as well as differing levels of perceived corporate risk from a given incident. Increasingly there may also be commercial conflicts of interest between different providers that make the notion of open collaboration very difficult to achieve. This becomes harder still where there are two or more different commissioners for service providers involved. Leading a multi-agency investigation is a significant challenge and for the most part this book aims to address conducting an RCA investigation within a single service provider. Nonetheless, the principles outlined would apply equally if a multi-agency investigation occurred.

7. BE TIMELY AND RESPONSIVE

Within the NHS and indeed in any regulated health system, time constraints are placed upon a formal investigation of a serious incident. It is customary to produce an initial report, generally no more than a statement of the basic facts with an outline of the proposed scope of the investigation, within 72 hours of an incident being recognised as having occurred. Following this an investigator has 60 days within which to complete a report. It is important to note that timelines are for guidance only. There may be compelling reasons why an investigation may take longer than anticipated. As long as commissioners, relatives and staff are informed of the reasons and assuming that the reasons are sound, then a delayed report is acceptable and even desirable if the delay leads to greater clarity.

Responsiveness essentially means that the investigation should not leave questions unanswered. In particular, it is important to ensure that in addition to covering the general technical questions that arise for investigators in all investigations – what, why and how – the investigation and report should also address any specific questions raised by the commissioner or the patient involved or their representatives. If these questions are beyond the reasonable scope or expertise of an RCA investigation, then this may be stated within the report, but ideally commissioners or a patient should be aware of this before a final report is drafted.

Now that we have some background, let us take a look at how to recognise a serious clinical incident.

3

How do we recognise serious clinical incidents?

CASE SUMMARIES

Baby Anna

Baby Anna is 12 months old. Her parents attend a GP out-of-hours service at 9:00 p.m. with a history that Anna has a fever, has been shivery and is not well. Dr King assesses Anna and diagnoses a viral upper respiratory infection and Anna goes home. Thirty hours later Anna's mother awakes at 3:00 a.m. to hear her grunting and calls an ambulance. Anna dies two hours later in the emergency department. Lumber puncture suggests a cause of death to be acute bacterial meningitis.

Carole

Carole is an 84-year-old lady who lives in a residential home. She has end-stage cardiac and renal failure and has expressed a wish to avoid extensive investigation or treatment in hospital. On Friday evening she develops a temperature and a productive cough. An out-of-hours GP sees her and notes a fever of 38.8°C, a pulse of 88 and a blood pressure (BP) of 120/80 and commences her on a course of Amoxicillin antibiotics for a lower respiratory infection. On Sunday morning the out-of-hours service receives a call from the home to say that Carole has been found to have died in the night.

Arnold

Arnold is an 89-year-old man who lives alone in a flat. He has meals delivered to his home seven days a week but is otherwise self-caring. He takes antihypertensive medication. On Friday morning he visits his GP with a history of a recent cold that he thinks has 'gone to his chest'. His GP identifies a temperature of 38.8°C, a pulse of 88 and a BP of 140/80, and commences him on a course of Amoxicillin antibiotics for a lower respiratory infection. At 8:00 p.m. Arnold's daughter phones the NHS 111 service reporting that his breathing appears laboured. His local out-of-hours GP service arranges to visit him at home. The GP arrives at 10:30 p.m. to find an ambulance on site. Arnold had collapsed and was not able to be resuscitated.

The first of many challenges that face clinicians or service managers who oversee clinical services is determining when a serious incident has actually occurred. We prefaced the chapter with three different cases that all have the same sad outcome – the patient died. In terms of patient-related outcomes one cannot get a worse outcome than death – so how can we decide which of these incidents may constitute a serious incident?

For the most part, the techniques explored in this book apply to serious incidents requiring investigation. That is to say, incidents that reach a threshold for reporting to regulatory bodies. In fact, root cause analysis can be used to investigate any clinical or service incident or complaint but it is important to understand how to recognise a case that needs referral to regulators. It is also important to remember that when we use the phrase 'serious incident' we are using a technical term that may have different meanings to different people. In particular, many GPs and primary care nurses may confuse the term with 'significant event'. This is generally an incident of concern identified and investigated within a practice but not reported externally. It is likely that many 'significant events' analysed informally in practices actually reach the threshold for regulatory reporting but remain hidden from wider scrutiny by ignorance of the process. Another important fact to bear in mind is that very few patients or patient representatives will be aware of what the term 'serious incident' means. While many will be gratified to think that an incident is recognised as 'serious', they are not likely to be familiar with root cause analysis and the principle of seeking to identify learning rather than apportioning 'blame'. Patients will often expect a serious incident report to identify someone to blame for a failing in care and may expect to see someone disciplined for any harm that may have occurred as a result of the incident.

So, when we think about the recognition of a serious incident it is helpful to remember that this comes with certain formal obligations in terms of reporting and investigation and potentially 'duty of candour', but also informal implications with regard to the need to ensure that both your colleagues and any patients or their representatives involved understand the process that you are about to embark upon.

RECOGNITION AND REGULATORS

Throughout the world most healthcare regulators have adopted a very similar approach to the matter of recognition of cases that should be reported and investigated using a formalised process such as root cause analysis. Within the UK the terminology has changed slightly over the past few years – previously regulators in the UK preferred the term Serious Untoward Incident to designate incidents that would require reporting. Recently, this has changed to Serious Incident Requiring Investigation (SIRI), although most people involved at the sharp end of healthcare governance in the UK simply use the term Serious Incident (SI) when they are dealing with a case that they believe reaches a threshold for reporting. Hence there is potential for misunderstandings to arise when investigators or staff in senior governance roles communicate with both patients and their relatives but also when they communicate with colleagues in primary or secondary care. This is especially so within primary care where the distinction between a SIRI and a 'significant event' is often not clearly understood.

REPORTING TIMELINES FORCE DECISIONS WITH INCOMPLETE INFORMATION

A characteristic of serious incident reporting systems is that they have timelines for both recognition and reporting of incidents and for completing investigations. There is an imperative to recognise as soon as possible that a serious incident has occurred. The reasons for this are fairly obvious and include the potential need for service providers to take immediate remedial action if the incident uncovers a previously unforeseen service risk. It is frustrating – to say the least – to investigate an incident for two months only to discover that a further patient has died in the same circumstances in the interim and noone is aware that an investigation is already underway. If an incident occurs, then a service provider must have systems in place to recognise a potential serious incident as soon as it comes to their attention and to decide if a serious incident has occurred within a matter of hours. (Timelines can range from 12 to 72 hours depending upon service type and commissioner stipulations.) This means that a decision about whether to declare an incident and launch a full-scale investigation with all that this entails must often be made before there is time to fully evaluate all of the information that one may wish to consider. There are definitions and guidelines to help and there are also custom and practice. Most regulatory bodies recognise that different service types will need to establish their own thresholds for recognising when a serious incident has occurred. In my own experience this particular exercise seldom occurs or, if it does occur, it is done informally and with considerable individual variation even within similar service types. While we may understand that an emergency department may have a different view of what constitutes an unexpected death to a general practice, it is not uncommon to find that one emergency department has quite different practices with regard to recognising a serious incident compared to another, even within a similar geographical area. General practices are more likely to have very little experience with regard to reporting serious incidents to regulatory bodies and frequently lack experience or resources to mount a high-level investigation into serious incidents even if they are recognised.

DEFINITIONS AND GUIDANCE

Although it is very difficult to define what constitutes a serious incident that warrants reporting and formal investigation, the NPSA has attempted to do this. The NPSA was a quasi-autonomous non-governmental organisation (quango) that was decommissioned by the government in 2012. Prior to this the NPSA had established the parameters for the recognition of patient-safety incidents including serious incidents. They also established a number of useful tools to help in the investigation and reporting of incidents that remain available today via their website, now hosted by the NHS England patient-safety domain. The NPSA had defined a patient-safety incident as 'any unintended or unexpected incident which could have or did lead to harm for one or more patients'. (www.npsa.nhs.uk/nrls/reporting/what-is-a-patient-safety-incident/, accessed 1 July 2016)

An incident was regarded as being serious when the harm suffered was severe. From this guidance it was surmised that the unexpected death of a patient following an episode of care would constitute a serious incident that would warrant reporting. Problems arose when one considered lesser degrees of harm. What is considered severe or significant harm by one person may not be regarded as serious by another. The amputation of a little toe, for example, could be seen as serious by some but less so by others.

A second issue that arose was the meaning of the word 'unexpected'. If a surgeon amputates your right leg when you were expecting your left leg to be amputated, we can all agree that this is an unexpected outcome. Most surgical and procedural interventions have a fairly clearly defined outcome with predictable results. It is relatively easy to see when they go wrong. In medicine, however, the issues may be less clear. In the case above, Arnold died following assessment and treatment by his general practitioner for a chest infection. Arnold was 89 years old and so his death was not a surprise to his GP – after all, elderly patients may well succumb to a chest infection. But not being surprised by an outcome is not the same as expecting it. Compare Arnold's case with that of Carole. Carole had significant underlying medical problems and when she developed a lower respiratory infection her condition deteriorated markedly. Her GP, considering Carole's known wishes and in consultation with her family, had instituted palliative care at home, keeping her comfortable with an expectation that the chest infection would be likely to result in Carole's imminent death. The guidance that a severe outcome that is unexpected may constitute a serious clinical incident is helpful in excluding Carole's case from reporting processes but it is less clear in the case of Arnold. The guidance suggests that Arnold's death should be reported and yet most practitioners would not regard the death of an elderly patient from pneumonia as a significant learning opportunity.

In its 2015 update to guidance of the recognition and reporting of serious incidents, NHS England wrote: 'Serious incidents are events where the potential for learning is so great, or the consequences so significant for the organisation or patients, that they warrant additional resources to mount a comprehensive response.' (NHS England Serious Incident Framework, p. 12, NHS England Patient Safety Domain, London.)

NHS England were trying to eschew the notion of hard definitions as it was felt that lack of clarity in the definition was leading to services either over-reporting incidents that were not valuable from a learning perspective or under-reporting incidents. (Services that proudly boast not reporting any serious incidents in the preceding one or more years are either brilliantly managed clinically or poorly managed from a governance perspective.) In particular, NHS England attempted to steer healthcare providers away from simply using an unexpected severe outcome of an event alone as a trigger for declaring a serious incident.

OTHER REASONS FOR REPORTING

Apart from regulatory imperatives to report incidents, there may be other reasons for reporting an incident. These may contradict the guidance from the regulator that an 'outcome is not an incident'. For some services there may be contractual reasons for certain types of incident to be declared to regulators or there may simply be pressure from commissioners to declare incidents, particularly when services are new. Services themselves may determine that certain classes of incident should be reported. If you are new in a governance role in a service it is worth checking to see whether there are incidents above and beyond what NHS England stipulate should be declared.

TRIGGERS FOR DECLARING AN INCIDENT

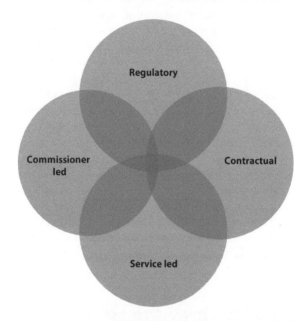

CAUSATION – THE NEEDLE IN THE HAYSTACK

At the root of this question of recognition is the issue of causation. Causation will recur again and again as the key element that is often lost sight of in incident investigation and reporting. The point about incident reporting and investigation is being able to identify and learn from those episodes of patient contact in which the actions of clinicians or service systems altered the natural progression of pathology in an adverse way. What this means is that the severity of the outcome for the patient is not actually the point. The outcome is just a trigger point to think about causation. The point is whether the healthcare intervention (or lack of intervention) did something to cause the death or severe harm suffered by the patient. The reason that the issue of causation is so crucial is that this has a direct link to whether learning may arise from the case. If a healthcare provider has done something that may have caused an adverse outcome, then identifying the causative action(s) (or lack of action(s)) may enable us to learn how to avoid doing (or not doing) the same thing in the future. The key element of the definition of a patient-safety incident are the words 'lead to', in the sense that an error of care (an act or omission) must not only have occurred but that this must also have led to the adverse outcome. An error of care may not lead to the adverse outcome. An adverse outcome may occur without there being an error of care.

RECOGNITION OF CAUSATION BY PROXY – THE TRADITIONAL APPROACH

Faced with the dilemma that one must recognise and report a serious incident as soon as possible and faced with the additional dilemma that the key element that matters from a reporting point of view is this issue of causation, many services had adopted a strategy of using the combination of two common proxies to act as triggers for recognising serious incidents. These proxies are proximity to the service and an unexpected severe outcome.

Proximity is important because it relates to the probability that the cause of an adverse outcome may be related to the service provider. It is basically an extension of the legal notion that the causation is likely to rest with the last provider to have contact with the patient. There is no hard-and-fast rule about proximity in terms of time but as a rule of thumb, a severe unexpected outcome within 24 to 48 hours of contact with a service should prompt a service to consider that potentially a serious incident may have occurred. In some cases, the timeline may extend for longer than this. A patient in whom a high-risk condition was either missed or inappropriately managed – that may include failure to provide adequate safety-net advice – may remain a potential serious incident even where an adverse outcome does not occur for days or even weeks after contact. (Consider in particular a missed DVT where harm may not arise for days or weeks following a clinical contact at which the diagnosis was missed.) Cases should be considered upon their merits and while a significant delay between contact and an adverse outcome makes the likelihood of causation much less, it would not in itself rule it out.

UNEXPECTED ADVERSE OUTCOMES

We have already noted that the issue of whether an adverse outcome is unexpected or not is a challenge. The way that this issue is tackled will vary from unit to unit. Ideally two or more senior clinicians should discuss the events and reach a consensus regarding the management of the case. This often comes down to a clinician taking a view as to whether they may have managed the case in the same way or not or whether they can spot any obvious errors of care. This is summed up by such phrases as 'I think that we did everything by the book . . .' or 'I would probably have managed the case the same way – I don't think we could have anticipated or changed that outcome'. While this approach has the merit of being functional and generally the opinions expressed are likely to be sound, it is an approach that is flawed in two key regards. Firstly, it lacks a formal structure or rationale and thus it is very difficult to ensure that decisions are consistent and that all potential areas of causation have been considered. Secondly, in an era of increasing scrutiny such decision making lacks both transparency and accountability. Should the patient death be subject to subsequent further investigation by a coroner or a medico-legal process, the reasons why a service decided that this particular case did not warrant investigation may be lost completely unless the responsible clinicians keep thorough notes of their deliberations.

A STRUCTURED APPROACH TO RECOGNISING SERIOUS INCIDENTS: THE SERIOUS INCIDENT RECOGNITION TOOL (SIRT)

The Serious Incident Recognition Tool (SIRT) is a tool that I have developed to help formalise the assessment of potential serious incidents. It can be used by service leads in any service line within 24 to 72 hours of the recognition of a potential serious incident to help identify whether an incident reaches the threshold for recognition as 'serious' as defined by regulatory bodies and for which an in-depth structured investigation using a technique such as root cause analysis should be initiated. It can also be used as a tool to formalise the initial assessments of serious complaints that may also warrant a robust investigation such as an RCA. The tool is an adaptation and development of a tool devised by the NPSA. The NPSA developed a tool called the Incident Decision Tree to help governance leads to assess the severity of a clinical incident. I have adapted this tool and used it to provide a structured and formal approach to the assessment of potential serious clinical incidents. The advantage of this approach is that the decision-making process attains an easily reproducible structure that addresses the key elements that may be implicated in any type of incident from the point of view of causation. Not only may the tool be used to structure the approach to assessing potential serious incidents but, once completed, it may also be stored and retained as a record of any decisions made in the event that the case is reviewed at any future date. This approach may be used by any service type, be it a general practice, a surgical unit or a telephone call centre. I have used the tool effectively in general practice, urgent care services including GP out-of-hours, urgent care centres, prison health services and NHS 111 services. It may also be used in secondary care services. The caveat for use is that service leads must consider each of the criteria as it applies to their service and there may be a need to provide guidance for staff on how to interpret aspects of the tool with reference to their specific service line. (See below.)

THE SIRT – SERIOUS INCIDENT RECOGNITION TOOL

The tool considers six elements related to the incident:

- Outcome
- Proximity
- Intention
- Capacity
- Foresight
- Substitution

The latter four elements are derived from the NPSA Incident Decision Tree. The tool may be used in a group meeting to assess an incident and both clinical and non-clinical staff may be involved in the assessment of the case. The assessment should be used by a senior member of staff who has had training in serious incident investigation and who is confident in the interpretation of each of the six elements. At least one senior clinician

Table 3.1 SIRT – Serious Incident Recognition Tool

This tool is designed to help clinical services recognise a patient-safety incident that may require a structured and in-depth investigation. It does not itself identify a causal link between an episode of care and an adverse outcome.

Case ID:. . . . .

Age:. . . . .

Sex: . . . .

Date of incident: . . . .

Date of review:. . . . .

This form must be completed by staff trained in its use. For clinical incidents, two senior clinicians should be involved in the consideration.

	Guidance	Comments
Outcome	Was the outcome both: Severe? Unexpected?	

Severe = Death or permanent disability. Severe outcomes may also include prolonged need for medical or psychological treatment as well as any outcome that the service itself or the patient or their representatives regard as being a severe outcome. A 'near miss' with a potentially severe outcome for the patient or service may be considered as a 'yes' answer at this stage.

Unexpected = Not arising naturally or directly from pathology that was identified and that the patient was being treated for at the time of the incident. If the pathology identified has a potentially severe outcome but a severe outcome was not anticipated at the time of treatment, then the outcome would be regarded as unexpected. (Not being surprised by an outcome does not mean that the outcome was expected.)

If the answer to both elements of the outcome question is unequivocally no, then the likelihood of a serious incident having occurred is remote and the incident should be investigated according to standard local protocols for non-serious patient-safety incidents.

If the answer to either strand of the outcome question is yes, then consider the further questions below.

Proximity	Did the incident occur within such a time frame within contact with service that the possibility of causation exists?	

This question must be answered by at least one named senior clinician and is based upon the balance of probability – that is, is the outcome more likely than not? If the answer is yes – proceed to consider the questions below. If the answer is no, then the likelihood of a serious incident having occurred is remote and the incident should be investigated according to standard local protocols for non-serious patient-safety incidents.

If response to both questions is yes, then proceed with assessment below.		
Intention	1. Are clinical actions different from those intended? 2. Is there any evidence of a deliberate intention to cause harm or to provide sub-optimal care?	
Is there an obvious error of intention? The clinician clearly intended to do X but did Y instead (for example, intended to prescribe erythromycin but prescribed penicillin). This suggests a 'slip' or mistake. Deliberate intention to cause harm is extremely rare but may occur in certain high-risk environments. If intention is suspected, senior service leads must be involved in assessment of risk.		
Capacity/ Capability	1. Was the service at risk due to capacity issues at the time of the incident? 2. Was the staff member involved acting outside their capability or impaired by any personal incapacity?	
A service-capacity issue refers to a mismatch between capacity within the service and demand upon it. The capacity–demand mismatch must be exceptional and severe and not simply be a reflection of a 'busy' day. Capability refers to a member of staff who may have been acting outside their competence levels – for example, students performing tasks normally undertaken by trained staff or staff in training acting outside a defined role limit. Consider also personal health/psychological issues impacting upon capability.		
Foresight	Did any individual deviate from guidelines, protocols or standard safe practice?	
This is a balanced judgement. Could the potential for a severe adverse outcome have been predicted because of failure to follow policy, guidelines, protocol or best practice? Must be based upon evidence available at the time of assessment.		
Substitution	Were actions of staff outside expected norms for role?	
Excluding foresight considerations (see above), would any other member of staff working in the same capacity have been equally likely to have acted in the same way? Base judgement upon 'average' staff – not best and not worst.		
Answering yes to any question above should trigger an in-depth investigation and consideration of declaration of SI to commissioners and NHS England.		
Risk assessment	Consequence = Likelihood = Risk = C × L =	

A risk score greater than or equal to 12 should prompt review of scoring and risk at the most senior clinical and managerial (legal) level in the organisation. A confirmed risk score greater than or equal to 20 should prompt board-level notification.
Use NHS risk matrix and guidance to complete a risk score.

Immediate action	Is any immediate action indicated based upon: 1. risk assessment? 2. individual staff actions?	

A risk score of 12 or more may indicate a need for action to reduce risk even before a full investigation has been completed.
Staff acting deliberately, beyond capacity, outside standard practice or outside expected norms for behaviour may require immediate individual risk assessment before being allowed to continue their next patient-facing work shift.

must form part of any team using the tool. The tool also incorporates an initial risk assessment and a prompt to consider the need for any immediate actions.

Before using the tool, it will be necessary to obtain as much preliminary information as possible. The format of the tool in Table 3.1 includes guidance on use and interpretation. 'Yes' answers trigger action.

The tool is intended for use in situations in which the potential for a serious incident to have occurred arises and a decision is needed as to whether to proceed to an in-depth investigation such as a root cause analysis and whether regulatory and commissioning bodies should be informed. Full guidance on use of the SIRT tool is provided in Chapter 4 with worked case examples and discussion of special circumstances and specific service considerations.

CREATING A SAFETY-FOCUSED LEARNING CULTURE USING THE SIRT

The SIRT enables a service to have a clear and transparent process for assessing potential serious clinical incidents. It provides a practical means of assessment that can be consistently applied across any individual service or group of services and that provides a rationale by which service leads may escalate cases that need further in-depth assessment or reassure themselves that an in-depth assessment using RCA is not likely to yield significant learning. Use of the SIRT does not preclude a standard patient-safety investigation from occurring and indeed, should further evidence arise that suggests that an RCA may be useful, then use of the tool may be repeated and any decision about whether to proceed with an in-depth investigation may again be made in a structured and consistent fashion. There are some procedural considerations that organisations may usefully take into account to ensure that this process works efficiently.

- Formalise the process for recognising serious incidents.
- Train staff about serious incidents – let them know what they are and why it is important to recognise them.

- Equally importantly, let them know what types of case are not serious incidents – inexperienced staff tend to misunderstand the notion of probability in healthcare and in a permissive safety environment often over-report certain types of frustrating minor incident as 'serious' because of skewed logic about the potential for them to cause harm.
- Create a protocol for a trained group within your service to assess potential incidents within 24 hours using a formal process such as the SIRT.
- Allow any member of staff to raise an incident (or series of incidents) to this SI recognition group for consideration.
- Train the group recognising serious incidents in how to use a formal process or tool such as SIRT for recognition.
- Ensure you have processes in place for recording and storing group discussion and actions as part of your incident investigation process.
- Ensure the group knows how to escalate serious incidents that meet the threshold to regulatory bodies.

TOP TIP

Meet with patient-safety and quality leads from commissioning organisations to discuss your approach to assessment. They are likely to be very supportive. Consider inviting commissioner representation to one or more of your SI recognition meetings to show them how you work and also to benefit from their input. Developing a shared understanding builds trust and mutual respect and makes it easier for commissioners and service providers to agree where subsequent investigations suggest that an incident may be downgraded from 'serious' status in the light of RCA findings.

Let us now look a little more closely at the recognition of serious incidents using some case examples.

4

Recognising serious incidents using the SIRT: Case studies

The following case examples help to demonstrate the value of using a formal process for recognising a serious incident that requires in-depth investigation. Once we are familiar with the basic principles of using the Serious Incident Recognition Tool we will move on to special considerations.

INITIAL EVIDENCE

An in-depth investigation will require the accumulation of a significant amount of evidence. However, at the outset and in particular at the time at which an incident is initially recognised, evidence is likely to be limited. Incidents will come to the attention of clinicians or service leads in a variety of ways and this will often determine the amount of evidence available. The key central evidence will always be the clinical notes but before a decision may be reached it is often necessary to rapidly obtain certain other pieces of information to enable a judgement about how to proceed.

TOP TIP

As soon as you find yourself considering whether a serious incident may have occurred, make a note of how it came to your attention. Formal serious incident reports require a brief account of how the incident was initially reported and it is easy to overlook this and then find it difficult some weeks into an investigation to track down how it first came to light.

A timeline is your best friend. Start to make a timeline as soon as information comes to hand. Include noting the date and time when the incident first came to your attention. In some important cases such information will matter and you will not know which cases are important until further down the line when your memory of events will have faded (Table 4.1).

Table 4.1 Initial evidence checklist

Evidence	Guidance	Additional considerations
Clinical notes	Obtain a copy that is date and time stamped.	Notes must remain unchanged – do not correct typos.
Patient evidence	Do you need to contact a patient or their next of kin to clarify details of the contact? If the case has come to light as a result of a patient complaint or comment, consider whether the information is sufficient to help form a decision – do you need to contact them to seek clarification?	Incomplete or ambiguous notes may make initial assessment difficult. Do not avoid early contact with the patient or their next of kin for fear of upsetting them. Most patients or families welcome sympathetic and sensitive contact when a service has recognised that an adverse outcome has occurred and are reassured that the service is looking at the case. (See Chapter 5 regarding openness and candour.)
Voice recordings	If the service makes voice recordings of telephone contacts, then these should be obtained within 24 hours.	Do not delay a decision if a copy of a voice recording is delayed.
Initial staff debrief	If clinical notes are unclear or ambiguous, contact staff as soon as possible to seek clarification.	A phone interview is acceptable. Make notes of date and time. Do not delay a decision if staff are not contactable within 24 to 48 hours. If using a voice-recorded telephone line, you should inform your colleague that the conversation is recorded.
Non-GP services – contact with GP	Urgent care or acute services may consider contacting the patient's GP for information or for assistance with information gathering.	Be aware of consent issues if seeking information. GPs may be very helpful in providing guidance about how a family may be coping with a bereavement and agree to act as an initial contact point in potentially sensitive cases to facilitate service contact with the family.

CASE STUDY: BABY ANNA

Let us consider the case of baby Anna. We will think about the case from the point of view of a clinical service lead who is presented with information and has to make a decision about whether this is a serious clinical incident requiring an in-depth investigation using root cause analysis.

CASE DETAILS

At 7:00 p.m. on a Monday evening the NHS 111 service passed the case of a 12-month-old girl, Anna, to the GP out-of-hours service. The patient was reported as having been unwell for approximately one day. She had had routine vaccinations four days previously.

The patient was seen at approximately 9:00 p.m. that evening, two hours after contact from the NHS 111 service.

Anna was assessed by Dr King who noted a history of the child appearing tired and unwell in addition to having a fever and shaking episodes. Dr King diagnosed a probable viral infection. Advice on home management was given and the child returned home.

At approximately 3:00 a.m. on Wednesday Anna's mother awoke and noted that her child appeared to be 'grunting' and called 999. Anna was transferred to hospital where she died later that morning.

The cause of death is believed to be bacterial meningitis based upon initial blood tests and lumbar puncture results.

You know Dr King to be a local GP partner who has worked for the out-of-hours service for several years.

The case was brought to the attention of the out-of-hours service lead by a phone call from the local paediatrician who had dealt with the case in the early hours of the morning.

TOP TIP

Outcome bias is a tendency to judge the merits of a decision or an action based upon its outcome rather than on the act itself. You will be affected by outcome bias as soon as a potential serious incident is brought to your attention. You must be aware that you will be biased. You must remind yourself to temper your initial reaction and to look at the evidence objectively before you reach a decision. It takes a lot of practice to overcome outcome bias – it is best to assume that it will affect you. The value of a formal investigative process, including a formal process for serious incident recognition, is that it mitigates the effects that outcome bias can have upon an investigation, and, importantly, upon both the patient and staff involved if it is not recognised.

Is this a serious clinical incident? Common sense suggests that the answer must be yes – after all, a baby has died within a very short time of contact with an out-of-hours GP. The outcome must be unexpected and it is certainly as catastrophic an outcome as one can get. At this stage it is vital to bring to mind and consider two key concepts that apply in this context:

- Outcome bias
- 'Serious' means it reaches the threshold for an in-depth investigation or reporting

Remember also that in this context 'serious' does not mean a tragic outcome. Serious means two things in the context of serious incident recognition:

1. That an in-depth investigation of the case is likely to reveal learning that is of significant value. Learning is more likely to arise where there is a causal relationship between the service contact and the subsequent outcome.
2. A service may determine that certain categories of adverse outcome are 'serious' and warrant formal reporting or in-depth investigation regardless of learning potential because of a strategic desire to ensure demonstration of best practice.

Use of a formal tool such as SIRT will assist with consideration of the potential for significant learning because it will help us to identify potential causality between events occurring and a final adverse outcome.

If a service takes a strategic view about use of in-depth investigation of certain designated case types (for example, all unexpected deaths in children or all moderate or severe episodes of self-harm within a given institution) then this should ideally be explicitly stated within internal policies or by provision of written guidance for service leads. Use of the recognition tool would still be helpful in guiding the direction of the subsequent investigation.

If we set aside outcome bias and review the death of baby Anna, we have evidence that Anna died within a short window of contact with an out-of-hours service. The parents of Anna had told the hospital consultant that the out-of-hours doctor had told them that Anna had a viral infection. It seems plausible that an out-of-hours GP may have discharged a child with a febrile illness with a diagnosis of a viral infection and given that the investigation in hospital suggested that the child in fact had a bacterial meningitis, it would appear that the GP diagnosis was incorrect and that, when seen by the out-of-hours GP, Anna was in fact suffering from a prodromal phase of bacterial meningitis. Thus we have a severe and unexpected outcome in close proximity to the out-of-hours service. We also appear to have a missed opportunity for diagnosis by an out-of-hours GP. Is this not a straightforward 'serious incident'? Is the potential for learning not evident from the fact that the out-of-hours GP clearly failed to make the correct diagnosis? Surely there must be significant learning to be gained from this incident?

The simple answer is that significant learning is not necessarily obvious in this case. We already know that a case of bacterial meningitis presenting in the prodromal phase may be indistinguishable from a simple viral infection. Thus on the evidence available thus far, an in-depth investigation of this case may tell us nothing more than we already know – that patients will sometimes tragically die as a result of the natural course of illness and for certain illnesses such as meningitis, even the best clinicians working in ideal environments may not be able to diagnose a condition early and prevent a tragic outcome.

In order to progress in making a decision we need more evidence and we need to look at the evidence in a more structured way.

Having spoken to the consultant paediatrician (and having made a note of the date and time of notification of this potential serious incident) you obtain a copy of the clinical notes. You discover clinical notes both from the NHS 111 initial telephone assessment service as well as from Dr King, who saw Anna in the out-of-hours service.

NHS 111 notes – time stamp 7:06 p.m.

The patient's reported condition states:

'12-month jab four days ago unwell – shaking one day'

During the NHS Pathways assessment, the 111 health adviser documented the following user comments:

'Shivering – whole body unwell few days had 12 month jab 4 days ago'

'Sleeping more than usual'

'Cold symptoms – last week'

Dr King's clinical notes from the out-of-hours IT system

Arrival time stamp: 9:00 p.m.
Consultation start time stamp: 9:05 p.m.

The clinical notes read as follows: (NB: Notes are copied verbatim from record and include typos and spelling mistakes.)

HISTORY

'had 12 month jabs 4 day sago, has been well, slightly unwell yesterday, today ahs been usual self til this evening when she felt very hot, nappy changed, was wet and dirty, then she vomited ×1 and has the shakes for about 1 min, then ok again. mum concerned she is very unwell, given ibuprofen at 20.00, is now tired.'

EXAMINATION

'temp 38.7, HR 170, resp rate high at about 40, chest clear, no recessions or nasal flares,'

DIAGNOSIS

'febrile fit and viral illness'

MANAGEMENT

'given paracetamol 5mls at 21.20, monitor temp at 22.00. encourage fluids, if temp falling then can go home, 1 hour later, pt sleeping colur better, temp down to 38.3, parebts reassured, hom eregular paracetamol and fluids, to call again if concerned'

FINAL DIAGNOSTIC CODE

'Viral infection NOS'

PRESCRIPTION

'Paracetamol suspension 120 mg in 5 mls, 500 mls, 5mls 4 × day as required.'

The available evidence enables us to go some way to assessing this case. We know that the outcome is catastrophic – a death – and that it was not expected. We know that it occurred within close proximity to contact with an out-of-hours service consultation, which raises a potential for a causative act or omission within the service. Can we answer the four supplementary questions regarding the management of a case that may help us determine if there may be a causal relationship between the service contact and the final outcome?

INTENTION

Intention is twofold. We have to consider whether the clinical events that occurred were the intention of the clinician involved. Did Dr King intend to send Anna home with paracetamol? The answer appears straightforward in this case as the actions are consistent with the notes and make sense from a clinical perspective.

Was there an intention to cause harm? In most services one may confidently assume that no intention to cause harm arose. There are situations in which this issue needs more careful consideration and this is dealt with below under 'special considerations'. In this case an assumption of no intention to harm is made.

CAPACITY

Capacity is also twofold. In this case we know that Dr King is a local GP partner who has worked for the out-of-hours service for several years and thus there is no issue of Dr King working outside of his level of professional competence. It would be useful to know that Dr King did not have any personal issues ongoing at the time of assessment that may have affected his performance. The only way to address this is to ask Dr King directly. At this point we must consider a phone call to Dr King.

The second strand of capacity is capacity within the service itself. Was the service so overstretched at the time that this in itself may have created pressure for the staff? For this to be a potential factor we must be considering a situation in which an exceptional mismatch between capacity and demand exists – not just a busy or very busy day. In this case we have two useful pieces of information. Firstly, Anna's parents contacted the telephone advice service at 7:00 p.m. and had an appointment booked at 9:00 p.m., only two hours later. Further, Anna was seen by Dr King just five minutes after appointment time. For the purposes of this assessment then it seems clear that service capacity was not an issue in this case.

FORESIGHT

Foresight is perhaps one of the hardest issues to address in incident assessment. There will always be a subjective element to assessing foresight, which is why the structured approach is helpful. We must consider only what the clinician knew or would reasonably have been expected to know at the time of the assessment. An important principle is that clinicians are not expected to get a diagnosis right every time. They are expected, however, to do all that is reasonably possible to establish a correct diagnosis or understanding of what is going on. At a very basic level, a clinician must do the following:

- establish a sufficient history of events
- perform a relevant examination
- formulate an opinion as to what is occurring
- provide management appropriate to the opinion they have formed.

> **TOP TIP**
>
> The difficulty with foresight assessments is that investigators always make them with the benefit of hindsight and it is very difficult to eliminate this. Try to imagine that you are reviewing the case as a simple routine audit and that the patient has fully recovered. Does anything in the notes stand out as being significantly outside normal occurrence such that specific feedback may be needed.

The principle for assessing the consultation and management is that it must be reasonable, not perfect. It is important to bear in mind that you are reading what Dr King wrote about the consultation. This is not likely to include everything that was said or done. Dr King appears to have obtained a reasonable history of what had happened. Given that we know the tragic final outcome, we can of course think of other things that we would like to see written down but there is certainly enough information to get a sense of what had been going on. The examination includes a number of relevant and important physical signs such that one can see that Dr King was looking for evidence of significant illness. The fact that some information that we may like to see is missing should be noted but this alone should not trigger a positive response to the foresight question. Failing to record every single potential symptom or sign does not in itself indicate a significant problem with the consultation and by inference imply a potential causality.

Dr King had written that his diagnosis was 'febrile fit and viral illness'. He gave Anna some paracetamol in the clinic and then reviewed her an hour later and noted that her temperature was slightly lower and that she was sleeping and looked a better colour. He advised paracetamol and to call back if there were any concerns.

Overall one could view this assessment as reasonable. The symptoms and signs were indicative of an infectious illness. The vital signs were a little abnormal but not strikingly so. There is no specific mention of rash nor meningism and it is possible that Dr King did not consider or look for this but a clinician who does note temperature, pulse, respiratory rate and other observations about a child is likely to have also assessed for meningism. A diagnosis of a viral illness seems reasonable.

TOP TIP

An incident investigator is not a medical lawyer – the rule 'if it is not written it did not happen' does not apply. You may form opinions based upon the balance of probability providing you have some evidence to indicate what swayed you one way or another.

The child seemed a little better after having some paracetamol, albeit that we have to read between the lines a little and assume that Dr King was reassured by factors other than simply the small temperature drop and better colour as he did not record any vital signs other than temperature at the second review. The management plan to return home and manage with paracetamol and seek review if there were concerns seems reasonable. On routine audit one may provide feedback about the need to record slightly more comprehensive notes of vital signs. One may also question the value of giving a febrile child paracetamol and reviewing after an hour, which is no longer regarded as best practice, but this in itself would not be significant in terms of the final outcome.

If you feel that something has been overlooked at this point you would be correct. A good habit to develop is that once you have reviewed the clinical notes, put them down for an hour, do something else and then have another look at them later – you may have overlooked something. As a general rule it is useful to have a minimum of two heads reviewing data, as it is easy to miss details that may be important. If this is not possible, then set the task aside for a time and take another look. When I did this with the baby Anna case I noticed that Dr King had written 'febrile fit and viral illness', and not simply viral illness. The issue of the febrile fit was overlooked. The fact that Dr King has recorded a diagnosis of febrile fit raises a concern because if that was the case, then Dr King should have referred baby Anna to the local paediatric unit for further assessment (as this is current UK recommended practice). There are mixed views about the value of this approach and it may well be that Dr King had a good reason for not referring Anna to hospital at the time but from the point of view of 'foresight' we have discovered a significant issue. According to current UK best practice guidelines, baby Anna should have been referred and not sent home. We cannot possibly know the significance of failing to refer at this stage as we do not know enough about the case. What we do know, however, is that based upon the documented notes that best practice was not followed. With regard to potential serious clinical incidents, whenever there is a clear deviation from best practice, especially when this is formulated within a national or local guidance or policy document, the potential for causation arises. This would constitute grounds for recognising the incident as 'serious' and warranting an in-depth investigation.

Substitution. Within any service line it is important to be able to establish a benchmark for the substitution test. Traditionally, substitution is based upon the opinion of an experienced colleague. This remains a valuable and valid approach; however, in many services a less subjective benchmark is possible, namely the service audit. Both out-of-hours and NHS 111 call-centre services use nationally validated audit template tools to audit the clinical work of their staff. Staff are trained and employed as auditors. Where formal audit does not exist, audit tools used in other similar services may be adapted and used for the purpose of establishing a more objective assessment for the purpose of the substitution test. For example, the out-of-hours audit tool may be used for a daytime general practice assessment. In this case Dr King's assessment was reviewed using the Royal College of General Practitioners (RCGP) out-of-hours GP audit tool. Dr King lost some points for failings considered above but overall his performance was within average range. The use of audit tools for assessing cases is considered further throughout the book.

TOP TIP

Do not personalise the review process. This can lead to development of blind spots. When assessing the baby Anna case, I initially evaluated the presentation by imagining how I might manage the case. I thought that the shaking episodes described were likely to have been rigors and not convulsions. I initially missed the significance of Dr King recording 'febrile fit' in the notes as I had mentally dismissed this as a possibility myself. When assessing a consultation try to avoid thinking through the clinical scenario from the point of view of how you would manage the case. Focus on discovering what happened.

How may the assessment above be recorded using the formal assessment tool? See Table 4.2 as an example.

It takes some time to explain the assessment process but one can see that in practice taking a formalised overview of a case and recording this does not take too long. It is important not to confuse the initial assessment of a case with a more in-depth analysis. There is much that we may want to explore about this case but the initial assessment is not the place to do this. The focus is primarily upon determining whether the case reaches the threshold to be declared serious.

Two further factors are considered at this stage. One is the risk assessment of the case and the second is the need for any immediate action.

Table 4.2 SIRT – Serious Incident Recognition Tool

Case ID: 12345
Age: 12 months
Sex: Female
Date of incident: 03/08/2015
Date of review: 05/08/2015

	Guidance	Comments
Outcome	Was the outcome both: severe? unexpected?	Yes – outcome = death Clearly not expected
Proximity	Did the incident occur within such a time frame within contact with service that the possibility of causation exists?	Yes – within 30 hours Did we miss a diagnosis that should have been made?
Intention	1. Are clinical actions different from those intended? 2. Is there any evidence of a deliberate intention to cause harm or to provide sub-optimal care?	No – Actions as intended No evidence of deliberate harm
Capacity/ Capability	3. Was the service at risk due to capacity issues at the time of the incident? 4. Was the staff member involved acting outside their capability?	None – based upon appointment time and time seen after arrival No – experienced GP Personal capacity issues not clarified at this stage
Foresight	Did any individual deviate from guidelines, protocols or standard safe practice?	Potentially yes – failure to refer following diagnosis of a febrile convulsion – acting outside national and local guidelines
Substitution	Were actions of staff outside expected norms for role?	No – scored within average range on standard audit
Risk assessment	Consequence = Likelihood = Risk = C × L =	(See below)
Immediate action	Is any immediate action indicated based upon: 1. risk assessment? 2. individual staff actions?	(See below)

RISK ASSESSMENT

Risk assessment is a key skill in both general governance and in particular in incident investigation. It is frequently poorly performed, mainly because of an all too human failing – our difficulty in understanding probability. A standard risk matrix is used in the NHS that categorises both outcome and likelihood or probability into five potential levels. Risk is an expression of outcome versus probability and hence a potential maximum risk score of 25 is possible.

Outcome is relatively easy to identify and potential outcomes are well described on the NHS risk tool.

Probability is more difficult. Make sure that you are specific with respect to the exact type of action you are determining the probability of. Further, the NHS tool has guidance for probability both in numbers and words. Try to think about probability in numbers rather than words because the words contain descriptors such as 'possible' that are so vague as to invite the unwary to choose them as safe middle options. In fact, 'possible' equates to a relatively high chance of occurrence and this can skew risk assessments. For most incidents the probability of recurrence score should be very low: one or two. If you find yourself scoring higher than this then you have either identified a very high risk within your service that needs immediate mitigation or, more likely, you have got the probability score wrong.

We know that our consequence score will be the maximum five as baby Anna died. We now need to consider the likelihood that this event will repeat itself. A potentially misleading factor is the ease with which it is possible for even an experienced clinician to miss a diagnosis of a condition such as meningitis, particularly when it presents in its very early stages. The tendency may be to adopt a logic that says that missing prodromal meningitis is common; you may recall or even look up data suggesting that as in as many as 50 per cent of cases of meningitis admitted to hospital there had been a previous

Table 4.3 Outcome or consequence

Level	Outcome
1	No harm
2	Mild harm
3	Moderate harm that is temporary – lasting less than 1–2 months
4	Severe harm that is temporary or Moderate harm that is permanent
5	Severe harm or death

Table 4.4 Probability or likelihood of risk recurrence

Level	NHS verbal descriptor	Comments	Probability score in numbers
1	Rare	Verbal descriptors are more likely to	1:1,500
2	Unlikely	lead to skewing the probability score	1:750
3	Possible	to a higher level than is realistic. Try to	1:500
4	Likely	convert probability into numbers, as	1:100
5	Certain	in the example below.	1:75

consultation in primary or emergency care in which the diagnosis had not been spotted. This may lead you to conclude that it is quite likely that another case will present in similar circumstances and have a fifty–fifty chance of being missed – which is quite high. It is certainly a 'possible' occurrence, perhaps even likely? After all, the probability of an event deemed 'likely' is 1 in 100 and we are considering a diagnosis that may be missed half of the time it presents. While it is true that there is a high risk of missing meningitis when it presents, this is not the risk we are assessing. The risk we must consider is actually twofold. Firstly, there must be a case of meningitis that presents and, secondly, it must be missed. Thankfully, meningitis is very rare. Many cases present very rapidly and aggressively and are recognised immediately and admitted either from a GP clinic or even via ambulance as alert parents summon emergency services directly. That leaves a segment of perhaps two-thirds of a very rare group of patients who may present – a very small number. Even if the risk of missing the diagnosis is relatively high, the fact that so few cases are likely to present means that the likelihood of the sequence of events that occurred in this case repeating itself is thankfully small. Think about the numbers. An average-sized county out-of-hours service will see in the region of 20,000 to 30,000 children in a given year. At least 10,000 are likely to have febrile illness. There may be as few as one or even no cases of meningitis presenting in a given year or there may be three or four. In other words, the likelihood is well under 1 in 1,500 and thus the probability or likelihood score will be 1. This gives an overall risk of five.

TOP TIP

Remember to try to convert likelihood assessments into measurable or estimable numbers and avoid verbal descriptors that can be misleading.

We had noted that it would be useful to talk to Dr King about any personal capacity issues that may have been affecting his judgement on the night in question. This point became moot in terms of the recognition assessment in this case as the foresight test was positive. It would still be prudent to call Dr King in any case just to let him know that baby Anna has died. Dr King is bound to be upset and may need some support and this issue is dealt with further in the section on openness and candour. However, there is another more pressing reason to contact Dr King. We have identified that Dr King failed to refer a child in whom he had diagnosed a febrile convulsion. This indicates that Dr King may have a significant gap in his clinical knowledge and, worse, that this gap may be putting patients at risk. It is important to clarify this point before Dr King sees any further patients. It is likely that Dr King is fully aware of the guidance for admitting children following a febrile convulsion and it is also likely that Dr King had a reason for not admitting Anna to the paediatrician on this occasion, but until this has been clarified a prudent approach would be to stand Dr King down from patient contact. The final part of the SIRT reads as per Table 4.5.

A formal approach to assessing and recording cases in order to recognise 'serious incidents' is valuable because it not only provides a formal starting point for a subsequent investigation but it may also provide an indication of how to determine the scope of the

Table 4.5

Risk assessment	Consequence = 5 Likelihood = 1 Risk = C × L = 5	Risk score = 5
Immediate action	Is any immediate action indicated based upon: 1. risk assessment? 2. individual staff actions?	No immediate action on basis of risk. Doctor who saw child stood down from clinical assessments pending further enquiry into actions in not referring case to paediatricians.

investigation or the terms of reference. A formal assessment of a potential serious incident is also useful in providing a record of deliberation when a decision not to declare a formal serious incident is taken. Consider Case study: Arnold. The details of the incident are as follows.

CASE STUDY: ARNOLD, 22 OCTOBER 2015

At 10:00 a.m. on a Friday morning Dr Khan sees 89-year-old Arnold at his surgery. Arnold has complained of a productive cough and shortness of breath following a brief episode of symptoms of sore throat and runny nose. Arnold has controlled hypertension, he is usually self-caring and independent and still driving his car locally to do shopping for himself.

Dr Khan diagnoses a lower respiratory tract infection and commences Arnold on antibiotics. At 8:00 p.m. on the same evening Arnold's daughter phones the NHS 111 telephone assessment service because she is worried about her father's breathing. The local GP out-of-hours service is contacted and a home visit is arranged. On arrival an ambulance crew is on site as Arnold had collapsed and sadly could not be resuscitated.

Dr Smith, Arnold's regular GP, discussed the case with the local coroner on Monday morning and it was agreed that a medical certificate of cause of death could be issued with the cause of death listed as bronchopneumonia.

On the following Tuesday the practice manager receives an angry call from the daughter of Arnold who is upset that her father had died. She wishes to lodge a complaint and states that her father would be alive if Dr Khan had admitted him to hospital.

Dr Khan is a locum doctor who qualified as a GP 12 months previously and who has worked in the practice previously on three occasions.

The senior partner in the practice, Dr Singh, completes a formal structured assessment of events to see if he can rapidly establish the significance of the case.

In this case evidence is available from the clinical notes on the practice IT system.

Practice IT record

Clinical record – time stamp 22/10/2015; 10:00 a.m. to 10:12 a.m.

'2/7 URTI sx, runny nose sore throat – now cough ++ with green phlegm. No chest pain. Mild soboe-on stairs. Feels hot. BM levels ok-10. Drinking ok, chest infection last year.

OE-T38.8, p98, bp144/84, HS I+II +0, Sats 96% on ari, rr 18, speaking sentences, orientated TPP, reduced AE RLL, dull to percussion.

Diagnosis RLL pneumonia.

Treatment – Amoxicillin 500 tds × 21

See sos if sig chest pain or sob. Call back next week if not settling.'

Table 4.6 SIRT – Serious Incident Recognition Tool

Case ID: Mr X		
Age: 89		
Sex: Male		
Date of incident: 22/10/15		
Date of review: 26/10/15		
	Guidance	**Comments**
Outcome	Was the outcome both: severe? unexpected?	Yes – outcome = death Yes – not a surprise but not expected at that time
Proximity	Did the incident occur within such a time frame within contact with service that the possibility of causation exists?	Yes – within approximately 36 hours
Intention	1. Are clinical actions different from those intended? 2. Is there any evidence of a deliberate intention to cause harm or to provide sub-optimal care?	No – actions as intended No intention to cause harm
Capacity/ Capability	3. Was the service at risk due to capacity issues at the time of the incident? 4. Was the staff member involved acting outside their capability?	None – routine workload None – fully qualified and experienced No known personal capacity issues

Dr Singh begins to complete the SIRT tool (Table 4.6).

Dr Singh has some difficulty with the foresight and substitution questions. Dr Singh felt that Dr Khan's assessment was thorough and that his notes were probably better than those that he would normally keep. Dr Singh was aware that his local out-of-hours service did clinical audits on work that he did when working for the service but he was not familiar with how to score the audits. Dr Singh decided that based upon the principles of sound practice Dr Khan had established a history that included relevant risk factors, had documented a thorough and relevant examination, had reached a diagnosis that seemed to fit with the evidence and had managed the case appropriately. Dr Khan had even documented safety-net advice. On this basis Dr Khan's actions were well within the norms expected of a GP.

This leaves Dr Singh considering the issue of foresight. It is well known that pneumonia, particularly in the elderly, is a potentially high-risk condition. Dr Singh feels that given the same findings as those documented by Dr Khan, he too would have managed Arnold in the same way and would not have admitted him to hospital. He cannot see any red flag signs or symptoms that Dr Khan had missed.

VALIDATION BY AFFIRMATION

One or more senior clinicians agreeing that the actions of a colleague are reasonable is essentially a process of validation by affirmation. Senior colleagues simply affirm that they would have done the same given these circumstances. Such affirmation has a long tradition in medicine and remains a cornerstone of assessment both in incident investigation and in medico-legal cases. The drawback of validation by affirmation is that there will always be cases where colleagues may disagree, particularly if hindsight bias creeps into the assessment. Validation by affirmation also raises the spectre of a profession protecting itself from external scrutiny.

OBJECTIVE VALIDATION – GUIDELINES AND PROTOCOLS

Whenever one considers the foresight test it is important to search both memory and other relevant data sources for policies, guidelines or protocols. A nationally validated and recognised guideline or policy is ideal. Local policies and protocols may also be relevant and very useful. In this case Dr Singh recalls that there is national guidance for the assessment and management of community-acquired pneumonia. A quick search on the Internet brings him to the National Institute for Health and Care Excellence (NICE) guidance CG191, published in December 2014 and guidance on the use of the CRB65 tool.

CRB65 score for mortality risk assessment in primary care

CRB65 score is calculated by giving one point for each of the following prognostic features:

- confusion
- raised respiratory rate (30 breaths per minute or more)

- low blood pressure (diastolic 60 mmHg or less, or systolic less than 90 mmHg)
- age 65 years or more.

Use clinical judgement in conjunction with the CRB65 score to inform decisions about whether patients need hospital assessment as follows:
- Consider home-based care for patients with a CRB65 score of zero.
- Consider hospital assessment for all other patients, particularly those with a CRB65 score of two or more.

Dr Singh is reassured that Dr Khan has acted in line with current national guidelines. Arnold scored one point for his age but was otherwise well within scoring thresholds of the CRB65 tool.

In completing the formal assessment tool (Table 4.7) Dr Singh has assured himself that the assessment of Dr Khan was reasonable and that despite the unexpected death of Arnold the outcome was almost certainly a sad reflection of the normal pathological process of pneumonia. Given that Dr Khan acted fully within his role remit and within national guidance for managing community-acquired pneumonia, an in-depth investigation is not likely to discover any significant learning nor any likely causation link between the assessment and management of Dr Khan and Arnold's subsequent death. Dr Singh may still choose to investigate the case but a full-scale RCA investigation is not likely to shed significant light on matters. In the event that Arnold's daughter is not satisfied with the response that Dr Singh makes to her complaint at a future date, Dr Singh will have a record of his consideration of the case and the reasons behind his decision not to launch any wider-scale investigation.

Further examples of use of the SIRT tool and the assessment of potential serious incidents can be found at www.PatientSafetyInvestigations.com

Table 4.7

Foresight	Did any individual deviate from guidelines, protocols or standard safe practice?	No – community treatment is in line with national guidance in NICE and CRB65 tool.
This is a balanced judgement – could the potential for a severe adverse outcome have been predicted because of failure to follow policy, guidelines, protocol or best practice? Must be based upon evidence available at the time of assessment.		
Substitution	Were actions of staff outside expected norms for role?	No – treatment consistent with best practice in primary care.
Excluding foresight considerations (see above), would any other member of staff working in the same capacity have been equally likely to have acted in the same way? Base judgement upon 'average' staff – not best and not worst.		
Answering yes to any question above should trigger an in-depth investigation and consideration of declaration of SI to Commissioners and NHS England.		

Once you have made a decision that a serious incident requiring investigation has occurred you should commence the process of a root cause analysis investigation. Before you do this, however, you need to consider how you will communicate with the patient or relatives involved and, indeed, with your own staff. In the next chapter we will briefly consider the issues of openness, candour and blame. Do we really aspire to have a 'blame-free' culture when it comes to incident investigation?

5

A culture of complaint: Openness, candour and blame

'To err is human – to cover up is unforgivable.'

Sir Liam Donaldson, former chief medical officer for the Department of Health (DH) speaking at the launch of the World Alliance for Patient Safety in Washington DC on 27 October 2004

Before embarking upon root cause analysis investigations it is helpful to understand the implications of Duty of Candour as well as to consider what we really mean when we talk about a blame-free culture with regard to the investigating and reporting of healthcare-related incidents.

- Any healthcare provider in England who is registered with the Care Quality Commission (CQC) is now subject to a statutory duty of candour.
- Most clinicians and service managers are aware of this fact but many struggle to understand what this actually means in practice.
- A serious incident investigation aims to identify learning and not to apportion blame.
- This last statement is not actually true.

DUTY OF CANDOUR

In every country you will find that healthcare regulators and professional governing bodies endorse, at least on paper, a notion of honesty and openness. If something goes wrong and a patient is harmed we (the healthcare provider) must acknowledge, apologise and fix any faults identified. In England the notion of acknowledgement has gone beyond the realm of professional guidance to become incorporated in legal statute. This has arisen primarily as a result of the Francis report into the events at the Mid Staffordshire NHS Foundation Trust and the subsequent report by Dalton and Williams with regard to the thresholds of harm that may be expected to trigger the duty of candour. The full details of the duty of candour are contained within regulation 20 of the Health and Social Care Act 2008 (Regulated Activities) Regulations 2014. I believe that it is worth noting the full details of regulation 20.

Regulation 20 of the Health and Social Care Act 2008 (Regulated Activities) Regulations 2014

20.—

- Registered persons must act in an open and transparent way with relevant persons in relation to care and treatment provided to service users in carrying on a regulated activity.
- As soon as reasonably practicable after becoming aware that a notifiable safety incident has occurred a registered person must –
  - notify the relevant person that the incident has occurred in accordance with paragraph (3), and
  - provide reasonable support to the relevant person in relation to the incident, including when giving such notification.
- The notification to be given under paragraph (2)(a) must –
  - be given in person by one or more representatives of the registered person,
  - provide an account, which to the best of the registered person's knowledge is true, of all the facts the registered person knows about the incident as at the date of the notification,
  - advise the relevant person what further enquiries into the incident the registered person believes are appropriate,
  - include an apology, and
  - be recorded in a written record which is kept securely by the registered person.
- The notification given under paragraph (2)(a) must be followed by a written notification given or sent to the relevant person containing –
  - the information provided under paragraph (3)(b),
  - details of any enquiries to be undertaken in accordance with paragraph (3)(c),
  - the results of any further enquiries into the incident, and an apology.
- But if the relevant person cannot be contacted in person or declines to speak to the representative of the registered person –
  - paragraphs (2) to (4) are not to apply, and
  - a written record is to be kept of attempts to contact or to speak to the relevant person.
- The registered provider must keep a copy of all correspondence with the relevant person under paragraph (4).
- In this regulation –
  - 'apology' means an expression of sorrow or regret in respect of a notifiable safety incident; 'moderate harm' means –
    - harm that requires a moderate increase in treatment, and significant, but not permanent, harm;
  - 'moderate increase in treatment' means an unplanned return to surgery, an unplanned re-admission, a prolonged episode of care, extra time in hospital or as an outpatient, cancelling of treatment, or transfer to another treatment area (such as intensive care);

'notifiable safety incident' has the meaning given in paragraphs (8) and (9);

'prolonged pain' means pain which a service user has experienced, or is likely to experience, for a continuous period of at least 28 days;

'prolonged psychological harm' means psychological harm which a service user has experienced, or is likely to experience, for a continuous period of at least 28 days;

'relevant person' means the service user or, in the following circumstances, a person lawfully acting on their behalf –

a   on the death of the service user,

b   where the service user is under 16 and not competent to make a decision in relation to their care or treatment, or

c   where the service user is 16 or over and lacks capacity in relation to the matter;

'severe harm' means a permanent lessening of bodily, sensory, motor, physiologic or intellectual functions, including removal of the wrong limb or organ or brain damage, that is related directly to the incident and not related to the natural course of the service user's illness or underlying condition.

- In relation to a health service body, 'notifiable safety incident' means any unintended or unexpected incident that occurred in respect of a service user during the provision of a regulated activity that, in the reasonable opinion of a health care professional, could result in, or appears to have resulted in –

    the death of the service user, where the death relates directly to the incident rather than to the natural course of the service user's illness or underlying condition, or

    severe harm, moderate harm or prolonged psychological harm to the service user.

- In relation to any other registered person, 'notifiable safety incident' means any unintended or unexpected incident that occurred in respect of a service user during the provision of a regulated activity that, in the reasonable opinion of a health care professional –

    appears to have resulted in –

    I.   the death of the service user, where the death relates directly to the incident rather than to the natural course of the service user's illness or underlying condition,

    II.   an impairment of the sensory, motor or intellectual functions of the service user which has lasted, or is likely to last, for a continuous period of at least 28 days,

    III. changes to the structure of the service user's body,

    IV.   the service user experiencing prolonged pain or prolonged psychological harm, or

    V.   the shortening of the life expectancy of the service user; or requires treatment by a health care professional in order to prevent –

        i.   the death of the service user, or

        ii.   any injury to the service user which, if left untreated, would lead to one or more of the outcomes mentioned in sub-paragraph (a).

This is quite a daunting set of regulations. From my perspective, the key details are contained within items one and two.

One: We must be open and transparent.

Two: Our duty of candour arises when a 'notifiable' safety incident has occurred.

Sections eight and nine do provide some clarification as to the thresholds of incident for which candour may apply and part of the anxiety and confusion arising from the statutory duty is the inclusion of moderate harm within regulation 8. Traditionally, incidents that resulted in moderate harm would not have triggered notification. When this new regulation is read in conjunction with the revised NHS England guidance on the recognition of serious incidents, one can see that the intention is to replace the emphasis upon the severity of the incident as being the key arbiter in terms of recognising when a notifiable serious incident has occurred. Much less severe incidents may be regarded as notifiable if harm is sustained or permanent. It is for this reason that I place so much emphasis on the need to formalise our process for recognition of incidents and in particular on being able to identify the issue of potential causation. In my opinion at least, we need to be able not only to recognise when a serious incident has occurred but also to be open and transparent with regard to how we reached this conclusion.

REMEMBER

A patient-safety incident arises where an act or omission on the part of the service provider causes harm to the patient.

An incident has not occurred if the harm, the unexpected adverse outcome, is the result of the natural pathological process from which the patient is suffering.

This means that you cannot know if a duty of candour exists until you have determined the issue of causality. (Unless the incident is a never event – in which case causality may be evident from the outset.)

So the full remit of candour – the acknowledgement, apology and remedy – will not be applicable until an incident investigation is complete or at least at a stage where the issue of causality is fully clarified. Ahead of this one should notify the patient or their representative that an incident has been recognised and is being investigated. It is quite right and reasonable to express sympathy and offer an apology when a patient has suffered an adverse outcome during or following contact with your service, without any acknowledgement that this has been caused by the service.

The regulations stipulate that contacting patients must occur following a notifiable incident. Contact with patients may be limited to those for whom notification to regulators has occurred but this does risk appearing to be less than open. I would suggest extending open contact with patients or relatives both when a notifiable serious incident has occurred and also when you identify an incident for which an in-depth investigation is launched (RCA or enhanced significant event analysis), even if notification to regulators has not been made. The small amount of extra work that this may entail will be more than compensated for by the integrity of the action. Dealing with the aggravated issues caused by a patient or relative belatedly discovering that an incident was investigated without their knowledge can be a very challenging and draining experience for which there is very little in the way of mitigating defence.

Guidance on patient contact is provided in Chapter 6.

NO-BLAME CULTURE

The repeated mantra of clinical governance is that serious incident investigation using RCA is all about learning and not about blame. Anyone who has been to a coroner's inquest and been subject to questioning by the coroner or by solicitors and barristers regarding an unexpected patient death may be forgiven for thinking that our learned colleagues have failed to get the message. When one considers the imperative to be open and honest, however, and particularly when one acknowledges the statutory duty of candour, you realise that it is actually clinical governance that has it wrong. *Incident investigation is all about blame.*

In subsequent chapters I will revert to message but I feel an indulgence is warranted at this point to try to clarify something that has certainly caused me a lot of frustration over the past ten years. Let me repeat, we have the opposite of a no-blame culture – our current governance culture is all about blame. And quite rightly so. It is just a pity that we do not own up to this so that we can be better prepared to deal with the consequences.

The Oxford online dictionary defines blame thus:

BLAME

Feel or declare that someone or something is responsible for a fault or wrong.

Assign the responsibility for a bad or unfortunate situation or phenomenon to (someone or something). ('Blame', http://www.oxforddictionaries.com/definition/english/blame, accessed 1 August 2016.)

The prime meaning of the word 'blame' is to hold someone or something responsible for the consequences of their actions. This is actually exactly the intention of the statutory duty of candour. This is exactly the intention of a root cause analysis. Both are about identifying and accepting responsibility for actions. And so they should be. Blame is not actually a bad thing. We must, as professionals, be able to accept responsibility for our actions, even if they are the result of accidental or unintended errors.

What we really mean when we talk about a no-blame culture with regard to incident investigation is a no-censure culture. We mean that we will not harshly judge or criticise someone for actions that are largely beyond their control – assuming that the harm arose because of unavoidable human or systemic error. Even this of course has its limitations. While an RCA investigation would not be expected to explore issues of clinically negligent behaviour, it would nonetheless be expected that any such behaviour would be identified and referred to the appropriate channels for investigation.

So, while I will continue to advocate for a 'no-blame' culture with regard to RCA investigations, I think it is important that we remain aware that 'no blame' does not mean no responsibility. We may aim not to criticise and judge our colleagues harshly for acts or omissions that any one of us may make in the same circumstances. But we certainly must be prepared to identify responsibility for what has gone wrong.

MANAGING YOUR RESPONSIBILITIES

Before you make contact or before you engage in discussions about incidents, ensure that you are very clear about the level of responsibility that exists for the incident.

Make sure that all involved agree about the nature and extent of any disclosure. Consider getting legal advice about the nature of wording used when acknowledging responsibility for harm. Where the level of responsibility is not determined or, where partial responsibility may exist, honesty is the best policy. Advise that the incident is being investigated or advise that the investigation has indicated that acts or omissions within the service appear to be, or may be, responsible for at least some of the harm suffered.

LITIGATION – THE ELEPHANT IN THE ROOM

Behind all of the fine words about openness and candour lies an anxiety on the part of both individuals and organisations that patients or their representatives will want to take legal action. They will want to seek compensation or pursue litigation for alleged negligence. There is considerable evidence that openness and candour does not increase the likelihood of litigation – people will either be minded to go to a lawyer (or be persuaded to do so) or they will not. It is a waste of time and energy to worry about such an eventuality. The issue of compensation and potential claims for negligence are specialist issues – as soon as they are raised they should be referred to legal advisers. The onus on clinicians and clinical governance teams is not to muddy the waters by straying beyond our areas of expertise and commenting upon such matters. There are some tips to keeping the divide between legal issues and our duty of candour.

TOP TIPS

In general, unless the issue of causality is absolutely clear, it is helpful to separate any failings in the service from the harm suffered.

- I am very sorry for the failings in our service.
- I am very sorry that you have suffered harm.

Avoid expressions such as 'I am very sorry that failings in our service led to you suffering harm', or 'I am very sorry that we did X and that you suffered harm'. These sentences imply that a causal link is being acknowledged between the act and the outcome.

Separation of what the service did wrong from the harm suffered will offer some protection to both clinicians involved and the service from any erroneous implication that actions caused harm. Candour works both ways – being honest doesn't mean acknowledging or apologising for things that you have not done. Having open, honest and adult conversations with both staff and patients or their representatives will pay dividends in the long run.

APOLOGY AND REMEDY

If errors have occurred, then there is a duty both to apologise and offer some sort of remedy. Apology is a sensitive issue so try to avoid formulaic responses. Saying that you are sorry that someone felt that they needed to complain is not really adequate. Try to see the issue from the point of view of the patient or relative, as and this may help you to make the apology both sincere and more personal. Try to identify details relevant to this particular incident to include within the apology to demonstrate that you understand the impact of the event on the patient.

Remedy is about being able to demonstrate that you have learned something from the event. Your learning and recommendations (see Chapters 13 and 14) should form the basis of your remedy in terms of demonstrating learning and how you acted upon it. In addition, however, you need to consider whether the patient may need further clinical treatment or care. This is another area where a sensible and compassionate mature conversation needs to be had. How is the patient now? How are the relatives? Are they receiving ongoing treatment? Do they need further treatment?

If a patient or relative needs ongoing treatment it is part of the duty of candour to provide reasonable assistance to achieve this. This does not mean that you or your service have to offer to pay for private treatments or provide care yourself if it is not within your area of expertise. What you may need to do is to contact the GP of the patient or, if you are their GP, to refer onward for further care.

RESOLVING CONFLICTS

Despite your best efforts, emotions may run high following certain incidents. Offers of remedy, particularly your learning and recommendations, may be seen as not doing enough by a patient or their representative. You will not be able to please everyone.

For less significant cases (near miss, say) where there are areas of relatively minor conflict that still cause vexation to a patient or their representative, consider offering a small donation in their name to a charity of their preference in acknowledgement of distress caused. This may be a compassionate method to enable someone to feel that their distress has been recognised and to accept what has happened and move on – a face-saving gesture of sorts.

Where a significant conflict exists you have available a number of strategies:

- Buy some time for reflection. Agree that at this stage you are not seeing eye to eye about the issues. Suggest that you both reflect further upon the issues raised and agree to meet again to discuss further in a week or a month. Time does help in calming raw emotions but it also does give opportunity for reflection and this works on both sides. You may find that your own point of view shifts. Ask someone in your organisation to take the side of the patient and view your actions and responses from their point of view. Do they feel that your actions are reasonable?
- Always ask the patient or their representative what they feel needs to be done to resolve the conflict. Do not assume you know what they want – they may have changed their viewpoint since earlier discussions.
- Seek an independent view. This may be combined with buying additional time. Local patient advocacy services may be helpful although, as the name implies, they are not necessarily independent. Other sources of support may include the local clinical commissioning group. Think about asking the patient-safety lead for the Clinical Commissioning Group (CCG) to assist in negotiations with the patient and in a sense checking your position.
- Follow your complaint-resolution process. This may include the offer of a meeting with a more senior member of your team.
- Provide details of how to contact the health ombudsman.

TOP TIP

Before allowing a case to be escalated outside your organisation, review how you have handled the case to ensure that all relevant regulations, including duty of candour, and policy guidance have been adhered to – particularly your own incident and complaint policy. The ombudsman will look closely at this if they take on the case.

6

Root cause analysis: What happened? The evidence

Root cause analysis is a simple process that can be difficult to execute. Each phase of the process has pitfalls for the unwary. Certain phases can go critically wrong and result in reports that are completely off the mark. Getting a report wrong may waste time and money but more importantly it may cause significant distress to clinical staff who may be wrongly implicated as having been the cause of an adverse event and it may cause unnecessary anguish to a patient or relative who is presented with misleading information. On top of this, opportunities for improving patient safety are wasted.

There are five basic phases to the RCA process:

1. What – identify what events happened – acts and omissions
2. How – identify how events happened – contributory factors
3. Why – identify the critical event – the root cause
4. Learning – what did we learn?
5. Recommendations – what needs to change?

This chapter is concerned with the first phase – understanding what happened.

STICK TO THE PROCESS

The strong temptation at the outset of an investigation will be to jump straight from an adverse outcome and a review of the clinical notes to identifying contributory factors or even a root cause – usually based upon one's own prejudices or experiences or personal hot topics of the month. Following the full RCA process will protect you from making significant errors.

TOP TIP

RCA is a process – stick to the process.

If you have used the SI Recognition Tool or have had a structured meeting to review initial evidence and formally recognise that a serious incident has occurred, then the scope of the investigation should have already been addressed. Hopefully you were part of that meeting but if not it is important from the outset that you understand the remit of your investigation. There are some important terms that you need to be aware of.

TERMS OF REFERENCE

Terms of Reference (ToR) is the definition of the task to be undertaken and the responsibilities of those involved. In a sense the ToR of an RCA is defined within the process itself and a formal ToR is not always included in a report for this reason. The ToR is to conduct an RCA investigation that will necessarily involve identifying what happened, how and why and what can be learned. It is important to remember certain negatives with regards to terms of reference – that is, you need to clearly understand what an RCA does *not* assess or consider.

CAUSE OF DEATH

It may seem paradoxical that identifying the cause of death is not an objective of an RCA investigation, given that we are often trying to understand if there is a causal link between what happened in a service and the death of a patient. In many cases, however, the cause of death is not clear and this may make identification of a root cause within an RCA very difficult. Investigators may spend much time trying to investigate or speculate about a cause of death in order to tie things together to complete a report but one must remember that responsibility to determine the cause of death of a patient lies with the coroner and not with the RCA investigation. Where a cause of death is not known it may not be possible to identify a root cause and this may be part of a narrative explanation of the case.

STAFF CONDUCT

At any time within an investigation the conduct of staff may raise concerns. Staff may have displayed improper conduct that reaches the threshold of disciplinary action or even referral to professional regulatory bodies. If such concerns arise then the investigator does not need to investigate this matter and should refer the issue to the relevant service leads and/or human resources department. Any investigation of misconduct takes place as a separate process to the RCA. Reference may be made to indicate that action of this nature has been taken but the outcome of this separate investigation is not part of the RCA report.

CLINICAL NEGLIGENCE

Once again, an investigator may identify care that falls so far below expected standards that they believe it may amount to clinical negligence. It is not appropriate to investigate or comment upon this matter within an RCA report other than to note that concerns exist and that actions have been taken to refer the matter to appropriate authorities. RCA investigations need to tread a fine line with respect to medico-legal issues but understanding ToR and following process and good reporting guidance will keep things on track.

TOP TIP

Understanding what is outside the remit of an RCA can save time and frustration.

Scope

The scope of the investigation defines which part of the 'patient journey' is the subject of the investigation. Generally, this will be limited to all contacts within the service in which you work but, as indicated previously, a multi-agency investigation may have a much wider scope. Sometimes an RCA may involve cooperation between two or more providers but in practice this may prove very challenging. If you are concerned about the scope of your investigation discuss this from the outset with your commissioner and the internal officer authorising the investigation. Remember that you may revisit the scope or indeed any aspect of an investigation at any time if new evidence comes to light.

A generic ToR and scoping statement may look like this:

- To investigate the circumstances of the contact between patient X and the Y practice/service
- To investigate using the principles of root cause analysis with the aim of identifying care delivery problems (CDPs) and contributory factors
- To establish any actions that can reduce or eliminate the risk of reoccurrence of any errors identified
- To formulate recommendations and an action plan from any items identified in the above terms
- To provide a report as a formal record of the investigation
- To provide a means of sharing the learning from the incident

Choosing an investigation team

An investigation team may be as small as one person or as big as your organisation can afford.

A solo investigation may be appropriate for certain cases and it may also be appropriate for small organisations with limited resources. If a solo investigator is used, then it is important that the investigator is very experienced and aware of the dangers of investigator bias. In RCA the old adage that two heads are better than one is generally true. If a solo investigator is utilised, then it is good practice for the investigator to meet with the person who is authorising the investigation to give regular feed back on progress so that a 'second head' can sense-check what is going on.

An ideal small team would be a team of three with two investigators and one person who may provide administrative support. At least one of the investigators should have had formal training in RCA techniques and, ideally, all investigations should involve at least one person who has received enhanced training or mentoring with regard to RCA investigation.

Teams need a lead investigator who can direct the investigation to ensure that process is followed and to mentor and support colleagues in the techniques of information gathering and analysis.

What happened? First steps – gathering evidence

There are three types of evidence available to investigators, each having advantages and disadvantages.

PRIMARY EVIDENCE

This includes:

- voice recordings
- contemporaneous clinical notes
- other evidence contemporaneous with incident: photographs, emails, instant messages and data from external sources recorded at the time of incident.

GP out-of-hours services, NHS 111 services and ambulance trusts record all phone contacts with patients. This data is invaluable in an incident but be aware that it can also be distressing to listen to, particularly for relatives of a patient who has died. A written transcript is essential but this may not reflect the empathy of a clinician or conversely may not reflect rudeness or a curt tone on either side. Where this appears significant, it is essential to highlight contextual issues within the report to ensure that the evidence is seen for its true value and does not distort an investigation or a report. (An appropriate analysis may be undermined by an unqualified transcript that may 'read' very differently from hearing the real recording.) Sharing voice recordings with family or relatives needs sensitivity and preparation. If you know that a clinician appears rude, or that an assessment is 'less than ideal', do give some degree of warning to this effect. Any apparent rudeness on the part of the caller needs to be addressed with empathy and compassion. They may well have been very distressed at the time of the call and this may be acknowledged ahead of listening to the call to indicate that you understand that any rudeness on a call may not have been intended or typical for the caller.

Primary evidence may exist outside your organisational records. While full cooperation may not always be possible in an RCA, it is often useful and feasible to seek clinical notes from an ambulance service, hospital or GP clinic if a patient was seen within a very short time frame of the incident in question. It may take some time to obtain this data so early identification of its value is important.

While we do not typically go to the trouble of seeking closed-circuit television (CCTV) footage to obtain objective evidence, it is worth thinking laterally in some cases. Do not forget to ask relatives if they took any photographs at the time of illness. Smartphones have made this practice very common, particularly when a patient has a rash.

Caution needs to be exercised if a patient claims to have a video or voice recording of a consultation. Apart from the potential for such information to breach information governance regulations there is also a problem with establishing the integrity of recordings – that is to say, you would not be certain that recordings have not been tampered with or edited in some way. You may decline to view such evidence at all or may agree to review evidence but make it clear that you may opt not to include such evidence in your report. You may need to seek legal advice regarding this type of evidence.

SECONDARY EVIDENCE – STAFF, PATIENT AND WITNESS STATEMENTS

Secondary evidence comes from those involved in the incident but obviously after the fact. This may come in various formats. The value of secondary evidence is that it is direct evidence from those involved. The two major disadvantages of secondary evidence are related to its reliability and its veracity.

Reliability: Secondary evidence may be unreliable because of failings in the recall of those involved. Considerable evidence is available that attests to the various factors that may bias recollections of events. Factors such as the time lag between event and recall, the emotional state at the time of the event, confusion of events occurring during the incident with events just before or just after and the impact of the event upon the individual concerned are all factors known to affect the reliability of recall. These factors are all functioning at an unconscious level and are beyond the control of those involved. Interview and debriefing techniques may help improve the reliability of recall as described below. The technique of triangulation is also essential in validating any secondary evidence as described below.

Veracity: Anyone involved in a serious incident may have reason to consciously manipulate information provided in a statement or interview. Reasons for conscious manipulation of information include a desire on the part of a patient or their representative to prove negligence or greater harm in order to help them secure compensation. Conscious manipulation may also occur on the part of clinical staff because of a desire to avoid what they may believe is evidence of poor standards of care, or simply anger at having their professional reputation questioned.

How often conscious manipulation of evidence or recall of events occurs is difficult to say and it is likely to vary greatly depending upon the clinical environment and any pre-existing relationship that exists between the patient and the clinician. It is important to be aware of the potential for this phenomenon to occur and, as described below, to always seek to triangulate evidence wherever possible.

TOP TIP

Where possible, triangulate – obtain a second source or fact-check key evidence. If this is not possible then 'sense-check' evidence – does what is being said to have happened make sense?

PATIENT/REPRESENTATIVE EVIDENCE

A patient or their representative may make a verbal or written complaint about service received and in this instance the complaint becomes secondary evidence. Where no such complaint arises it will be necessary to contact the patient or their representative to seek further information. If a patient has died this may mean contacting their next of kin. Apart from the issue of needing to do this sensitively, it is also vital that you ensure that you are liaising with the true representative or 'next of kin' of the patient. The best way to achieve this is to ask them about their relationship and whether there are any other relatives who may share next-of-kin status and to document that you have done so and the response, in your notes. This initial contact forms part of your professional duty of openness.

STAFF INTERVIEWS AND STATEMENTS

Staff involved in incidents are usually requested to provide a statement of their recollection of events that they both date and sign. While this may be of some value, I would suggest that it is preferable to interview staff and take notes. This has the advantage that you can be more specific about areas that you would like to clarify and it also ensures that all relevant information is obtained. A second or even third interview may be needed if further information comes to hand or clarification is needed.

A staff interview also provides an opportunity to assess the reaction of staff involved in an incident and to ensure that they are aware of avenues to get support should they need it. Colleagues may be very anxious or upset following an incident and compassion and empathy are required at all times. If a member of staff needs support to deal with the emotional impact of an incident or if they are anxious about the consequences in terms of their job or professional registration, it is important that these concerns are noted but are directed away from the investigation team. This is difficult when the investigator is also a service lead and in some circumstances, for example in a small GP practice, it may be necessary for an investigator to attempt to 'wear two hats', as both investigator and service lead. In general, however, try to identify a colleague who may be able to support staff. This may involve asking a colleague in a neighbouring practice or service to act as a support in a quid pro quo arrangement with you offering to do the same if the situation were reversed. See the communication section below for examples of initial letters to staff.

WITNESSES

Witnesses are third parties who were not involved in the incident per se but were present at the time and may have seen or heard what happened. Witnesses can be helpful in confirming or challenging information provided by the main protagonists or in adding context to an incident. Keep witness statements in mind and think laterally as they can be a valuable resource and you may not always think of them. For example, if a strong element of patient concern was that the doctor whom they saw on a Monday evening was rude and rushing to get through the consultation, you may consider contacting patients who the same doctor saw before and after the event and asking them to complete a patient-satisfaction survey form. You may then follow this up with more specific questions about the demeanour of the doctor.

KEEPING RECORDS

When interviewing it is important to keep records. There are various ways to do this depending upon the perceived seriousness of the case and the resources available to you. At one extreme an interview may be recorded and a transcript produced that is sent to the interviewee afterward and signed and returned as a true record of the interview. This is a bit extreme, however, for most incidents and may even be counterproductive in giving the impression to the interviewee that they have entered into some sort of formal legal process, engendering unnecessary anxiety. It is generally acceptable to take notes during the interview and to maintain these and refer to them in the report. Notes may be taken by a third party to free up the interviewer. Where a case may be sensitive or if resources allow, a non-interviewing investigator should sit in on the interview and make observations of key issues or discrepancies in the account. This can be very helpful when evaluating information later. Apart from conducting a structured interview to determine what happened during an incident, it is also important to ask the patient or their representative if they have any specific questions or issues that they would like to ask you to address in the investigation. Any issues raised should be acknowledged and addressed in the final report. They constitute evidence that the investigation is open and responsive.

While a face-to-face interview is ideal this is not always practical and a telephone or video/phone call is an acceptable way to conduct interviews.

If you are recording an interview then it is important that you remember to disclose this fact to the interviewee at the outset – including those who work for a service that routinely records calls, such as out-of-hours services, ambulance trusts and NHS 111. Interviewees may ask for a transcript of the call afterwards.

When considering how you obtain and record information, it is important to remember the context of your investigation. Your aim is to identify significant learning in order to improve patient safety. You are not performing a staff performance interview nor are you performing a medico-legal investigation. Formal written statements and in particular transcripts of recorded interviews, when reviewed at later times or in different contexts (a conduct interview or medico-legal proceeding) can be damaging for your clinical colleagues. I personally feel that an investigator has a professional obligation to colleagues to help them to explore and reflect upon incidents in a compassionate and positive manner and for this reason I have increasingly felt that recordings of interviews may place colleagues at a disadvantage. Ill-chosen or offhand comments seen in a transcript may be difficult to defend when viewed later in a different context. On the other hand, taking notes during a debriefing or interview allows the investigator to record responses that are appropriate and filter comments or asides that do not help the investigation. Ambiguous comments may be clarified to ensure that meanings are apparent. The caveat is that should an investigator become concerned about the attitude or comments expressed during an interview then they may raise these via the appropriate line management or human resource channel.

COMMUNICATIONS – LETTERS AND INTERVIEWS

CONTACTING PATIENTS OR REPRESENTATIVES

Remember that at this stage the full extent of duty of candour may not be apparent but we would still wish to contact the patient or their representative. We may not yet have established whether anything has actually gone wrong and, even if we are already aware of some failings, we would certainly not know if any of the things that went wrong actually caused the patient to suffer harm. A basic structure for a phone or written contact may look like Table 6.1.

Table 6.1 Template letter or phone contact to a patient or relative advising them of a RCA investigation and inviting their participation

Comments	Specimen
Introduce yourself – give your name and role	Dear Mrs Smith, My name is X. I am a senior doctor [your role title] in the county out-of-hours GP service.
You can express sorrow and condolences over the outcome. Do not link the outcome to events within your service – you have no evidence to do this yet.	I am aware that you contacted our service regarding your daughter Anna on the evening of Monday, 6 August. Dr Pink from County Hospital has contacted me to tell me that Anna tragically died in the early hours of Wednesday morning at County Hospital. I am so sorry that Anna has died – please accept my sincere condolences.
Say that you are investigating events within your service line as a matter of routine in response to an unexpected event. The combination of 'formal' and 'routine' is deliberate in this context. A formal investigation is reassuring for the patient or representative – it indicates that you are taking the event seriously. The fact that a formal investigation is routine for your organisation should also be mentioned as it reassures both patient and commissioners that your service is well governed and recognises its obligations to improving patient safety. Let them know what the letter is about – you are aware of the incident. You may let them know how you became aware of the outcome. It is also reassuring to indicate that you will be following a standard investigation protocol.	I wanted to let you know that as part of our routine internal response to an unexpected event such as this, we are launching a formal investigation into the management of Anna within our service and I will be leading this investigation. We will be following a standard NHS protocol for such investigations, which is called a root cause analysis.
Let the person know that you will both ask questions and listen to concerns.	It would helpful to me if I could ask you some questions about your recollection of events on the night and I would also like to take note of any concerns that you may have regarding your visit to our service.
Provide a named contact point and a means of contact.	Our patient services manager, John Jones, will act as a contact point and John is available on [phone and/or email address].

Comments	Specimen
Try to keep the initial contact letter brief. You may advise the patient or representative that they may have support at a meeting and discuss where a meeting may occur or alternatives to a meeting such as phone contacts or liaison via a third party but this could be saved for a follow-up contact as you would not wish to overwhelm on first contact.	Once again, please accept my sincere sympathy, Yours

CONTACTING STAFF

While a complaint letter may engender a certain dread in all clinicians, the notification that you have been involved in a serious clinical incident can also be very distressing and communication of this fact needs to be managed sensitively. Staff directly involved should be contacted as soon as possible by phone or email. Contact should be both supportive and informative.

Dear

You may recall seeing a baby Anna whilst on duty for the Out of Hours service on Monday, 6th August. I am sorry to advise you that baby Anna died some 24 hours following this consultation and as a result of this unexpected adverse outcome we have decided to launch a formal serious incident investigation. This is a routine procedure in such circumstances with the aim of identifying what exactly happened and whether there is any learning which may arise as a result of the investigation.

I am aware that you may be both shocked and upset at this unexpected outcome. I have asked Dr Anwar Ali to be available to offer support to you if you feel you need it. Anwar will contact you in any case.

I will be leading a Root Cause Analysis investigation which is a routine procedure following significant unexpected adverse outcomes such as this. I will need to speak to you to conduct a debriefing interview and I may also need to speak to you a further time to try and get more information. I will be liaising with the family in this case and they may raise specific issues which I would need to discuss with you.

The purpose of the investigation is to fully understand what happened with a view to identifying any learning that may arise.

As a matter of routine best practice I would advise that it would be prudent for you to take notes of your recollection of events and any reflections you might make about the case and also to inform your indemnity provider of this event.

Yours truly,

INTERVIEWING

Interviews generally take two forms, a debriefing interview and a 'cognitive' interview. Debriefings are conducted early and the primary aim of a debriefing is to find out what happened. Debriefings require minimal preparation in terms of structuring questions but be aware that they are done when emotions may be raw and one may need to give time to allow staff or patients to vent emotions during the interview.

Cognitive interviews require more thought and preparation. The aim is to move beyond simple questions of what happened and to try to also establish how events transpired as they did.

DEBRIEFING INTERVIEWS – WHAT HAPPENED AND WHEN?

- Keep interview focused upon what happened.
- Do not venture into how or why – you may come back to this.
- Focus upon establishing a timeline of events.
- The three words you need are 'what', 'where' and 'when'.
- Make a note of discrepancies or issues you may wish to come back to but try to avoid delving into other questions until you have established what, where and when.
- Construct an initial timeline (see below) from any clinical notes that are available and fill in any blanks from there.
- Details matter in some cases – explore timelines in detail.

COGNITIVE INTERVIEWS

Cognitive interviews are a technique employed to explore an event in more depth in order to understand how certain events came about. The technique is very useful in the exploration of potential contributory factors. There is obvious overlap between debriefing and cognitive interviews – you may move from debriefing into a cognitive interview within the same session and you may repeat cognitive interviews as needed as more information comes to light.

Cognitive interviews recognise that recall of events is not a faultless linear process. Not everyone will recall information in the same way. Cognitive interviews involve using multiple gentle approaches to questioning to elicit recall including asking people to remember feelings, emotions and sensations as well as events. Recalling weather, lighting, sound and so on can all help to prompt memory recall. Do not expect a linear narrative; take notes and be prepared to wander around events a few times to try to ensure that all relevant information is retrieved. Encourage people to reflect and contact you if they think of anything else.

Let us review primary evidence available for baby Anna and some secondary evidence.

PRIMARY EVIDENCE

NHS 111 notes

The patient's reported condition states:

'12 month jab 4 days ago unwell-shaking 1 day'

During the Pathway assessment, the 111 health adviser documented the following user comments:

'Shivering-whole body unwell few days had 12 month jab 4 days ago'

'Sleeping more than usual'

'Cold symptoms – last week'

CLINICAL NOTES FROM ONLINE CLINICIAN SECTION OF ADASTRA

The clinical notes read as follows: (NB: Notes are copied verbatim from record and include typos and spelling mistakes.)

HISTORY

had 12 month jabs 4 day sago, has been well, slightly unwell yesterday, today ahs been usual self til this evening when she felt very hot, nappy changed, was wet and dirty, then she vomited ×1 and has the shakes for a bout 1 min, then ok again. mum concerned she is very unwell, has older son and is pegnant, given ibuprofen at 20.00, is now tired.

EXAMINATION

temp 38.7, HR 170, resp rate high at about 40, chest clear, no recessions or nasal flares,

DIAGNOSIS

febrile fit and viral illness

MANAGEMENT

given paracetamol 5mls at 21.20, monitor temp at 22.00. encourage fluids, if temp falling then can go home, 1 hour later, pt sleeping colur better, temp down to 38.3, parebts reassured, hom eregular paracetamol and fluids, to call again if concerned

FINAL DIAGNOSTIC CODE

Viral infection NOS

PRESCRIPTION

Paracetamol suspension 120mg in 5 mls, 500mls, 5mls 4 × day as required.

[NB: Dr King would also have had access to NHS 111 notes.]

Following a review of the notes, an interview was undertaken with both Baby Anna's parents and Dr King. Notes containing the key points from these interviews are provided below. This constitutes secondary evidence.

SECONDARY EVIDENCE

NOTES FROM INTERVIEW WITH PARENTS

Parents advised they took Anna to see the doctor because she had a temperature and had had a seizure and was sick. She was not responsive that night and her feet were very cold and she was limp. She was not eating or taking fluids and they knew that she was very sick.

The doctor just checked her temperature and put something on her finger and then said she had a virus.

We asked if the doctor was sure that she did not have meningitis and the doctor said no. We asked if he was 100% sure it was not meningitis and the doctor said he was 110% sure it was not meningitis. The doctor gave three options

Attend hospital where they would just give Paracetamol

To A+E where they would give Paracetamol

Stay in OOH clinic and have Paracetamol and see if temperature came down – parents preferred to stay in OOH

Parents waited for just over an hour and doctor took temperature again. It had gone down by 0.4 degrees and the doctor said he was happy with that and to go home

Doctor also said it was hard to see how responsive Anna was because it was her bed time

They intend to take matters further

They do not understand how meningitis was missed

They do not understand how doctors can work in their roles and get a diagnosis of meningitis wrong

NOTES FROM INTERVIEW WITH DR KING

Remembers case well – was not rushed at time and saw child quickly

Well in self at time – busy at work but no more than usual

Remembers mum and dad being very anxious

Was in two minds about whether child had had convulsion – did say it might have been a febrile convulsion initially but on review felt this was not certain.

Thought about paediatric referral but no in house paediatricians where he was working and it would be an 8 mile drive to local hospital where paediatrics was located and thought Anna may well be just sent home after a review there anyway.

Recalls seeing baby feeding ok in WR whilst it was waiting for review.

Acknowledges did not record all observations made but confirms had noted absence of rash and meningism and Cap refill. Also had noted respiratory rate when child reviewed and believes this was back to normal.

Felt that parents were not keen to go to paediatricians and were looking for reassurance.

Did not recall offering them three options – he recalled offering a paediatric referral or the option of Paracetamol and then a review later within OOH clinic.

Told them to see own GP next day for review.

When asked Dr King said he had no recall of being asked if the child had meningitis. He said he would never use a phrase such as 'I am 110% certain . . .' with regard to any medical condition.

Dr King is familiar with guidance to refer all first febrile convulsions to paediatrics but believes that if this occurred the paediatric services would be overwhelmed. He is not certain that all GPs do this all the time.

Dr King was not aware of NICE guidance suggesting use of Paracetamol and review 1 hour later had potential to be misleading.

TRIANGULATING EVIDENCE

We can see that in the baby Anna case there is secondary evidence that either contradicts or qualifies primary evidence available from the notes. How do we evaluate evidence? The key is to use a technique called 'triangulation' (see Table 6.2).

Table 6.2 Triangulation and evaluation of evidence

Parental comments and concerns	Commentary
She had a temperature and had had a seizure and was sick. She was not responsive and she was limp. She was very sick.	Notes available from both the NHS 111 service and Dr King support a view that the baby had vomited and was shaking. They also indicate that the mother feared that Anna may be very unwell. She was also noted to be tired. Comments from the parents that Anna had had a seizure and was limp are not supported. They may suggest a degree of confusion between events that occurred following assessment and what happened when Anna was seen.
The doctors just checked her temperature and put something on her finger and then said she had a virus.	This suggests a concern that Dr King did not perform an adequate examination. Notes made at the time of examination indicate that Dr King did more than was suggested and was observing a number of key clinical parameters as well. This does not support the parents' assertion about Dr King's examination.
We asked if he was 100 per cent sure it was not meningitis and the doctor said he was 110 per cent sure it was not meningitis.	Dr King said he would never use a phrase such as 'I am 110 per cent certain . . .' with regard to any medical condition. This is a 'he said/she said' conundrum. We cannot know what was said but we can 'sense check' the information. It seems implausible that any clinician would use the phrase attributed to Dr King.

Parental comments and concerns	Commentary
The doctor gave three options.	Another he said/she said scenario. In this case the parents recall three quite specific options presented to them. Even though Dr King does not recall this it does seem more plausible that Dr King may forget the exact details than that the parents would invent a third option.
Doctor also said it was hard to see how responsive Anna was because it was her bed time.	We have no evidence to support this comment but it should be noted as it sounds like a plausible detail. It may also reflect the internal logic being used by Dr King to support his own formulation of what was going on. Such comments may support views about potential human factors at play such as thought biases (see later chapters).
Dr King's comments	
Was not rushed at time and saw child quickly.	This is consistent with the timeline of events.
Did say it may have been a febrile convulsion initially but on review felt this was not certain.	We cannot triangulate such evidence but it does seem plausible.
Thought about paediatric referral but thought Anna may well be just sent home after a review there anyway.	This is just an opinion from Dr King but it does indicate how Dr King may have been thinking about the case at the time.
Recalls seeing baby feeding OK in waiting room while it was waiting for review.	We could ask the parents if they recall feeding Anna in the waiting room. But, again, this evidence really speaks to Dr King's frame of mind at the time. Dr King is recalling clues that he relied upon to formulate a judgement at the time. They may help us to identify human factors such as thinking biases that may have been at play during the consultation. See later chapters.
Acknowledges did not record all observations made but confirms had noted absence of rash and meningism and cap refill. Also had noted respiratory rate when child reviewed and believes this was back to normal.	Dr King's note keeping is not the worst you may see but it is not good. Apart from being sloppy with a lot of typographic errors the clinical details are skimpy. Nonetheless, there is quite a lot of detail in the history and key vital signs are noted. A clinician who is astute enough to note pulse and respiratory rate will almost certainly have looked for a rash and meningism as well. Writing bad notes does not equate to performing a bad examination and, as stated previously, an investigator is at liberty to form a view based upon the balance of probability. In this case, the rest of the examination notes may service as sufficient evidence to allow one to believe that Dr King did make the other observations that he claimed.

We can see that there is some evidence that we can confirm by noting more than one source for the same information (triangulation) and some evidence that we may decide to believe because it is plausible – it makes sense. There is also evidence that we may not be able to verify one way or the other.

TERTIARY EVIDENCE

Tertiary evidence comes in two forms. Firstly, there is policy, guidance or protocol – that is to say, formally described guidance or protocol. In order of merit these are ranked as:

- National: NHS policy, NICE guidelines, nationally recognised protocols and so forth
- Local: Policies, guidance or protocols adopted by local commissioning groups or trusts
- Service/Practice: Policies, guidance or protocols used within a specific service or practice.

Always check events and actions against national policy or guidance if such exist. Verify whether there is local variation – some services expect staff to go above and beyond or, conversely, there may be explicit reasons why certain guidance may not apply. While it is important to be aware of national guidance, do not be afraid to challenge it. NICE guidance, for example, is often a valuable resource but it is not without fault. NICE guidance NG17 regarding the management of type 1 diabetes in adults, for example, is a very large and comprehensive document. Keeping up to date with all NICE recommendations is very difficult. All NICE guidance comes with a summary of stakeholder comments. In the 2015 version of NG17 stakeholder comments include this from the RCGP: 'The draft guidelines are welcome but are sizeable and are unlikely to be widely read in primary care.' (NICE NG17 Type 1 diabetes in adults: diagnosis and management, p. 14, NHS England, London.)

Awareness of this type of feedback enables an investigator to not only consult tertiary evidence but also to put it into context when it comes to assessing the actions of colleagues working at the coal face of clinical medicine. This was tucked away on page 14 of 260 so it may take some digging but when explaining why a GP may not have been fully familiar or compliant with NG17, a personal view that no GP could reasonably be expected to keep up to date with all available guidance at least has some valid backing in the form of the comments from the RCGP.

Do not forget to include checking policies governing how incidents or complaints are dealt with. Your own report may be subject to scrutiny and this includes adherence to a wide range of potential policies including information governance, equal opportunities and your service incident management policy.

A second source of tertiary evidence is expert opinion. This may take the form of evidence from reputable and reliable text or electronic sources of information or it may occasionally take the form of personal testimony or opinion from an external expert.

Most investigations may rely upon published data from reliable sources and this has the advantage of being readily accessible. Use nationally recognised standard textbooks or websites and quote your sources if you access data.

STRUCTURING THE EVENTS – TIMELINES

As you amass evidence of what happened, you will need to structure it to create a picture of what happened. One of the most useful tools associated with RCA and my first go-to tool is the tabular timeline.

There are three useful types of timeline template that you may use, depending upon the nature of the incident. These are the simple tabular timeline (Table 6.3), an enhanced tabular timeline (Table 6.4) and the time person grid (Table 6.5).

Some incidents are very simple in structure – a patient has contact with a single clinician and an adverse outcome follows. Few other contact points exist with any other service. In such cases a very simple timeline may suffice (Table 6.3).

The timeline presented in Table 6.4 is based upon NPSA templates but I have added a few tweaks based upon my experience and preference. Most standard templates, for example, have a single or dual column for date and time. I strongly advise that the day of the week is included as well as this may be relevant when considering events leading up to the index event.

A further enhancement is adding a time gap row between events. Timelines matter, more so in some cases than others and in some cases the time between events can be significant. Note that you may calculate the time lapse from the primary or index event as well as the time lapse from one event to the next as both of these factors may be relevant.

With regard to who was involved, remember that names will be anonymised in a report so you need to allocate a code to staff involved. If you include the timeline in the report (and you generally should) you may delete the real names from the version in the report. Keep a copy of the original timeline with real names on it for reference.

The timeline may become a key working document storing the details of both events as well as your evolving thoughts about what is going on as you progress. You may remove columns containing comments or supplementary information or other early speculative comments from the final timeline that may appear in a report.

THE TIME PERSON GRID

Sometimes, when several people are involved, an event is quite complex. In such circumstances a time person grid may be helpful. This places people and locations against time. Time person grids can be helpful in institutional settings where several people may be involved in the care or supervision of a patient.

Time intervals may be as narrow or as broad as is needed. Noting the location of key staff in the lead up to and at the time of an incident can be very helpful and the grid makes this easy to visualise.

Table 6.3 Simple tabular timeline

Date and time	Event	Comment

Table 6.4 Enhanced tabular timeline

Date	Day	Time	Time gap	Event	Supplementary information	Care/service delivery problems	Who was involved		Information source	Comments – further questions, learning points and so on
							RCA code	Name		

Table 6.5 Time person grid

Person	9:00	9:15	9:30	9:45	10:00	10:15	10:30
Nurse 1							
Nurse 2							

Once you have gathered evidence of what happened and when it occurred you need to begin to dig a little deeper and discover whether anything that occurred constituted an error – something that was done that should not have been done, or something that should have been done that was not. Such errors are called care or service delivery problems. How you identify them is the subject of the next chapter.

7

RCA – What happened? Care and service delivery problems

We have recognised that an adverse patient outcome has occurred and that it warrants an in-depth RCA investigation. We have gathered evidence and composed a timeline of events.

TOP TIP

Remember to stick to the process and to avoid bias.

The next stage of the RCA involves identifying whether something went wrong with the care or service delivered. Remember outcome bias? We are not looking to find what went wrong – we are looking to see *whether* something went wrong. This is an important distinction.

DID SOMETHING GO WRONG? WAS THERE A CARE DELIVERY PROBLEM?

Remember that it is essential to stick to a process when doing an RCA and, within that process, identifying the care delivery problem (or service delivery) is the first step once you have evaluated the evidence and structured it in a timeline.

A simple way of thinking about care or service delivery problems is to view them as acts or omissions.

- An act is something that was done that should not have been done.
- An omission is something that was not done that should have been done.

A care delivery problem (CDP) is an act or omission involving the direct clinical care of the patient.

A service delivery problem (SDP) is an act or omission involving the organisation of clinical care but not the clinical act itself. (This may include scheduling rotas and appointments, training and preparation of staff or equipment, including premises, IT and vehicles as well as clinical equipment.)

The CDP or SDP is the 'what' element of an RCA. These are the things that went wrong that may or may not have led to the adverse outcome for the patient. The CDP or SDP are things that were either done or not done that deviate from normal procedure or best practice.

TOP TIP

A CDP/SDP is the act or omission only – it is not the reason behind the act or omission – reasons come later – stick to the process.

Identifying an accurate CDP or SDP is vital to the rest of the investigation. If you get the CDP or SDP wrong, you will end up on the wrong track. This can lead to frustration, wasted time, confusion and, worst of all, the production of erroneous conclusions.

OBVIOUS CDP OR SDPs

Sometimes an act or omission appears obvious from the outset. Examples may include:

- Dr Pringle prescribes penicillin to Miss Kemp. Miss Kemp is allergic to penicillin and has an anaphylactic reaction and suffers hypoxic brain injury.
- Dr Kipling prescribes an inappropriate regime of insulin for a diabetic patient who subsequently has a year of poor diabetic control thought to be contributory to worsening of an underlying liver condition.

Both cases appear to be simple prescribing issues with obvious care delivery problems:

- Prescription of penicillin to a penicillin allergic patient
- Prescription of an inappropriate insulin regime

Review of the case notes confirmed that Dr Pringle had seen a patient who had a documented history of penicillin and they had diagnosed acute tonsillitis. They prescribed penicillin despite the warning in the notes. The identified care delivery problem seems appropriate and needs little justification.

In the case of Dr Kipling, however, a review of the notes reveals that Dr Kipling had seen a newly registered patient who had arrived in the UK from Hungary. The patient was on an insulin regime that included a long-acting Lantus insulin as well as a shorter-acting insulin that was not available in the UK. Dr Kipling identified an insulin that he thought was appropriate and prescribed this instead of the unavailable short-acting insulin. Unfortunately, Dr Kipling chose an intermediate-acting insulin and this should not be prescribed at the same time as a long-acting insulin. This is a prescribing issue but in this case greater precision is needed. Dr Kipling was actually substituting one insulin for another. This is a different task from initiating a new prescription. The process of logic and deduction is different from that used when prescribing insulin de novo. There is certainly overlap but the differences are significant, as is the frequency with which such tasks occur. In this case it is better to be more precise in describing the care delivery problem as: insulin prescribing – inappropriate insulin substitution. This gives greater clarity to the issue and will provide a better steer for where the investigation should be heading. It will also guide you further on where to look for normal or best practice. It will not be of much value to outline the steps for prescribing insulin de novo when this was not the task that Dr Kipling was undertaking.

INCORRECT DIAGNOSIS – CDP OR NOT?

It is tempting to think that an incorrect diagnosis must be a care delivery problem. Certainly, from a patient perspective this is likely to be the main concern. The doctor got the diagnosis wrong. In some cases, failing to make a diagnosis may be appropriate as a CDP, particularly if the diagnosis seems to have been obvious from the outset. In general, however, even if you list an incorrect diagnosis as a CDP you will need to qualify it by seeking to understand how it was that the incorrect diagnosis came to be made. You will need to look more closely at the consultation itself. We must remember that on many occasions we can only know that a diagnosis was incorrect with the benefit of hindsight. Clinicians may do all that they reasonably can to assess a patient and, in spite of this, may get a diagnosis wrong. It is more helpful to look at the consultation process as a whole first to see whether the overall episode of care met 'normal' standards before considering the implications of missed diagnosis. This helps to avoid hindsight bias.

IDENTIFYING AND CLARIFYING CARE AND SERVICE DELIVERY PROBLEMS

There are two methods for determining or clarifying care and service delivery problems. The most useful for care delivery problems is a process called change analysis. The second method, nominal group technique, is useful for certain situations where a clear process or the usual best practice is not easy to establish. Even if a CDP or SDP seems obvious it can be useful to see if you can apply change analysis to the case to confirm that you are on the right track.

CHANGE ANALYSIS

Change analysis is deceptively simple but there are pitfalls and it is easy to get tied up in knots. The technique is to compare the events that occurred on the day with events that should occur within an 'idealised' encounter – what did happen versus what should have happened.

A standard change analysis tool is suggested for use in the NHS by the NPSA.

A key problem with this type of tool, however, is that the investigator needs to establish 'normal/accepted procedure' and this may be quite difficult. Consider the case of baby Anna. Dr King examined Anna but how may we begin to look more deeply at his

Table 7.1 Standard change analysis tool

Normal/Accepted procedure	Actual procedure at time of incident	Was there a change? (Y/N)	If yes, what was the CDP/SDP that contributed to the incident?

consultation to identify where things may have gone wrong during the encounter? What is the normal procedure that we are expecting Dr King to follow? Further, where an investigator does establish a 'normal' procedure, their version of normal may be subject to challenge and so must be carefully considered and justified. A simple and consistent approach is to utilise tools that already exist and that define 'normal' for you. The ideal tool for this purpose is a service audit tool and there are two very useful audit tools that can help us. The first tool is the RCGP audit tool that was designed to enable audit of out-of-hours GP consultations. This makes an excellent template for performing change analysis with regard to a primary care consultation. It is designed for an out-of-hours environment where access to patient records is not present and so it is not immediately applicable to a general practice in-hours consultation but the tool can easily be adapted by removing some of the descriptors. The benefit of using such a tool is that the investigator is using a template for normal that is derived from an authoritative source and that is applicable on a national scale and not just a local one. As such, the investigator would not need to justify the template and can be confident that they are assessing a patient encounter fairly. For those unfamiliar with use of such tools there is a need to define how each descriptor is assessed and potentially to ensure that scoring is benchmarked for a given service. Audit tools do come with guidance on their use but it is important to ensure that anyone using them is doing so in a fair and consistent fashion. Within out-of-hours services this is an exercise that is well understood and incident investigators who have not used audit tools such as this may get advice and support from colleagues who have regularly performed audits. If you are going to do regular incident investigation then clinical audit is a skill well worth acquiring.

Let us look at the baby Anna case using the RCGP audit tool as a template for normal. The tool breaks down a GP–patient encounter into seven parts that essentially correspond to a standard model of a primary care consultation.

TOP TIP

Remember the process. At this stage you are just looking to establish what happened and in particular where actions deviated from normal or best practice. This will direct you to where the learning may arise. Do not try to second-guess learning at this point. If something occurs to you, make a note to explore it in more detail later.

CHANGE ANALYSIS USING RCGP AUDIT TOOL TO DEFINE 'NORMAL' BABY ANNA CASE

The comments in the Table 7.2 summarise a review of the evidence to hand. It is important to remember that use of tools such as change analysis have an important function in helping us to identify potential points of learning. There is not necessarily a right or wrong approach to how an action is broken down or how evidence is interpreted per se – the key element is to continually consider how the breakdown of the evidence may help in understanding where a patient contact may have broken down and hence to find a point at which we may usefully learn something. Not all points at which things deviate from normal will be relevant to the final outcome but they may still be useful from a learning point of view. In this case, for example, we have identified three areas in which Dr King appeared to have deviated from 'normal' or best practice. Each of these are 'acts', 'omissions' or care delivery problems. For instance, we see that Dr King did not fully explore the symptoms of shaking in a way that would make him confident about whether they represented febrile convulsions or whether they may just have been rigors – simple muscle fasciculations (twitches) in response to a fever. More skilled questioning may have helped but in a sense this does not matter with regard to the final outcome as, even if there was uncertainty, Dr King could have still referred baby Anna for a paediatric opinion. He did not have to be certain of whether it was a convulsion or not to have made this decision. This type of care delivery problem is a type of omission. Dr King could have asked more questions about the nature of the shaking episodes but he omitted to do so.

The decision not to refer for a paediatric opinion is also an omission and this decision is more significant in terms of the outcome. Dr King had raised the question of a febrile convulsion and had written it in the notes. He was concerned enough about Anna to offer the option of a review by the paediatrician but then presented easier options to the parents instead – they could simply stay in the out-of-hours clinic and have paracetamol and a review. The question as to whether this was a balanced and reasonable decision is not at issue at this point; what we must simply identify is that Dr King had a reason to refer and he had considered it and that ultimately a referral did not occur. An opportunity for Anna to be reviewed by another clinician in a specialist unit was thus missed. This was another omission – something that arguably should have happened but did not. Incidentally, do not worry about hindsight bias at this point. We are trying to simply look at the evidence that exists in a neutral way. Bias needs to be eliminated later when we interpret the reasons why actions occurred as they did.

The third issue or CDP we identified was also related to the management of Anna and it was the decision to give Anna paracetamol and review her after an hour. This was something that was done – an act – that the tertiary evidence that was consulted confirmed should not have been done. This approach is no longer regarded as being clinically relevant or useful according to expert opinion within guidance from NICE on the management of febrile illness in children. In terms of the impact upon the outcome, the significance of this act probably falls between the two other CDPs in that as an act in itself it would not do any harm, but harm may arise if the act leads to a false reassurance for a clinician that enables them to rationalise and justify another unsafe action. In this case the act helped Dr King to justify not referring Anna to the paediatricians.

TOP TIP

We are looking to link actions and outcomes. The degree to which a CDP or SDP is potentially linked to an outcome is also a reflection of the degree to which learning may arise from the incident. This should direct your endeavours to understand 'why' care delivery problems arose.

Identifying care and service delivery problems is not just an academic exercise. The purpose is to help direct your efforts in understanding what really led to the incident occurring. If you get the CDP wrong, you will be looking for learning in the wrong place.

Change analysis is a very simple tool to use in principle but do spend time teasing out what happened in sufficient detail for it to make sense. If you feel that the descriptors you have chosen are too broad, you can refine them by splitting actions even further into their component parts.

The RCGP tool is very useful for primary care consultations either in hours or out of hours. Another similar tool that I have used successfully is the NHS Pathways audit tool for NHS 111 call audit. This tool is used for routine analysis of NHS 111 telephone calls either by health advisers or clinicians and it can be very useful to use it when assessing serious incidents within the NHS 111 service. There are further examples of using this tool on my website: www.PatientSafetyInvestiagtions.com

Where an audit tool does not exist it is very helpful to consider the nature of the clinical encounter and identify whether there are any guidelines or protocols that apply to that specific scenario. National guidelines or protocols are best but local ones may also apply in certain scenarios. Within the UK, NICE is a good source for guidance but it is important to assess the degree to which guidance is known and adhered to. A very useful alternative or additional tool for assessing a consultation for children is the NICE traffic light guidance tool for assessment of children aged under five presenting with a fever. The tool could be used as an alternative change analysis template for children who have presented with a fever or as an additional tool to tease out what happened in the encounter. The value of this NICE tool is that it is very widely known and utilised in primary care.

NICE TRAFFIC LIGHT GUIDANCE ADAPTED TO BECOME A CHANGE ANALYSIS TOOL

This tool compares the assessment against 2013 NICE guidance on the management of feverish illness in children under five. NICE guidance is in blue. Evidence of events on the day may be from any source but the source should be documented in the comments column.

Examples of use of the NICE tool can be found on my website.

Other tools that can be of value either alone or in conjunction with a general consultation tool are items such as ABCD2 scoring, Wells scoring, CRB65, local DVT management protocols and surgical checklists. The key point is that they must be guidelines or protocols that are in general use and are well known to staff.

Table 7.2

Normal/Accepted procedure	Actual procedure at time of incident	Was there a change? (Y/N)	If yes, what was the CDP/SDP that contributed to the incident?
Clearly elicits reason for contact	Notes indicate key symptoms of shaking, reduced responsiveness and fever; concerns of parents that child is unwell	N	
Identifies red flags	Clinical notes are incomplete but contain sufficient key vital signs to indicate that red flags were considered	N	
Appropriate history taking	There is a lack of clarity with regard to history of shaking episodes – further information may have helped to distinguish between rigors and febrile convulsions	Y	Limitations of clinical history – did not clarify symptoms of shaking to enable certainty as to nature of symptoms
Full examination performed	The clinical notes lack evidence of certain vital signs but sufficient evidence exists to believe that examination was adequate	N	
Makes appropriate management decisions	The doctor had not excluded a febrile convulsion but did not refer to pediatricians	Y	Failed to refer to paediatric services following first febrile convulsion
	Gave paracetamol with a review at one hour – an action that is not consistent with current best practice	Y	Performed a reassessment at one hour following a dose of paracetamol – an action no longer regarded as best practice
Appropriate prescribing behaviour	Not relevant – addressed above	N	
Safety netting	Did provide advice to review patient next day with GP	N	

Table 7.3 NICE guidance

	Actual events at time of incident	Did change occur? Y/N	What was CDP that contributed to incident?	Comments
1.2.1 Life-threatening features of illness in children				
1.2.1.1 First, healthcare professionals should identify any immediately life-threatening features, including compromise of the airway, breathing or circulation, and decreased level of consciousness. [2007]				
1.3.1.2 Children whose symptoms or combination of symptoms suggest an immediately life-threatening illness (see recommendation 1.2.1.1) should be referred immediately for emergency medical care by the most appropriate means of transport (usually 999 ambulance). [2007]				
Below are the five key criteria that NICE promote as essential for assessment of poorly children. The guidance is referred to as 'Traffic light' guidance as symptom severity is ranked Green, Amber and Red and further action depends upon the colour of key symptom descriptors.				

	Green	Amber	Red	Actual events at time of incident	Did change occur? Y/N	What was CDP that contributed to incident?	Comments
Colour (of skin, lips or tongue)	Normal colour	Pallor reported by parent/carer	Pale/Mottled/Ashen/Blue				
Activity	Responds normally to social cues Content/Smiles Stays awake or awakens quickly Strong normal cry/not crying	Not responding normally to social cues No smile Wakes only with prolonged stimulation Decreased activity	No response to social cues Appears ill to a healthcare professional Does not wake or if roused does not stay awake Weak, high-pitched or continuous cry				
Respiratory		Nasal flaring tachypnoea: respiratory rate >50 breaths/minute, age 6–12 months; >40 breaths/minute, age >12 months oxygen saturation ≤95 per cent in air Crackles in the chest	Grunting tachypnoea: respiratory rate >60 breaths/minute Moderate or severe chest indrawing				

(continued)

	Green	Amber	Red	Actual events at time of incident	Did change occur? Y/N	What was CDP that contributed to incident?	Comments
Circulation and hydration	Normal skin and eyes Moist mucous membranes	Tachycardia: >160 beats/minute, age <12 months >150 beats/minute, age 12–24 months >140 beats/minute, age 2–5 years Capillary refill time ≥3 seconds Dry mucous membranes Poor feeding in infants Reduced urine output	Reduced skin turgor				
Other	None of the amber or red symptoms or signs	Age 3–6 months, temperature ≥39°C Fever for ≥5 days Rigors Swelling of a limb or joint Non-weight bearing limb/Not using an extremity	Age <3 months, temperature ≥38°C Non-blanching rash Bulging fontanel Neck stiffness Status epilepticus Focal neurological signs Focal seizures				

1.3.1.3 Children with any 'red' features but who are not considered to have an immediately life-threatening illness should be urgently assessed by a healthcare professional in a face-to-face setting within two hours. [2007] NICE guidance on remote assessment

DIFFICULTY IN ESTABLISHING 'NORMAL': NOMINAL GROUP TECHNIQUE

There remain many areas of medicine where establishing best practice or 'normal' practice remains difficult. In such circumstances it is useful to utilise the wisdom of crowds – or at least a group of experienced clinicians working in the field. This is essentially what is meant by a process called nominal group technique (NGT). In fact, NGT can be used both to establish a norm and also to directly identify care delivery problems but the nature of the group that is selected may differ in each case. If you are just seeking to establish what is normal practice for a general clinical encounter in a particular service, then it is important to select a group that is representative of the service with both experienced and new clinicians involved. Within bounds of resources, both time and money, and proportionality, the more clinicians involved in the group the better the outcome will be. On the other hand, if you are trying to pin down what CDPs or SDPs may have occurred within an incident then it is important that you have staff of sufficient length and breadth of experience. In this case quality is more important than quantity. If the incident involves both clinical and non-clinical aspects, then both clinicians and non-clinicians should be involved and if the incident is primarily a service issue then it may be that the group is composed of administrative staff only.

HOW TO PERFORM NGT

NGT works best when a group can be gathered together at one time and in one location as members may feed off one another's ideas. This is not always possible, however, and it is still possible to perform the technique by speaking to staff in several small groups or even individually. It all comes down to facilitation. Introduce the group to as much of the incident as seems relevant and then ask the group to help by proposing ideas in a free-form fashion. You may do this by writing ideas as suggested by members of the group on a flip chart or by asking the group to write ideas down on paper or 'sticky' notes. Do not allow the group to analyse or dismiss suggestions – this will come later. Allow the group to 'brainstorm' or 'brainwrite' ideas even if they think that they may be too harsh, too critical or too perfectionistic.

After a period of working through the incident you should have a group of headings either on a flip chart or on sticky notes that may be stuck on a wall. You now need to organise these to eliminate duplicates, clarify ambiguity and remove red herrings. Go through each of the headings that you have with the group with the aim of reducing your list of headings to a manageable amount – perhaps six to a dozen.

Remember that you may be asking your group to describe the essential steps to perform a given procedure or you may have asked the group to look at the events of a particular incident in some detail and then asked them to identify what they thought may have been done wrong or things that had not been done but should have been done (acts or omissions).

You will be left with what the group regards as the dozen or so key steps within a given process, or perhaps half a dozen or more potential care delivery problems that the group think may have occurred within a particular incident. What you need to do now is to refine this list down to the key elements. When identifying a process, you may be left with about six to ten steps. For CDPs or SDPs there is likely to be between two and four key acts or omissions that seem to be the most important. Both preparation and flexibility are important here as it is up to you as the facilitator to determine how much you wish to cull the list. At the outset you may have an idea that a given process was relatively straight-forward and that you just wanted to highlight the key six steps within it. Be prepared for your group to convince you otherwise. Likewise, you may have viewed evidence and been seeking help to pin down what you thought were likely to be just two CDPs only to find that the group identified a dozen and that you may need to give the group greater scope when narrowing the list down.

In any case, what you must do is narrow things down and to do this you present a revised list of the process points or CDPs and ask each member of the group to select the top six or the top three or even just the top one item from among the list. If trying to estab-lish a normal process, then ask for the top six steps in a process in order of importance. For a CDP ask for the CPDs identified to be ranked one to three in order of importance.

Finally, it should be noted that you can use NGT after you have identified a selection of CDPs by change analysis, as a method to pin down which are the most significant in a given case.

NGT IN PRACTICE

Assume you have selected a group of eight experienced colleagues working within the out-of-hours service to look at the baby Anna case. In this case, by facilitating a meeting and asking colleagues to think about things that they think could have been done dif-ferently on the night in question you come up with a list of the following care delivery problems.

1. Did not clarify history of shaking episodes – were they convulsions or not?
2. Did not document capillary refill time, absence of rash or meningism
3. Did not document any signs other than temperature when reviewed child an hour later
4. Lots of spelling errors in notes
5. Did not refer to paediatricians
6. Gave paracetamol and reviewed after one hour – no longer best practice
7. Safety-net advice is not the three-phase advice advocated by RCGP

CHALLENGING YOUR CARE DELIVERY PROBLEMS

Use of NGT offers you an opportunity to challenge CDPs or SDPs within a group. This type of challenge can be done in isolation if necessary but two heads are better than one and assembling your co-investigators to consider CDPs or SDPs early on is an important step in the process.

Each of these care delivery problems ought to be considered within the final report but are they all relevant? Do they all warrant further in-depth analysis to determine con-tributory factors? Significantly, will they all yield new or significant learning in this case?

If you challenge your group to consider each item in turn, then you can get a better sense of the issue and any learning that may arise.

CDP 1 suggests that the clinician did not clarify the history of shaking in this case. Could this have been done differently and would it have made a difference? In the debrief notes Dr King admits that he was not certain that Anna had suffered true convulsion. He wrote it in his initial notes but after reflection he changed his mind. He suggested a referral but then presented an easier option to the parents of a review in the clinic after some paracetamol. Experienced colleagues in the group point out that more skilled questioning of the parents with regard to the shaking episodes may have given Dr King more confidence about whether convulsions had occurred or not. Asking the parents about whether they had watched Anna closely during a shivering episode and whether she had appeared to lose consciousness during such episodes may have been helpful. This type of question is a bit like a D-dimer test or urine dip-stick test – it has reasonable sensitivity but is not very specific. Nonetheless, had Dr King thought to clarify this then it may have been useful in either persuading him that a convulsion was actually likely, in which case the level of risk for the child would elevate significantly, or leaving the likelihood of convulsions still uncertain, in which case the risk would have remained undetermined. This seems like an area where further learning may arise.

Care delivery problems two, three and four relate to how Dr King documented his examination. He missed some key vital signs and he made a lot of spelling errors. How significant is this? In his debriefing Dr King admitted that he had not documented all of the findings that he had observed. He commented that he had assessed CRT and excluded a rash and meningism and that he had checked the pulse and respiratory rate when he had reviewed Anna before sending her home but had neglected to document these. He admitted that he had always struggled with spelling and typing and was quite slow on the keyboard and he sometimes kept notes brief to try to ensure that he did not run behind in clinics.

It is important to remember that a root cause analysis is not a medico-legal enquiry. We are not trying to establish liability and thus we may take a different view on evidence from the lawyers. Just because Dr King did not write down his full findings does not mean that he did not do things. We may take evidence from his recollection of events and judge its value. In this case, given that Dr King did document a number of key vital signs it is reasonable to believe that he identified others that he did not document. It seems reasonable to believe that Anna did not appear to be significantly unwell to Dr King based upon his observations and findings and therefore the fact that he did not record everything that he saw would not have altered the outcome in any way. There is certainly some learning here of course. Clinicians are frequently warned by medico-legal advisers that they should write more comprehensive notes and include key negative findings. This case illustrates how this practice is valuable because it would certainly place Dr King in a better position medico-legally if his notes had been better, but in this particular case this is likely to be the extent of the learning from the RCA point of view. This is a lesson that is already well established and it is not likely to bear much fruit to analyse this aspect of the case much further.

CDP 5 – not referring to paediatricians – certainly appears to be a key omission. However, it too is open to challenge. It illustrates how easy it may be to get side-tracked within an RCA onto the wrong course. This is usually due to hindsight bias. See below.

> **TOP TIP**
>
> It is vital within RCA reports that CDPs or SDPs are not erroneously linked to outcomes in a way that may falsely attribute causality. Beware of hindsight bias.

I have indicated that when identifying a CDP it may be necessary to ignore hindsight bias and simply look at guidance and protocol. We have identified that national guidance exists which indicates that an infant presenting with a first episode of febrile convulsion should be referred to the paediatricians. In this case, baby Anna was not referred and she later died of meningitis. It is easy to follow a false logic at this point.

- All babies with convulsion should be referred to a paediatrician.
- Baby Anna had a convulsion and was not referred and subsequently died of meningitis.
- All babies who have convulsions and are not referred to paediatricians will die of meningitis.

This is certainly how the parents of baby Anna are likely to view events. The reason why babies are referred to paediatricians is to stop them dying of meningitis and because Dr King did not refer, he allowed Anna to die of meningitis.

This, however, is faulty logic. It would only apply if the following were true:

- All babies with convulsions have a high risk of having meningitis.

We know that this is not actually the case. We do not refer babies with febrile convulsions to paediatricians in the expectation that they will diagnose meningitis. The reasons for referral are complex but are generally related to managing parental anxiety and education with regard to what to do in the future. It may include a screen for infectious source in cases where a clear origin of the fever is not clear and meningitis would certainly be on a diagnostic radar but it is not the primary reason for referral. The vast majority of babies with febrile convulsions are sent home perfectly well after about four hours in hospital and very few will progress to a diagnosis of meningitis. The significance of this issue is considered further when we discuss contributory factors and the identification of a root cause. The point is to keep in mind cause and effect. We have identified a key omission but did this cause the final outcome?

CDP 6 is the decision to administer paracetamol and review after an hour. It has been pointed out that this practice is misleading and can provide false reassurance. If Dr King was falsely reassured, then this would seem to be a significant CDP. It is also clear from the debrief interview that Dr King re-evaluated his diagnosis and management plan while he was waiting to observe the effects of paracetamol.

Finally, we have CDP 7. It is noted that Dr King did not follow current RCGP guidelines on safety-net advice. Dr King did advise parents to follow up with their regular GP the next day and we believe that they did. He told them to call back in the night if they had any concerns. On initial review using change analysis it was felt that safety-net advice was adequate. It is clear that advice was not specific with regard to what symptoms to monitor for nor for any advice about whether to allow Anna to sleep through the night or whether to wake her and check her ability to be aroused or to check how she looked or felt to the parents in the night. Such advice may have been ideal but it seems to be so only with the benefit of hindsight. The case may serve as a reminder of the current guidance upon safety-net advice from the Royal College but the evidence does not suggest that more explicit advice may have altered the outcome, particularly as Anna was seen by another GP prior to her death.

After some discussion, the group have whittled down care delivery problems from a potential seven to just three key CPDs. As stated, the report may mention learning arising from all seven CDPs but it seems likely that only three will warrant further in-depth exploration:

- Limitations of clinical history – did not clarify symptoms of shaking to enable certainty as to nature of symptom
- Failed to refer to paediatric services following first febrile convulsion
- Performed a reassessment at one hour following a dose of paracetamol – an action no longer regarded as best practice

The next phase of the RCA is to look at contributory factors and these are the three CDPs for which you will proceed with further in-depth analysis. Before you proceed you may wish to pin down the CDPs even further and identify the one CDP that seemed to have most potential for impact upon the final outcome. You may do this with your group by asking each member to nominate the single most important CDP. This can be done openly with the group being able to observe one another's voting and by offering members the opportunity to change their mind based upon viewing their peers' choices. This approach does allow for the possibility of peer pressure and so you may choose to do this process in a blind fashion by asking colleagues to write the single most important CDP on a piece of paper and then collecting their answers and counting them separately. The final result may be tabulated as per Table 7.4.

Depending upon the scale and complexity of the case and the make up of the NGT group, the scoring charts used may become part of the record of the assessment, usually in appendices. If this is not part of the formal record, then do keep good notes of the process and the outcome in case any aspect of the report is challenged at a later date.

Table 7.4 NGT to identify which CDP is of most significance

CDP	Instructions: Place a 'star' against the CPD identified below that you believe contributed the most significantly to the final outcome.
Limitations of clinical history – did not clarify symptoms of shaking to enable certainty as to nature of symptom	*
Failed to refer to paediatric services following first febrile convulsion	* * * * *
Performed a reassessment at one hour following a dose of paracetamol – an action no longer regarded as best practice	* *

SUMMARY

Accurately identifying the care and service delivery problems in a case is essential to a good root cause analysis. It will set the course for the rest of the investigation and honing down the most important CDP or SDP will ensure that you know where your investigatory efforts are likely to be focused.

In themselves CDP and SDP are not of much value to the RCA process as they are just a matter of stating what happened. As important as it is to get this right, there is not really much to learn from knowing what happened. The really useful component of an RCA is being able to understand *why* things happened as they did. To understand why we need to consider the factors that contributed to the CDP or SDP occurring. This is where the key learning will occur. Contributory factors are explored in the next chapter.

8

RCA – Understanding why

> ## CASE SUMMARY
>
> Dr MacDonald assesses Mrs Agrawal. She is 77 years old and has presented to him complaining of indigestion and asking for stronger antacid medication. She has burning in the throat and chest and it is worse when she lies down. Dr MacDonald notes that Mrs Agrawal was seen in the chest clinic two weeks ago due to worsening episodes of shortness of breath and had an electrocardiogram (ECG) that she was told was normal. Dr Macdonald doubles the dose of proton pump inhibitor that Mrs Agrawal takes and reassures her that her symptoms should improve. Five hours later Mrs Agrawal suffers a fatal myocardial infarct.

Following further investigation, it was determined that the following care delivery problems arose in this case:

- Inadequate exploration of presenting complaint
- Failing to identify symptoms presented as those of acute coronary syndrome

The CDPs tell us what Dr MacDonald did – that is to say, Dr MacDonald failed to explore the presenting history fully and missed a diagnosis of acute coronary syndrome. But they do not tell us why Dr MacDonald missed such a common condition with symptoms that may have triggered more alarm in other colleagues. The CDPs that have been identified suggest that the root of this error may lie in the way that Dr MacDonald obtained information and, further, with the way Dr MacDonald interpreted the evidence. To learn something of more value we need to dig deeper.

With the baby Anna case we have similar CDPs relating to exploration of the history and interpretation of evidence.

- Limitations of clinical history – did not clarify symptoms of shaking to enable certainty as to nature of symptom
- Failed to refer to paediatric services following first febrile convulsion
- Performed a reassessment at one hour following a dose of paracetamol – an action no longer regarded as best practice

We may also remember Dr Kipling who provided an inappropriate insulin prescription.

- Insulin prescribing – inappropriate insulin substitution

We know what Dr MacDonald, Dr King and Dr Kipling did – the question now is, why?

CONTRIBUTORY FACTORS ANALYSIS

Contributory factors analysis is the core of root cause analysis because this is where the questions of why something has occurred are resolved. More importantly, this is where we learn how we may avoid making the same errors a second time. For an investigator the exploration of contributory factors may be the most interesting part of an investigation as it provides real challenges in terms of understanding how clinical and operational processes, protocols and guidance work in the real world when they are confronted with the people who are required to use them.

Analysis of contributory factors requires combinations of certain attributes:

- Time
- Experience
- Aptitude

Aptitude and experience may compensate for a lack of time but having more time will not compensate for a lack of experience or, more importantly, a lack of aptitude. Being able to interpret evidence and explore potential contributory factors is a skill that will improve with experience but that is not a universal attribute. Service leads should bear in mind the experience and aptitude of those asked to complete RCA investigations and not simply delegate by role or availability.

There is no required format or process for identifying contributory factors and investigators may simply brainstorm their way through a case identifying contributory factors, but unless the individual in question has considerable experience of investigating incidents, they are unlikely to consider the full range of potential factors that may be contributory. Furthermore, if an investigator does not use a recognised process or technique for arriving at conclusions then the validity of their efforts may be questioned by the audience who read the report. Fortunately, considerable work has gone in to identifying and categorising potential contributory factors and the NPSA has even produced a very useful framework classification of contributory factors. I would strongly recommend studying and using this tool when investigating serious clinical incidents. Even after many years of experience I still use the tool in all cases to help guide my investigation. Other tools do exist and some may prefer the Ishikawa fishbone diagram as an aide-memoire. Nonetheless, the NPSA classification is a must-read for investigators.

THE NPSA CONTRIBUTORY FACTORS FRAMEWORK CLASSIFICATION

Use of the NPSA Contributory Factors Framework Classification tool has the advantage that it is both comprehensive and it has credibility. The full tool may be found at the NPSA website www.npsa.nhs.uk and it is worth study. A copy is also available from my website, www.PatientSafetyInvestigations.com along with other worked case examples.

The NPSA identified nine categories of contributory factors and within the framework classification each is broken down further into contributory parts. The nine categories in the order in which they appear in the framework are as follows:

- Patient factors
- Individual staff factors
- Task factors
- Communication factors
- Equipment factors
- Work and environment factors
- Organisational factors
- Education and training factors
- Team factors

I prefer to structure them into three broad categories as this makes the task of identifying contributory factors easier (Table 8.1). The three areas of contribution are:

- Patients – what factors do patients bring?
- People – Human factors among clinical/service staff
- Systems and tasks – what we do and how we do it

TOP TIP

At the point of considering contributory factors it is easy for investigators to introduce factors that seem relevant because they relate to the overall issue at hand. This is erroneous practice. The contributory factors must be linked to the CDP identified and should not be arising new at this stage of the investigation.

Table 8.1

Patients = patient factors	People = human factors	System and task factors	
		Task factors	System factors
The clinical condition	Individual personal, physical and psychological factors	Design of task at hand	Equipment – design and function including fail-safe protections
Physical state at time of incident	Cognitive factors	Value of policies and guidance	Work environment
Social and psychological factors	Team dynamics	Decision-making aids	Organisational issues including organisational culture
	Communication factors		Education and training issues

Patient factors

The 'Top Tip' above comes with one exception. Before you consider factors that may have contributed to the care or service delivery problems identified you have to consider an issue that has not formally arisen until this point but that is vital to the investigation – the patient. The issue of patient factors in healthcare RCAs is both a complex and sensitive one. It is also one that is the grit in an otherwise good process because patient factors do not fit neatly into the RCA model. The other contributory factors can all be seen as issues that would follow on from any logical assessment of a safety or quality incident – they follow from the CDP identified. Human, task and systems factors would apply when assessing the root cause of quality issues in a vehicle production line or the root cause of an aviation disaster but patient factors are unique to healthcare incidents and actually have the potential to disrupt the RCA. They need to be understood and managed carefully.

The issue is that an RCA is a tool designed to find the root cause of a failure in a process that should operate perfectly every time: a series of machine processes should produce a perfect engine component and a plane should take off from airport A and land at airport B. When something goes wrong we can expect to find an error in the industrial process or an error in the operation of the plane. There may be a problem with the plane itself but this would actually come under a problem with the process of ensuring that the plane was airworthy. In medicine, a patient presents to us because something is already wrong; that is, they have some underlying pathology, and that is why we are seeing them. Sometimes that pathology may be very serious and even with our best efforts the outcome for the patient may not be good. In addition to the issue of pathology, the patient will bring with them a range of psychological and social issues that may impact upon the clinical process either at the time or just after. Patients are capable of misunderstanding, misinterpreting or just disagreeing with what a doctor or nurse has told them and this can have an impact upon incident outcomes that may be difficult to quantify but is nonetheless important when considering why an outcome arose.

> **TOP TIP**
>
> It is very important to *consider* patient factors fully in any RCA but *investigating* them fully may be impossible.

Great care must be taken and sensitivity is needed to ensure that there is not a perception of blaming the patient. Most people, and especially most people who may read an RCA report, are unaware of the impact of biases such as outcome and hindsight bias. Even fellow healthcare workers will often examine an RCA report and find blame rather than explanation. Think how much harder it is for a patient or relative to read a report or be on the receiving end of probing questions about their own conduct without feeling that they are being blamed. So, consider fully but be circumspect about the degree to which certain patient factors are directly addressed. Bear in mind comments made in Chapter 5 about blame – we are not seeking to censure patients, just to identify where responsibility for outcome may arise.

THE PATIENT'S UNDERLYING CONDITION – DR MACDONALD AND ACUTE CORONARY SYNDROME VERSUS DR KING AND MENINGITIS

Both Dr MacDonald and Dr King failed to accurately diagnose the patients that they had seen. Mrs Agrawal, a 77-year-old, had presented complaining of indigestion. She had burning in the throat and she had also complained of increasing shortness of breath in the month prior to seeing Dr MacDonald. Dr MacDonald had asked Mrs Agrawal if her symptoms worsened when she lay down and she had said yes, an indicator to Dr MacDonald that the symptoms may be being caused by acid reflux disease, a condition that Mrs Agrawal was known to suffer from. Dr MacDonald had noted that Mrs Agrawal had been seen in the chest clinic two weeks earlier for her shortness of breath and had had an ECG taken that was normal and had had her inhaler dose increased. This reassured Dr MacDonald both that a cardiac cause for indigestion symptoms was unlikely and that Mrs Agrawal's underlying lung disease was causing her shortness of breath.

Dr MacDonald had made an assessment and reached a plausible diagnosis as to what was going on. With the benefit of hindsight, we know that Dr MacDonald's diagnosis was wrong. What we have to do now is to consider what we know about Mrs Agrawal's underlying condition and the way it presented and ask whether this in itself may have been a factor in Dr MacDonald making the wrong diagnosis. We need to consider two questions:

1. What do we know about the presentation of acute coronary syndrome (ACS) in general?
2. What do we know about the way that acute coronary syndrome was presenting in this specific case?

To answer question one, you must consult tertiary evidence. This may include an expert witness in some cases but more commonly one may use standard national or international reference sources. These may include current standard textbooks or professional Internet reference sources. Remember that this evidence should be cited in your report.

The response to question one may be something like this:

- ACS is a common presentation in primary care. Risk increases with age. Symptoms suggestive of ACS include typical symptoms of crushing central chest pain radiating to neck and arm, associated with sweating and nausea, as well as frequent documented atypical symptoms that may include presentation with throat pain, burning in the throat, shortness of breath or upper limb pain only. Atypical symptoms are more common in elderly patients.

The answer to question two may be:

- Mrs Agrawal presented with atypical symptoms of ACS, burning throat pain and shortness of breath.

When trying to formulate a balanced view it is important to try to follow a consistent pattern of evaluation. My view of what is reasonable and balanced may differ from a colleague's view, and thus in a report I will try to show my working out. From this point my logic would be as follows:

ACS is a common presentation, both in primary and secondary care. There are very rare presentations that will and do catch clinicians out but in this case the presentation, while atypical, is not a rare atypical presentation. Burning throat pain, particularly when associated with shortness of breath, is a documented atypical presentation and is noted to be more likely in the elderly. For this reason, the underlying condition of the patient, an atypical presentation of ACS, may be regarded a contributory factor to Dr MacDonald missing the correct diagnosis but it should not be considered a major contributory factor. That is to say, it is unlikely that this atypical presentation alone could account for Dr MacDonald being unable to identify the symptoms presented as being those of acute coronary syndrome.

So in the case of Dr MacDonald, patient factors are noted to have some relevance but would not be regarded as highly significant.

What about Dr King and baby Anna? We know that baby Anna died of meningitis.

1. What do we know of how meningitis presents in general?
2. What do we know of how meningitis presented in this case?

In response to question one, we may note:

- Meningitis presents rarely. Tertiary evidence suggests that meningitis may present with a rapidly fulminating case with obvious clinical signs or that it may frequently present with an insidious presentation with signs and symptoms that mimic a common upper respiratory infection. As many as 50 per cent of children later diagnosed with meningitis will have already presented to primary or emergency care services and been sent home with an alternative diagnosis before representing with a deteriorating condition. In its prodromal phase, it may be impossible to accurately diagnose meningitis. The outcome for patients with meningitis is frequently poor regardless of the stage at which they are diagnosed.

In response to question two:

- Anna presented with non-specific symptoms of fever and shaking that may or may not have been due to convulsions. There was no evidence of meningeal irritation or typical rash associated with meningococcal sepsis. There were some mildly elevated physiological markers that did appear to settle over the course of one to two hours.

In the baby Anna case we note that meningitis is a rare presentation. There are no typical features of acute meningitis present and it is well recognised and documented that if a child or infant presents in the prodromal phase of meningitis then the condition may be impossible to diagnose. Notwithstanding concerns about the consultation of Dr King already noted that need further exploration, the fact that baby Anna presented with what

TOP TIP

Conditions that are both rare and present atypically or in very early phase of illness may represent significant 'patient factors' in that they would be very difficult for any clinician to identify. A condition that is common would need an exceptionally rare or atypical presentation for this factor alone to be regarded as significant. This may be a difficult judgement so seek guidance and support from colleagues if in doubt.

appears to be the prodromal phase of an illness known to be difficult to diagnose and that also may have a poor outcome is highly significant.

While it is ideal to try to weigh the significance of any contributory factor, it may be that you are not certain as to how significant the patient's underlying condition is. In this case simply provide a narrative along the lines of those above but do not speculate as to the significance of the underlying condition. Note it as a contributory factor the significance of which is difficult to determine.

The issue of prognosis arising from the patient's underlying condition is a further complexity that is considered further when we look at root causes. That is to say, in either of the cases discussed above, would Mrs Agrawal or baby Anna have been more likely to have survived had Dr MacDonald or Dr King made the correct diagnosis or referred the patient to hospital?

I have developed a tool to help determine the likelihood of patient factors being the root cause of an incident and this is described in Chapter 12.

THE PATIENT'S BEHAVIOUR – DR KIPLING AND INSULIN PRESCRIPTION

The medical condition of the patient should be fully explored in order to determine the degree to which it may contribute to a missed diagnosis or to difficulty in interpreting evidence available to a clinical team. The behaviour of a patient is both a more sensitive issue and difficult to determine accurately. Evidence may not be readily available and probing patients or relatives on this issue may be difficult. Nonetheless, patient behaviour is important and one should not be discouraged from sensitive exploration if it seems relevant. If you think that exploration of patient behaviour may be difficult then you may specifically exclude this from the scope of the investigation. When this happens it is important that you explicitly document this within the narrative of the report.

The Dr Kipling insulin case raised some interesting questions about patient behaviour. The case details are as follows:

Mr Havel was a 25-year-old Hungarian patient who presented to a GP seeking repeat medication for his type 1 diabetes. He was on Lantus insulin and Humulin R, a rapid-acting insulin.

Dr Kipling found that Humulin R is not available in the UK and substituted Humulin I instead. This was an error as Humulin I is an intermediate-acting insulin and should not be co-prescribed with a long-acting insulin.

Mr Havel also suffered from fibrosis of the liver of unknown aetiology.

Mr Havel presented to the surgery on 12 subsequent occasions for medical review or repeat prescriptions and had contact with seven different doctors in this time. He also presented to his local emergency department twice. At no time was the inappropriate insulin prescribing noted.

The surgery attempted to manage his diabetes without specialist support despite the fact that blood markers (HbA1c) indicated worsening diabetic control as well as worsening liver function.

Mr Havel was referred to a liver specialist because of his worsening liver function and the liver specialist immediately noted the error in the insulin regime.

The liver specialist had indicated that a consequence of the inappropriate pre-scribing was poor diabetic control and that this in turn may contribute to worsening fibrosis of the liver.

The contributory factors in this case were numerous and interesting and a number of these are discussed later. What struck me about Mr Havel, however, was the lack of engagement he had demonstrated with his GP practice.

When first seen Mr Havel had run out of his Humulin R a month previously and had only been using Lantus insulin.

After his first assessment with Dr Kipling he was advised, in the presence of an inter-preter, that his blood results showed poor control of his condition. He was supplied with blood-testing equipment and the new, albeit erroneous script, and asked to return for review in two weeks with results of blood tests. Mr Havel did not produce any finger-prick blood-test results on review but he told Dr Kipling that his results were OK.

When Mr Havel was confronted with abnormal full blood-test results he insisted that he was modifying his diet and exercise regimes. However, he missed three subsequent clinic appointments.

After referral to the specialist clinic, Mr Havel missed two appointments at the hos-pital, delaying his assessment by three months. When I was investigating the case, Mr Havel had already seen a specialist and had had his insulin changed. Dr Kipling had met with him and advised him that he had made an error in prescribing his insulin that had now been corrected. He had apologised and explained that this may have affected Mr Havel's diabetic control and that it was important to monitor his condition closely. Despite the change in insulin regime, the blood markers for insulin control had only slightly improved in the three months since change in treatment. Despite the emphasis on improving diabetic control, Mr Havel once again turned up in the clinic seeking a repeat of his new short-acting insulin and informed Dr Kipling that he had run out of his short-acting insulin two weeks earlier and had not managed to find time to get to the surgery.

It seems obvious that Mr Havel's lack of engagement with the service is significant. Even the best of medical advice and care will count for little if a patient, for whatever complex reasons, simply does not engage or follow through with treatments or advice.

Remember that we are looking both for learning and for causality, as a consequence of acts or omissions on the part of the clinical team. In Dr Kipling's case, whatever the impact of his error in prescribing insulin may be, it is surely worsened significantly by the fact that Mr Havel was clearly not engaged and compliant with treatment. This makes the behaviour of Mr Havel a contributory (patient) factor in this case. The degree to which it contributes is considered later when we come to root causes but it is important to note that both the underlying condition and the behaviour of a patient may have an impact upon the outcome in any patient-safety incident.

HUMAN FACTORS

Human factors are the various psychological and behavioural factors that affect the judgement and actions of individuals or teams. Human factors as contributory 'people' factors are the subject of Chapters 10 and 11.

TASK FACTORS – GUIDELINES AND PROTOCOLS

Task factors are issues relating to the technical difficulty of the job in hand and the support available to do it in the form of guidelines, protocols or decision-making aids. In most clinical cases task factors are not highly significant as contributory factors. They become so when the clinical scenario is rare or unusual or is a novel or new procedure. In this context the rarity of the scenario does not refer to the rarity of the underlying condition of the patient but to the technical processes being utilised by the clinician. For example, when a clinician consults with a patient about their condition, regardless of how rare the condition is, the consultation process is a well-defined and well-described process for which the clinician will have had ample training – assuming that they are acting within their competency levels. Even complex encounters such as surgical procedures are generally well described and the procedure is clear to the surgeon performing the operation. If a surgeon undertakes to perform a new and pioneering operation, however, the task of the surgery itself would become a factor because we would not be confident about what constitutes 'normal' and for such pioneering surgery this risk would be made clear to patients at the time of consenting to the surgery. Think about Dr Kipling and the request by Mr Havel to resupply his insulin, however. Dr Kipling may be familiar with repeating prescriptions for insulin initiated by specialist colleagues. He may also be familiar with prescribing insulin for type 2 diabetic patients. Substituting one type of insulin for another of equivalent effect, however, is a task that is much less common for generalist doctors. When one considers the vast array of different types of insulin as well as the different types of insulin regime that a patient may be on, the issue of how common or easy the task of substituting one type of insulin for another is, becomes significant.

Let us think in terms of analogy. Imagine that the process of a standard medical consultation is akin to driving a car. When we learn to drive we have to go through a period of apprenticeship until we are confident to drive unsupervised. We have to make reference to standard guidance about various types of encounter we may meet on the road that is contained within the Highway Code. The Highway Code also contains advice on driving in adverse conditions as well as the various laws with which we must comply. Once we have mastered driving to a certain level and have demonstrated an understanding of the rules of the road (such as stopping distances and turning procedures) and the laws of the land, we are given a licence to drive and away we go. We drive during the day or at night, on quiet roads and busy roads, on town roads and motorways. But we are not licensed to drive a bus or a large truck. We are not licensed to drive on a race track. We are also not trained or skilled in driving off road or on ice or snow – and yet the occasion may arise in which we may feel compelled to do just this. Although we have never been trained to drive in the snow and may never have done it before, the day will arrive when snow lies thick on the roads and we still have to get to work or to a family event. Do we cancel the journey or take the risk? These are situations when a task such as driving a car, something that may be a familiar and everyday occurrence in which you are quite skilled, becomes a much more difficult task and one for which you have little experience or skill.

> **TOP TIP**
>
> Where a clinician is faced with a situation that is novel or significantly outside of usual day-to-day practice, they must rely on guidelines and protocols for support. The availability and adequacy of such guidance, protocols or decision-support tools may be a significant contributory factor.

Consider Dr Kipling working in his surgery and finding himself confronted with a patient who is taking an insulin type with which he is unfamiliar. Dr Kipling is used to prescribing insulin for patients. He is familiar with a small range of the many insulin types available but has not actually had to swap one insulin type for an equivalent one before. This is actually a novel task for him. It is like a driver who has to confront a new type of driving condition for the first time. How should this new task be tackled? Is it reasonable to even try to tackle it?

What guidance or support does Dr Kipling have with regard to substituting insulin? Is there any evidence that this in itself is a challenging task?

As an investigator faced with these questions I checked standard reference sources. I looked in the British National Formulary and found that there was no guidance on insulin substitution. Current NICE guidance offered no specific guidance either. I wondered if any of the typical online training courses in diabetes that a generalist doctor may do to keep up to date covered this so I did a few courses myself and found that none mentioned the issue of substituting one insulin type for another. An online search did reveal that one Acute Hospital Trust in the Midlands does publish guidelines for substituting insulin but the guidance is for staff working in hospital with in-patients and it only includes insulin types available in the UK.

Thus, in the case of Dr Kipling getting his insulin substitution wrong we have identified that Dr Kipling was doing a task for which there appears to be no guidance or protocol available for generalist primary care doctors and only limited availability of guidance for staff working in secondary care. This is a task where Dr Kipling is on his own – he has to work out his own way to deal with this. That is not to exonerate Dr Kipling from any decisions he may make – his actions still have to be examined critically – but it does put the position of Dr Kipling in to context. Dr Kipling had no support to help him make a decision and this increases the potential for human error to occur. This is definitely a contributory factor in Dr Kipling's case and one from which learning may derive. It is not likely to be the major factor or root cause but it is certainly of importance.

TASK FACTORS – TASK DESIGN

The value of a given task is only as good as its design. The United States military coined a useful term for the robustness of product design when selecting items that may be incorporated into general military use – 'Grunt proof'. 'Grunts' was the name given to soldiers working at the basic and entry levels of the service – the infantry men and women who comprise the largest volume of the military workforce. At this level of service would be the people who were competent enough to serve but who may have the least training, experience or aptitude. If a product or system was to be of value it must be able to be used by any of the Grunts. Not just once, but every day and in any situation in which a Grunt may find themself. An assault rifle, for example, must be able to operate not just on a firing range but also after having been carried across a swamp or after a desert march. It must keep firing all day if it has to, and be able to tolerate being dropped and not accidentally discharge. The designer of military equipment has to be very mindful of the type of person using their equipment and the environments in which they will use it so that they can make it 'Grunt proof'. How does this apply to medicine?

Doctors, nurses and paramedics as well as receptionists, call handlers and other ancillary health workers are constantly confronted with both equipment and services that have been designed. Modern healthcare is renowned for the speed with which new services may be formulated and introduced. Latent or hidden risks may exist due to unforeseen limitations of the design of the new service or equipment. If you wish to truly learn from clinical incidents, then you must be able to recognise and explore design flaws. This is not to criticise or blame colleagues who may have worked hard to develop a new service; it is to act as a 'critical friend', helping to identify weaknesses or glitches that may need to be improved to help to avoid future incidents. At the end of the day it is the safety of the patient that counts. We can explore this with two more case examples from primary care.

Dr Simpson and the DVT

Saturday 20 September, 5:30 p.m.

Dr Simpson is working as an out-of-hours GP. He is a young GP partner and had only recently commenced doing out-of-hours shifts.

Dr Simpson visits a 74-year-old man, Mr Cohen, at his home. Mr Cohen has been undergoing investigation for altered bowel habit and weight loss. His mobility is limited by arthritis of his knees and hips but today his daughter has noted that he has developed a painful swelling of his right calf.

Dr Simpson diagnoses a deep vein thrombosis. He consults guidance produced by the local Clinical Commissioning Group on the community management of DVT. The guidance advises that given Mr Cohen's circumstances, low molecular weight heparin may be administered ahead of a confirmatory Doppler ultrasound that may be organised in regular working hours.

Dr Simpson provides a prescription for low molecular weight heparin based upon Mr Cohen's weight and asks the service manager to arrange for the district nurses to come to administer it. Mr Cohen's daughter obtains the medicine and returns home to await the district nurse.

The district nurse arrives at the home at 8:00 p.m. and asks Mr Cohen where Dr Simpson left the form providing directions for administration of the medication. No such form has actually been left. The nurse phones the out-of-hours service advising that she cannot administer medication without the form and leaves the home.

The case is passed to another out-of-hours GP to visit but the service has a lot of urgent visits that evening and it is after midnight when the out-of-hours service GP phones the home to advise that he is on the way to the home to administer the injection. Mr Cohen's daughter asks if this can wait until tomorrow as Mr Cohen is now asleep.

On Sunday morning the case is put back on to a visit car for a further visit and a different out-of-hours GP visits and provides the injection and writes up a form to enable the district nurses to administer further doses.

On Monday evening Mr Cohen suffers a fatal pulmonary embolism.

Mr Cohen's family complain about the out-of-hours service and the delay in administration of low molecular weight heparin, expressing concern that this may have contributed to Mr Cohen's death.

INVESTIGATION FINDINGS

The community DVT policy adopted by the out-of-hours service and consulted by Dr Simpson was written from the perspective of a clinician working in daytime practice. No consideration was given to events occurring out of hours. While the treatment principles remain the same, the liaison between out-of-hours clinicians and the district nursing service is different. Out-of-hours district nurses are not working directly for a specific GP practice and are not able to consult practice patient records to determine treatment plans and hence need a specific treatment regime written up for each patient. The authors of the guidelines did not consider the full range of its application when it was designed.

Further, this lack of detailed advice was overlooked by the management of the out-of-hours service when they adopted the guidance for use by their service.

Dr Simpson acted correctly in consulting guidance on how to act but was let down by the design of guidance that lacked sufficient detail to cover all potential circumstances in which it may be used.

The design of the task that Dr Simpson had to complete was not robust enough to manage the various circumstances in which it may be used – it was not Grunt proof. This would be a significant contributory factor in the DVT case in accounting for the delay in receipt of heparin and it is a very useful learning point for the service. Note that this is a contributory factor with regard to a service delay but is not necessarily directly related to the death of Mr Cohen despite the concerns of the family. The issue of whether the short delay in heparin administration was a factor in Mr Cohen's death is a more complex issue and may be beyond the scope of an investigation.

NHS PATHWAYS – DRIVING THE CAR

In a previous medical director role, I was involved with the introduction to the UK of the NHS 111 telephone clinical assessment service. NHS 111 is a telephone support system designed to work at national scale from multiple regional call centres. Anyone in England can phone 111 and the call will be answered promptly by a trained health adviser who will utilise a specially designed computer-aided protocol to ask callers about symptoms they may be experiencing in order to determine the severity of their condition. The service uses a computer protocol called NHS Pathways that consists of a series of question sets for specific symptom groups, each designed to safely identify the level of clinical risk associated with a given symptom. NHS Pathways is in turn linked to a database of all NHS service providers and it is able to select an appropriate service for the patient-based upon their symptom severity and where they are calling from. It may even give the option of booking an appointment for some urgent services. It is a very clever and sophisticated system. Health advisers do not have any clinical training but do undergo a robust training course in how to 'drive' the system. They are supported within the service by clinical advisers, experienced nurses and/or paramedics, who may give advice or take over calls if necessary. I spent many an afternoon or evening meeting colleagues and explaining how the new service would work. A useful analogy was to describe NHS Pathways as a car that would take the caller – the patient – on a journey starting from the point of their call and delivering them to 'the right place at the right time'. We described the health advisers as the drivers of the car. We talked about the need to ensure that our 'drivers' were trained well and could drive the car to the best of their ability.

It is fair to say that the launch of NHS 111 did not go smoothly. Much of this was due to operational issues but from the outset and ongoing to this day was a concern about cases where the assessment seems to go disastrously wrong.

- Mrs Kent calls with an episode of chest pain that, to the clinician reviewing the voice recording, sounds typical of acute coronary syndrome and yet the pathways outcome is to contact a doctor within a 24-hour time frame.
- The mother of 14-year-old Chloe calls. Chloe is faint and dizzy and with blurred vision and is heard on voice recording to be deteriorating rapidly as the call progresses, vomiting, groaning and at one point collapsing. The pathways outcome is to see a doctor within two hours and yet the girl collapses and dies 20 minutes after the call ends.
- Eighty-two-year-old Mrs Huntly calls about an episode of acute abdominal pain. She is given a disposition to see a GP within 24 hours and yet a few hours later she is conveyed to hospital by ambulance and at the end of the evening she is on an intensive care unit (ICU). Within 36 hours she has died from complications of mesenteric ischaemia.

Driver error. This was the initial impression from each of the cases. The car was working fine; the health adviser drivers were having an off day. They did not probe the questions sufficiently and hence chose the wrong answer. If you choose the wrong answer you are in effect steering the car to the wrong destination. The learning was that we needed to improve our staff training, or re-train staff, or remind staff of training already undertaken. In short, we needed to make the drivers better.

Driving is a good analogy for any medical task. Clinicians are like drivers of a car and we must take care to ensure that we drive as well as possible as this will reduce the chance of us having an accident and harming our patients. The only problem is that road safety does not work like this – so why should medicine?

More than two-thirds of road-traffic accidents may be attributed to driver error and yet the greatest advances in road safety have not arisen as a result of improved driver training. In fact, this is likely to have virtually no impact upon road safety. The greatest advances in road safety have come from improving cars or improving the roads they drive on. One could argue that the greatest contribution to road safety is the seat belt. You may not be able to stop people driving into a tree but you can reduce the chance of the accident being fatal by making them wear a seat belt. You can't stop people driving their cars too fast but you can design roads with smoother bends, better lighting and better road surfaces.

So the driving the car analogy led me to thinking about how NHS Pathways was designed and the tasks we were asking our health advisers to undertake when they used it. How easy is the car to drive? What safety features does it have? If Pathways is the car, what constitutes the 'road'? What are the weather conditions that may affect driving? It may sound whimsical but this approach led to significant insight into the system and, more importantly, into how the system may be improved.

Both Mrs Kent and Mrs Huntly presented with one symptom each – chest pain and abdominal pain, respectively, with little else going on. When the question sets used by the health adviser in each case were examined in detail it became apparent that the response to a single question in each case determined the outcome. A 'Yes' instead of a 'No' in each case would have resulted in the case being escalated to either an ambulance or an urgent response. The health advisers pointed to the supporting advice for the relevant questions and one could immediately see that a strict interpretation of this advice could only lead to the answers that the health adviser selected. The problem was not the driver but, to expand upon the analogy, misleading information from the control panel of the car. This information was fed back to NHS Pathways and designers within the service were able to refine the way that questions are asked and the supporting advice given. Small changes, perhaps, but this type of insight and feedback is vital to improving services and demonstrates the value in being able to explore task design when looking at clinical incidents.

The case of 14-year-old Chloe was different again. In this case the health adviser started using a question set based upon the initial symptoms presented but this brought them to a result that seemed incongruous so they paused and sought advice from a more skilled driver. In the interim Chloe's condition deteriorated and she developed new symptoms. The health adviser tried to adjust the question sets to suit the symptoms and to get through the questions to reach an outcome. Chloe's case raised some very interesting questions for us about the impact of human factors in NHS 111 cases and this is explored later, but it also identified another problem. Chloe's call took three times longer than average and the health adviser changed tack three times within the call as well as seeking help once. In the heat of the moment we know that humans will miss the significance of events like this but machines do not. The time clock on the IT system kept counting and the IT system also dutifully recorded the pauses in assessment and the changes of direction. And yet the fact that what it was recording was significantly outside of normal for a Pathways assessment did not trigger any sort of warning or alarm that may have prompted the health adviser to review what they were doing. It is like driving a car that does not have warning lights to indicate that the engine is overheating. Without such a relatively simple device you will end up with an engine catastrophically overheating and seizing and it is indeed these hard lessons that led to safety devices such as engine heat sensors in cars. They were not part of the original design; they were lessons learned from mishaps. So too in healthcare; we can identify lessons from exploring contributory factors and in a case such as Chloe's the lesson is that IT systems should be designed to recognise deviation from normal behaviour and to deliver appropriate warnings to help us identify that we may be entering into difficult conditions.

Task design factors require some lateral thought and some effort to analyse but they are worth it. Changes in task design can have a significant impact upon patient safety. So too can changes in service systems. Analysing systems to identify contributory factors is the subject of the next chapter.

9

Understanding why: System factors

We have identified that contributory factors in incidents may be divided into three broad categories: patients, people and 'systems and task factors'. We have looked at patient factors and tasks. New we turn our attention to system factors. System factors include the following issues:

- Equipment – design and function including fail-safe protections
- Work environment
- Organisational issues, including organisational culture
- Education and training issues

Examining systems factors requires us to expand our analysis to potential factors beyond the event in question and to consider the event in its wider context within a healthcare system. Some readers may remember a serious incident that came to public attention some years ago in which a patient died at home following a home visit from an out-of-hours GP who gave him an injection of 100 milligrams of Diamorphine in treatment for an episode of renal colic. The doctor in question had flown over from Germany to act as a locum GP for the out-of-hours service. The patient had told him that he had previously been treated with 100 milligrams of pethidine for renal colic. The GP gave him the same dose of diamorphine that was carried by the out-of-hours service but he did not appreciate that the relative strengths of the two drugs were significantly different. The GP clearly made a catastrophic error of judgement that had its roots in individual factors both cognitive and educational. What about wider system issues?

- Equipment – The service carried 100 milligram of diamorphine ampoules for palliative care patients and it was one of these that was used by the GP. Does carrying such high-dose medication constitute an equipment risk?
- Work environment – Why was a service using a GP flying in for a weekend shift from Europe? Was this an innovative human-resourcing move or simply an attempt to shore up an understaffed service? The answer to this question may give an indication as to whether the GP was joining a well-organised and innovative service or a service that was struggling to deliver safe care.
- Organisational issues – Was the organisation aware of risks associated with diamorphine prescribing? Had other incidents occurred? Had any learning been derived? Had the organisation anticipated any particular problems with using European locum GPs? Was any mitigation put in place?
- Education and training issues – What type of induction did the GP have before starting his shift? Was his education and training sufficient to prepare him for work in England? Did he receive any specific training to prepare him for the English work environment?

The case in question was a high-profile case that attracted much media attention. It occurred in the context of emerging concerns regarding the way that GP out-of-hours services were coping with an increasing number of daytime GPs choosing not to work for out-of-hours services. In this context the broadening of the enquiry into wider systemic questions was quite appropriate. There is a danger, however, that a search for 'systemic' issues within a clinical incident may become a generalised fishing expedition at risk of trawling up general service issues that are not necessarily relevant to the case in question. Alternatively, it may become an excuse to allow an investigator or service lead to embark upon a personal crusade with regard to issues that are only tangentially relevant to the case. So try to make any exploration of systemic issues relevant and specific.

DR KIPLING – SEEING THE LARGER PICTURE

I have previously mentioned the case involving Dr Kipling. Ostensibly this was just a case in which Dr Kipling made an error in substitution of one type of insulin for another. We have considered task factors in detail, noting that the process of substituting one type of insulin for another is a specific task that had factors related to the degree of support and guidance available that may have impacted upon Dr Kipling's actions. Are there wider systemic issues as well? How do factors such as equipment, work environment, the organisation and education and training fit in?

The key lessons that we learn from other safety-critical industries is that humans will make errors. Where possible we must design systems and develop equipment that recognise this fact and provide as much support as possible to minimise the risk of error. So look at systems issues from the point of view of whether they may have helped the people involved avoid making errors or whether they hindered them, or were they just neutral in this regard?

Let's think it through.

TOP TIP

Remember to link your analysis of potential contributory factors to the care or service delivery problems identified or directly to the patient outcome. Do not get side tracked by factors that may be related to the patient's condition but that are not directly related to the case.

EQUIPMENT

Dr Kipling kept notes on his practice computer and he also prescribed the medication and printed off prescriptions. The practice used a well-known general practice software package that enables note keeping, appointments and prescribing. It may seem that IT systems are neutral – that they just do what we tell them to but this is not so. IT systems are designed to be as functional as possible and designers may incorporate a number of factors into a software design to help users. These include decision-support aides, condition-linked guidance within the general note-keeping section and medication alerts within the prescribing module. Was there anything in the software system that may have been directly relevant in this case? We have already established that there is no reference to insulin substitution in the British National Formulary and little published guidance elsewhere, so apart from general advice about diabetic control there is no likely prospect of guidance specifically relating to insulin substitution to be available in a general note-keeping module within a general practice software system. What about the prescribing module, though? Whenever you prescribe medications electronically there will always be pop-up warning windows appearing advising the prescriber of potential contraindications or interactions, particularly if the prescribing module is linked to a list of medication that the patient is already taking. If it is clinically inappropriate for Dr Kipling to prescribe two different long-acting insulin types together at the same time, would it not be reasonable to think that the software system would generate a warning if you tried to do it? Did Dr Kipling overlook this warning? After all, we know that we can become blind to repeated warning signs and dismiss them automatically without really noticing them.

A review of the prescribing module for the specific IT system revealed that no warning appears when two inappropriate insulin types are co-prescribed. The IT system is therefore allowing Dr Kipling to make an error by failing to warn him of potentially high-risk prescribing. Other high-risk prescribing actions trigger a warning window to pop up that halts the prescribing action until such time as the prescriber acknowledges the warning and closes down the screen but this system did not have a warning for this interaction. This appears to be an oversight by the designers of the IT systems. What significance might this have?

We know that in this case Dr Kipling provided an inappropriate script but, further, this script was repeated another 11 times by up to seven other colleagues within the practice. While Dr Kipling may have overlooked a warning even if it were present, a warning system would potentially have given 11 other opportunities to spot the error subsequent to the first mistake. Furthermore, the prescription was taken to a pharmacy and dispensed by a pharmacist. Additional checking also revealed that the dispensing software used by the pharmacist also failed to flag a warning when the two insulin types were recorded in the pharmacy and dispensed. Thus, if we include the pharmacy IT system as part of our equipment review, a total of 24 opportunities to identify the error were missed due to the IT systems in both the pharmacy and the GP practice not having a warning window in recognition of inappropriate insulin prescribing. This fact alone would be enough to suggest that this equipment issue was a significant systemic contributory factor in this case but it becomes even more significant when it was identified that at least one national supplier of primary care IT software does flag a warning to the prescriber when an attempt is made to prescribe the same two insulin types that were prescribed in this incident.

In this case then, by carefully reviewing how the IT equipment is used not just in the practice but also in the pharmacy where the patient collected his prescriptions, we can see that a safety feature that may have alerted Dr Kipling to his error in prescribing was not present. We have identified a system factor that may have contributed to the prescribing error in this case.

WORKING ENVIRONMENT

One may consider the support Dr Kipling had within the practice. Did the practice have a lead for diabetes within the practice – someone who may have had further advanced training to whom Dr Kipling may have gone for advice or support? Beware – because it may be a particular bias of the investigator who has a strong interest in developing such a role to suggest that a GP with a special interest in diabetes working within the practice may have prevented the incident. Perhaps they might if they had seen the patient but unless the practice insists that a specialist GP reviews all patients with diabetes it would be highly speculative to suggest that it may have made any difference. Dr Kipling could have made a specialist referral if he felt he was out of his depth with the prescribing issue, so an in-house specialist is not really essential.

Other factors considered would include appointment scheduling, systems for patient recall and availability of interpreters, given that Mr Havel had poor English. In fact, all such issues were reviewed and found to be within the norms for any general practice with no obvious pressures on appointments and good availability of translators when needed during consultations. In this case, then, there were no significant work-related factors but one can see that there may be a lot of separate issues to consider when determining if work-environment-related issues may be a factor in an incident. Don't be afraid to go into details of how things work in practice; this is where learning may arise even if the contribution to an event is not significant. In delving into the detail in this case I noted that Mr Havel had a number of missed appointments both at the hospital and in the practice. Two of these were in relation to appointments made to discuss abnormal blood-test results. We have already noted that Mr Havel had difficulty in engaging with the service and that this was a 'patient factor' that may have contributed to his poor diabetic control and his liver complications. When I asked about missed appointments the practice manager talked me through the process for GPs raising concerns to the administrative staff when patients failed to turn up. There was a good follow-up system in place to re-contact the patient by phone and letter; however, if the patient still failed to respond there was no further action triggered. Hence it was possible for the patient follow-up process to fail if the patient simply did not respond to contacts. There was no mechanism to keep a file open on the patient. If someone did not remember the follow up it could be lost. It was a small point and actually not likely to contribute in this case, as Mr Havel did eventually turn up for further insulin prescriptions, but although not a significant contributory factor, it was still a useful learning point that the practice could act upon to tighten up its recall system.

ORGANISATIONAL FACTORS

Was the organisation at fault in any way? The organisation may be limited to an individual practice or it may constitute a larger body such as a group of practices, a GP federation, an independent provider organisation or even a clinical commissioning group. Think about who is responsible for employment of staff and creation of policies and protocols and who is responsible for investigation of incidents or complaints. An organisation may contribute to an incident by failing to effect reasonable due diligence in its overall management of the service.

Good questions to ask to get you started would be around policies or protocols and also regarding complaints and incidents.

- What policies and protocols do you have that are relevant to this incident?
- Have you had any previous complaints or incidents of a similar nature before?
- If there are no policies or protocols, is that reasonable?
- Should there be a policy or protocol in existence?

It may be reasonable for there not to be a policy or protocol already but perhaps a learning point from your investigation may be that there should be one. Incidents or complaints about the same subject may indicate a trend or underlying problem that had been previously identified but not addressed by the organisation. The worst-case scenario for an organisation would be for an investigator to discover that exactly the same thing happened two years ago and that recommendations designed to prevent a recurrence had not been acted upon.

Sticking with the Dr Kipling case, I was interested in the following areas:

- Does the practice have medicines management policy?
- Does the practice have a protocol for management of diabetic patients?
- Does the policy or protocol address issues of insulin prescribing?
- Is there a protocol for management of repeat prescriptions?
- Is there a protocol for use of interpreters?
- Have there been previous medicines management incidents involving insulin prescribing?
- Have there been any complaints involving insulin-prescribing issues?
- Does the practice have a formal mechanism for sharing learning arising from significant clinical incidents?

Asking such questions may appear threatening to a practice as the question may imply that there should be a positive response – yes, of course we have a policy covering this issue. This is not the point, however. You are not trying to catch anyone out. This is just about finding out why things happen and whether we can learn anything. A review of the organisational issues may look like Table 9.1.

One can see that there may be areas where policies or protocols do not meet the challenges thrown up by this case but this does not mean that they are at fault. It is a fact that there is no specific guidance on substitution of insulin subtypes so it is important to note this but this does not imply that there should have been guidance in place. This will depend upon the relative risk of the incident arising and whether this type of risk had been anticipated and mitigation measures initiated previously. We have seen in our analysis of task factors in Chapter 8 that insulin substitution is a task seldom undertaken in primary care and that guidance is not readily available for this. The fact that the practice did not have specific guidance makes it just like any other practice and thus any deficiency is not likely to be a contributory factor even if we may identify it as a potential learning point. Similarly, the fact that the practice did not have a very good mechanism for sharing learning following incidents is something that the practice may learn from but it is not something that would have contributed to the incident in this case. It would only have been relevant if a similar episode had occurred two years ago and was mentioned at a practice meeting but no follow-up action occurred to improve the service.

Table 9.1

Organisational questions	Organisation response	Investigator comment
Does the practice have medicines management policy?	Yes	Generic policy – similar to most practice policies. Generally fit for purpose
Does the practice have a protocol for management of diabetic patients?	Yes	Protocol outlines processes for assessment and follow up. Structures follow up appointments and diabetic reviews in line with NICE guidance.
Does the policy or protocol address issues of insulin prescribing?	Yes	It only gives very general recognition of insulin as a potential high-risk medication. No specific guidance or provision for particular sub-groups of patients (for example, not initiating insulin prescribing for type 1 diabetics in practice). No guidance on insulin substitution. This, however, is in line with most practices.
Is there a protocol for management of repeat prescriptions?	Yes	Deals with process only – who does what and when. No clinical element to this.
Is there a protocol for use of interpreters?	Yes	Good provision of interpreter services. Everyone knows how it works.
Have there been previous medicines management incidents involving insulin prescribing?	No	None on record or in memory of senior staff
Have there been any complaints involving insulin prescribing issues?	No	None recorded or in memory of senior staff
Does the practice have a formal mechanism for sharing learning arising from significant clinical incidents?	Yes	Covered at monthly practice meetings; however, minutes of meeting limited and if staff not present they will not receive follow up

In summary, do not make a policy or protocol a contributory factor just because it may omit something that you think is relevant unless you can link it directly to the incident. If you identify a deficiency that did not directly impact, you may note it as a learning point without its being a contributory factor.

Furthermore, when investigating issues such as policy and protocol provision it is important that these are assessed in their proper context. If you consider a GP practice medicines management policy or diabetic protocol it should be seen in the context of what is a normal policy or protocol for a general practice and not compared with a hospital policy or protocol, for example. If you are not sure of whether a policy or protocol is typical for a particular service, you may need to call on colleagues to provide advice or support and most will be happy to help.

EDUCATION AND TRAINING

Education and training issues may be specific to individuals or may be a general issue for the organisation. In some cases, you may identify issues that extend beyond the individuals or organisation concerned and may be applicable to much larger sections of a health economy or even of national importance. Education and training issues concern not just potential or identified gaps in individual knowledge but also how an organisation ensures that staff are suitably trained for their role and how they maintain their level of competence. Issues that may arise include how an organisation determines educational competencies for a given role, how this is verified at selection and recruitment, how staff are inducted into the customs, practice and culture of an organisation and also how ongoing competency for the role is maintained.

Training issues become apparent in an incident when care delivery or service delivery problems indicate that a member of staff did not know the correct way to do something. The clue to this may have arisen in your initial assessment of the case if you undertook a foresight or substitution test. Did someone fail to follow standard protocol or national guidelines or accepted best practice? Did someone act outside the expected range of behaviour for their role? Essentially any actions or omissions by members of staff that suggest that they did not know how to do something should suggest a training or education issue.

In the baby Anna case Dr King failed to refer Anna for a paediatric opinion when he had identified that she had or may have had a febrile convulsion. Was he ignorant of the guidelines or did he know them but deliberately ignore them? For Dr King it was the latter; he was aware of guidance but chose to ignore it for reasons that were plausible even if they were wrong. But Dr King also made a further management error that demonstrated lack of awareness of current guidelines. He gave baby Anna a dose of paracetamol and then reviewed her after an hour and appeared reassured by the drop in temperature. Guidance from NICE has suggested that this technique, familiar to many doctors and nurses working in urgent care settings, is no longer regarded as best practice. Dr King was unaware of this change in guidance and had commented that he had used this technique since working in accident and emergency (A&E) departments as a junior doctor. It is clear that Dr King had not kept fully up to date with the latest available guidance and this raises a very real challenge with primary care. National guidelines are frequently promulgated by the great and the good and disseminated via various methods to clinical staff but there is evidence to indicate that clinical staff simply cannot keep up with the volume of updates and guidance that come their way. Is this then just an individual training issue for Dr King or is this a reflection of a wider educational problem for all GPs? If you are a clinical lead you may have a notion of what the answer is based upon observing colleague practice or auditing clinical notes. If not, however, a discovery such as this may prompt you to conduct a mini-survey of your staff to identify whether this is a common practice or not or whether there is awareness of NICE guidance on this matter or not. This may help to guide later consideration as to the learning value of this observation. You may identify that Dr King was one of only two out of fifty doctors and nurses who still did this practice. In which case, the knowledge gap and subsequent educational need is quite small and limited to a few individuals. If 50 per cent of staff were unaware of current NICE guidance and still use this outdated method, then a greater education need for the organisation arises. If you are not sure whether an incident involves an isolated educational learning need or a wider one, you may address the point by performing an audit as part of your investigation as indicated above. If this is challenging due to time or other logistical constraints, you may simply indicate that you have identified a question within the RCA that needs further exploration. You may recommend addressing the individual educational need with Dr King but also performing a wider audit as an action to complete after the incident investigation is finished with responsibility devolved to someone else.

What about Dr Kipling and his colleagues at the practice who made and perpetuated the mistake in insulin prescribing? Dr Kipling substituted the wrong insulin but this was also missed by several colleagues who followed up Mr Havel and repeated the same prescribing error. Mr Havel had had multiple contacts with five different GPs in the practice between registration and receipt of information indicating that a prescribing error had occurred. In addition, Mr Havel was seen at least once in a local accident and emergency department and yet the original insulin substitution error was not spotted.

We have already noted that insulin substitution is not a common task for a general practitioner but what are the educational points at stake here? In this case any inherent difficulty with insulin substitution is compounded by the fact that the insulin type that Mr Havel was taking, Humulin R, was not available in the UK and hence UK prescribers and dispensers would be unlikely to be familiar with it.

Dr Kipling has confirmed that he keeps up to date with ongoing professional development and this includes doing regular online refresher training modules on the management of diabetes. These, however, had not prepared him to be fully familiar with the various different types of insulin. Thus, in three subsequent consultations Dr Kipling remained unable to note the prescribing error.

Mr Havel was also seen by or had repeat prescriptions from Dr Darzi on five separate occasions. An interview with Dr Darzi indicates that they too keep up to date with professional development but were also ignorant of the range of different insulin types such that they failed to notice that the insulin combination was inappropriate.

Given that five different GPs and at least one doctor in an A&E department also failed to notice an inappropriate prescription it would seem that a lack of knowledge of insulin types sufficient to easily spot this kind of prescribing error is widespread. When faced with this level of lack of knowledge it is clear that this is not an individual knowledge gap; there is a bigger problem identified here. It is helpful to look at some of the training available. The author has reviewed online training available on commonly used training sites for GPs and although the sites do provide training on management of diabetes, the training focuses upon management of complications and does not focus upon insulin management. The few courses that do focus on management tend to focus on managing specific regimes and do not cover substitution of insulin. Thus, although a clear knowledge gap is identified by this case it does not appear to be due to a lack of ongoing training but rather the fact that we are dealing with a niche area of medicine that is simply not covered by standard training regimes. This is interesting from a learning perspective but it does not necessarily implicate a lack of training per se as a contributory factor.

KNOWN UNKNOWNS AND UNKNOWN UNKNOWNS

Educational and training factors in serious incidents raise an interesting phenomenon related to knowledge gaps among staff that is exemplified by the Dr Kipling case.

- We know that we cannot know every clinical fact.
- We know that there are unknown facts that may create risk.
- But we do not always know what we do not know.
- **Unknown unknowns pose a particular risk in clinical practice.**

UNCONSCIOUS INCOMPETENCE

As part of the Kipling case, I reviewed insulin types available in the UK and identified that there are more than 60 different brand names and sub-types of insulin device on the market in the UK at present. Within the British National Formulary there are 13 different types of insulin with 27 variants of delivery mechanism. A knowledge gap among doctors regarding insulin substitution and prescribing is thus not surprising.

Added to this is a confusing nomenclature among insulin sub-types that has arisen for historic and commercial reasons. In the UK, for example, we now recognise two types of insulin that provide a quick response and are suitable for use as part of a 'basal-bolus' regime, taken before meals. The insulin types are called 'Short acting' and 'Rapid acting', the former being active within a few minutes of injection and hence can be taken immediately before a meal while the latter take 20 to 30 minutes to act and need to be taken half an hour before a meal. When it comes to nomenclature, however, a clinician is faced with a mixture of brand names and insulin 'type' names that are at times counterintuitive. For example:

- Novorapid – is a rapid-acting insulin.

   But:

- Insuman Rapid – is actually a short-acting insulin
- Human actrapid – is actually a short-acting insulin

Further:

- Humulin S – is a short-acting insulin but the S stands for soluble – not short.
- Humulin R – (Mr Havel's original insulin, not available in the UK) is a rapid-acting insulin but the R stands for regular – not rapid.

Humulin R is the insulin that Dr Kipling was trying to substitute. If you Google Humulin R one of the first sites listed mentioning it is Drugs.com – this describes Humulin R as a 'fast' acting insulin, using yet another type of nomenclature again. Does 'fast acting' mean a rapid or short-acting insulin in English parlance?

Eli-Lilly's own product literature for Humulin R describes it as 'Regular' and it is only in the section on pharmacokinetics that one can read that its time of onset is approximately 30 minutes and hence it would fall into the UK designation of a rapid-acting insulin.

And further still, Humulin, Humalog, Hypurin and Insuman insulin types all come with a variety of sub-types or combinations that may include rapid or short-acting as well as intermediate or mixed formulations using the name Humulin, Humalog, Hypurin or Insuman as the prefix – thus making it very difficult for clinicians to retain a clear notion of which type of insulin is which at any given moment.

It is not just that this area is a complex minefield for the non-specialist who has to try to maintain a working knowledge of insulin types; the concern is that this area of medicine is so complex that the degree of one's ignorance is very difficult to gauge. Until I investigated this case I did not realise quite how complicated insulin prescribing was and how much I did not know. My own ignorance of my level of ignorance is a risk factor that amplifies the risk associated with my level of ignorance. Unconscious incompetence is a risk but two American psychologists, Dunning and Kruger, describe a phenomenon that may make this factor even worse. (Kruger, Justin; Dunning, David (1999). "Unskilled and Unaware of It: How Difficulties in Recognizing One's Own Incompetence Lead to Inflated Self-Assessments". *Journal of Personality and Social Psychology* 77 (6): 1121–34.) See Chapter 10 for more information about human factors in clinical incidents.

SYSTEMIC RISK FACTORS IN YOUR SERVICE

It helps to be prepared for investigation of incidents and to this end thinking about specific aspects of your service is helpful. Some services are more prone to systemic failings than others. Primary care is classically regarded as a sort of one-man band. Doctors, nurses or paramedic practitioners see patients in individual consultations and take responsibility for the whole of the encounter. If something goes wrong the obvious source of error is likely to be human error – errors in judgements on the part of the practitioner concerned. While human error is very important – indeed, we explore this in a lot of depth in subsequent chapters, it is actually just a small aspect of a wider problem. Just as road safety will only be increased to a small degree by improving driver performance, so too will healthcare safety only be improved to a marginal degree by tackling human error by improving the training of doctors and nurses. Individual awareness of risks associated with human error and consequent improved performance is an important step to take but bigger improvements are likely to be made by recognising when tasks or systemic issues are involved. So what is your service like?

Think about the following questions to evaluate your service systemic risks.

- What equipment do you use (including IT systems)?
- Are all staff competent to use it?
- Is it cleaned, maintained and calibrated regularly?
- Is your service new or established? (New urgent care services often put staff in positions where 'normal' is difficult to gauge, for example, NHS 111, paramedic emergency practitioners and autonomous nurse practitioners and the new physician assistants' roles.)

- What is your staffing profile and patient profile?
- Do you have a robust induction process?
- Do you require staff to do mandatory training?
- Do they do it?
- Do you undertake regular service audits? If so, are these clinical-performance audits or service-development audits?
- How do you manage medicines in your service?
- Do you have a medicines policy? Is this one that staff are familiar with? Is it functional or just for show?
- Can you identify how many times high-risk drugs were used in your service in the past month?
- Do you have policies and protocols for staff to follow? Are these bespoke to your service or have they been 'cut and pasted' from other sources? If so, are they really fit for purpose?
- Do all staff know how to raise patient-safety concerns?
- Do you have a complaint and incident policy?
- Can you evidence learning from previous incidents?
- How would you feel if you learnt that the Care Quality Commission (CQC) were visiting your service next Monday?

10

Human factors Part 1: The key to enhanced learning

'We're blind to our blindness. We have very little idea of how little we know. We're not designed to know how little we know.'

Daniel Kahneman, Nobel prize-winning psychologist and author of *Thinking, Fast and Slow* (Penguin, 2012)

Here are some things that we know about human behaviour:

- Humans make mistakes.
- It is a myth to think that if you punish people sufficiently for a mistake then they will never make a mistake again. (The punishment myth)
- It is a myth to think that if you practice hard enough at something then you will never make a mistake. (The perfection myth)

Despite knowing this, however, we still tend to react to human errors in the following way:

- surprise, disbelief and anger
- a desire to punish the person that made the mistake
- a desire to train people harder so that they do not make the same mistake again.

Following a serious incident, enlightened observers may manage to avoid surprise, disbelief and anger and even manage to seek to learn and not to blame – but surprise, anger and a desire for punishment will remain the primary reaction seen from most patients and relatives and perhaps even from commissioners and colleagues outside your organisation. However, even enlightened observers will still often tend to want to seek a training solution to a human error problem. After all, what else can you do to make human performance better other than to train? Is this not the lesson from learning to play a sport or a musical instrument or even our times tables? Practice does make perfect. Certainly, practice makes you better but you only have to observe the English football team in a penalty shoot-out to know that practice does not eliminate mistakes. That is because we are humans and the rule is: humans make mistakes. There is no qualification to this; it is not 'only some humans make mistakes' or 'only lazy or stupid humans make mistakes' (although they may of course make more than average). Practice makes you better but it does not make you perfect.

When investigating serious clinical incidents, the challenge is not just to identify human error, but to also identify where human error may be reduced in the future by better training, and where it is necessary to identify that humans will never stop making this particular type of error and to think about whether one could redesign a system to remove the human element from it. The British psychologist professor James Reason, world renowned for his work on understanding human error in clinical medicine, has famously stated:

> 'You cannot change the human condition; but you can change the conditions under which humans work.' (Reason, J, 2000, Human error: models and management, *British Medical Journal*, p. 769)

To return to the road-safety analogy, we must always consider how much an incident (a road accident) can persuade us that drivers need better training and how much an incident may tell us that vehicles or roads need better design. When vehicle-safety specialists realised that drivers keep crashing into one another even when they are experienced and driving in apparently optimal conditions, they took human error out of the equation and put seat belts into cars, with massive improvements in safety as a result. Understanding and learning from human error is vital but we must remember the need to find a solution to human problems in the wider context of the systems in which human clinicians are working.

HUMANS WORKING ALONE AND HUMANS WORKING IN TEAMS

The potential for human error is complicated by the fact that healthcare is provided by a mixture of individual human interactions and decision making as well as interventions provided by teams. We are lucky in that considerable research has been undertaken with regard to how individual humans make decisions and what factors may lead to them making errors. There has been less academic research but, nonetheless, a lot of practical experience of how certain types of team operate in safety-critical environments. Both sources of material provide very useful background theory and context for the investigator of clinical incidents. The military and the aviation and space industry in particular have invested heavily in understanding how teams function and how to improve team performance.

Table 10.1 Factors that influence human performance

Individual human factors	Team or group factors
Hubris – pride	Communication
Fatigue	Authority gradients
Distraction	Different mental models
Overload	Silo mentality
Confidence	Group thinking
Mental models	
Cognitive biases	
Situational awareness	

The list in Table 10.1 is certainly not exhaustive. Some sources will cite other factors or will split some factors further into constituent parts. For our purposes this is not really that important. Remember that we are exploring the matter not for academic purposes but to help us to understand the causes of incidents that we are investigating. The key point for investigators is the value of these concepts in understanding and learning from serious incidents. What is difficult during an incident investigation is the process of determining which of the many potential human factors that may have been involved are actually relevant.

HOW PEOPLE THINK

Three theoretical constructs are very useful when conducting incident investigations. They have been much quoted and utilised by incident investigators working in the health-care field. They are not mutually exclusive theories and all three approaches may be used either singly or together within an investigation. It depends upon what has happened and which theory helps the investigator to understand and learn from the incident. The three key theories are the constructs of Rasmussen and Reason with regard to learning and performing tasks, the work of Daniel Kahneman with regard to heuristic logic and critical decision making and the work of NASA with regard to safety-critical behaviour in high-risk environments. For the sake of simplicity, I have categorised these three useful theoretical constructs as follows:

- How we learn to perform tasks
- How we think and make judgements
- How we act in high-pressure environments

RASMUSSEN AND REASON: HOW WE LEARN TO PERFORM TASKS

Jens Rasmussen was a Scandinavian industrial psychologist who studied the learning mechanisms of workers in factories. (IEEE Transactions, May 1983.) He developed a model of learning that is called the Skill, Rule, Knowledge (SRK) model. It describes a hierarchy of learning in which the degree of active thinking or cognitive effort diminishes as someone moves from being a novice to becoming a skilled operator. At the outset a large amount of knowledge needs to be acquired and retained requiring a high level of cognitive effort and attention. Think about how much concentration it takes when you first learn to drive a car or play a musical instrument. As you progress, the degree of conscious thought diminishes as the basic knowledge base becomes consolidated and you rely on sets of rules to direct and maintain performance. Active recall of the full range of processes involved in overtaking another car, for example, may be replaced by recall of simple 'rules' such as '300 metres clear ahead' and then 'mirror signal manoeuvre'. Finally, an operative becomes skilled at a task and the degree of conscious attention to the task may diminish to virtually zero. You may drive a car or play a complex piece on

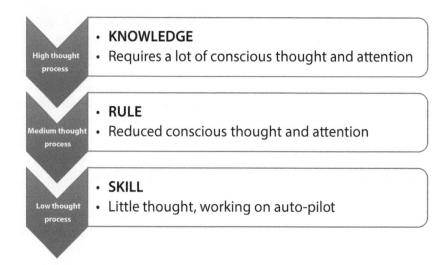

Figure 10.1 SKR model – diminishing conscious thought

an instrument without even thinking about it – your training and experience simply take over and you go on to automatic pilot.

Professor James Reason is a British psychologist who has contributed a great deal to our understanding of clinical error (see: Reason J. *Human error*. New York: Cambridge University Press, 1990). He famously proposed the 'Swiss cheese' model to illustrate how barriers to patient harm may, like a piece of Swiss cheese, develop holes. When a series of holes align, a risk may pass right through and lead to patient harm. He also recognised that Rasmussen's model of how we learn would also represent a model of how we make mistakes. Reason proposed that we make Skill-based errors, Rule-based errors and Knowledge-based errors (Figure 10.2).

Consider applying this to a common error – a clinician prescribes penicillin to a patient who is allergic to penicillin. The patient takes the medicine and dies from an anaphylactic reaction. What type of error may this be within the Skill, Rule, Knowledge model?

Skill-level errors – these are failures due to slips or lapses. Knowledge is present, the question is asked and the answer is recorded and yet the clinician still prescribes penicillin. A distraction or a mental 'slip' can easily lead to such errors.

Rule-level errors – these are failures to follow standard rules of operation. Standard procedure in taking a medical history is to ask whether the patient has allergies to medication – particularly when prescribing antibiotics. Failure to ask a standard question is a 'rule'-based error.

Knowledge-level errors – these are failures to know the facts. In this scenario, the clinician would have to be unaware that penicillin may cause allergic reactions – this is highly unlikely but may be relevant in some circumstances.

Among experienced clinicians skill and rule-level errors are relatively common when faced with common conditions. But experience does not preclude knowledge-level errors. Faced with a rare or uncommon presentation then even a very experienced clinician may make an error due to lack of knowledge about the presenting condition.

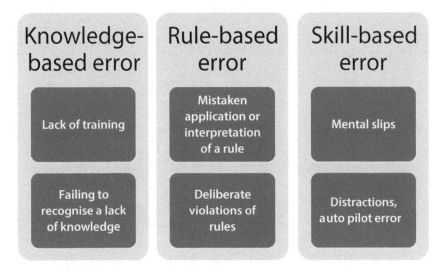

Knowledge-based error	Rule-based error	Skill-based error
Lack of training	Mistaken application or interpretation of a rule	Mental slips
Failing to recognise a lack of knowledge	Deliberate violations of rules	Distractions, auto pilot error

Figure 10.2 Active error types

A key learning point is that one's position on the Skill, Rule, Knowledge model is not fixed and one may fluctuate from case to case or even within a single patient contact. The inherent danger for clinicians is in allowing oneself to work for long periods at a 'Skill' level, on auto-pilot, with little conscious thought. In such a state a short lapse or distraction can lead to error. Flexibility of thought is essential in medicine and the ability to recognise cues to increase the level of thought in a particular case, to return to rules or protocol, even to return to the books (or the Internet) to acquire a little more knowledge is vital and represents a true skill.

ACTIVE FAILURE: INTENDED ERRORS, MISTAKES AND VIOLATIONS

Reason further breaks down human error into sub-types of either 'Intended' or 'Unintended' and then breaks these sub-types further into 'Slips', 'Mistakes' or 'Violations'. He has generally referred to these types of errors as being 'Active'. Active errors are opposed to 'Latent' errors that are errors arising due to potential design flaws residing within systems as a result of service or procedural design. (In the Dr MacDonald case of delayed heparin prescription, the failure to include provision for out-of-hours prescribing in the community DVT protocol was a latent error – an incident waiting to happen.)

In Reason's model it is not the error that is intended, of course; it is the action. For example, if we look at the same case as above, the clinician prescribing penicillin, the first question is, did the clinician intend to prescribe penicillin? A review of the notes may reveal that the clinician had written an intention to prescribe erythromycin but then, following distraction, had automatically selected penicillin from a drop-down menu 'without thinking'. This is an 'unintended' error.

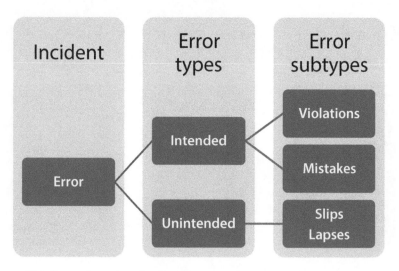

Figure 10.3 Error sub-types – after Reason

Taking the example of prescribing penicillin in error a little further, let us look at three possible scenarios.

CASE A

Dr A asks the patient if they are allergic to penicillin and records that they are. He makes a note that he will prescribe erythromycin but instead prescribes penicillin.

During investigation of the incident Dr A admits that they were busy and thinking of their next patient during the consultation and was rushing to finish the consultation. Without thinking they 'automatically' prescribed penicillin as they had done this several times already in the same clinic. The doctor said they were working on automatic pilot and not really thinking about what they were doing.

CASE B

Dr B asks the patient if they are allergic to penicillin and records that they are. He makes a note that they had a rash as a child after penicillin 30 years ago.

During the investigation Dr B said he deliberately chose to prescribe penicillin despite the history as they believed that the history was not consistent with a true allergy.

CASE C

Dr C does not record whether the patient has an allergy to penicillin and the patient's mother later testifies that Dr C did not ask the question.

At the inquest Dr C contends that this was their first out-of-hours shift and that they were used to working in a practice in which the patient's medication history and allergy status were known and recorded and that their practice computer would alert them if they prescribed a drug to which a patient was allergic. Hence, they did not think to ask about allergies.

In case A, the error was 'Unintended'. Dr A did not intend to give penicillin. Because of a distraction Dr A acted on auto-pilot and made an unintended mistake or mental slip. Error sub-types = Unintended Slip.

In case B, the error was 'Intended'. Dr B deliberately gave penicillin despite a history of allergy in the mistaken belief that the allergy history presented was incorrect. He intended the action but it was based upon a mistaken belief. Error sub-types = Intended Mistake.

In case C, the error was intended. Dr C deliberately gave penicillin but he also failed to perform a standard clinical protocol in not asking about allergies. Failure to follow a standard clinical protocol is a 'Violation'. Error sub-types = Intended Violation.

Slips and mistakes are relatively common – after all, humans make mistakes. 'Violations' are less easy to forgive and certainly from a medico-legal point of view it would be much harder to defend practice that is outside standard clinical practice.

And yet, 'violating' standard protocol is something that many of us do frequently. Experience does allow us to determine when it is safe to take a 'shortcut' or to overlook a rule for the sake of expediency. The key lesson from Reason is not that a 'violation' or deviation from standard practice should never occur, but to be aware of the risks associated with such actions. Reason posits that clinicians may make human errors of this type because within the context of a busy clinical practice we 'forget to be afraid' (Reason, J, Human Error: models and management, *BMJ* 2000, 320, pp. 768–770).

DANIEL KAHNEMAN: HOW WE THINK AND MAKE JUDGEMENTS

The Nobel laureate Daniel Kahneman and his colleague Amos Tvesky have made a massive contribution to the field of cognitive psychology – the study of how humans think and make judgements. Kahneman's initial work has helped us to understand the process of heuristic logic as applied to decision making. This in turn led to explorations of bias in thinking – innate tendencies toward certain types of thought pattern that can skew our judgements.

HEURISTICS AND BIAS

When humans think about a problem and seek a solution we use a particular type of logic. It is a short-cut system called heuristic logic. Rather than spend a lot of time and effort analysing all of the data in front of us, our brains have evolved to rapidly search for and identify patterns. We have learned to form conclusions and to make decisions without all the facts and without considering all of the different angles. We make a 'best guess' at something and act on this best guess. Heuristic logic is a type of best-guess logic that enables decisions to be made with much less information than a computer would need to make an accurate decision based upon the Algorithmic logic of the computer. Heuristic logic is an evolutionary advantage for animals and humans alike – it is vital for making quick, potentially life-saving decisions. The problem is that many clinical decisions often need a more deliberate and considered approach. Quick heuristic judgements are much easier to make and the tendency to make quick decisions can become habitual. This leads us into making errors. Certain types of heuristic thought patterns are so ingrained in humans that they occur time and time again in a way that recognisably biases our thinking and ability to make judgements.

A COGNITIVE MODEL OF CLINICAL ERROR: A TRIAD OF BIASES

Kahneman and colleagues have described a wide range of cognitive or thinking biases but certain types seem to be particularly common in medical incidents. Consider this model that I find a useful construct to walk through incidents (Figure 10.4). It posits that clinical errors are at the centre of a triad of biases affecting:

- attitude
- attention
- cognition (thought processes).

ATTITUDE

We all bring an attitude to anything that we do in life. It sets the tone for our engagement with the world and it may vary considerably depending upon how we feel at the time and due to unconscious factors related to our personality. As clinicians we are frequently

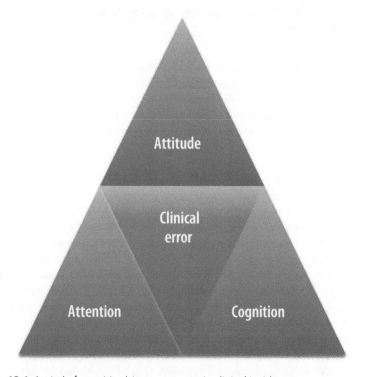

Figure 10.4 A triad of cognitive biases common in clinical incidents

beset by two common attitudinal heuristic biases – anchoring and availability. These are biases that will influence our immediate sense of what is going on with a case and, unfortunately, if they go unrecognised they are very difficult to eliminate. They do not usually cause the final error in decision making – they just set up the clinician to make further errors of attention or cognition.

The anchoring heuristic

Anchoring involves a mental fixation upon the very first visual or verbal impressions received. We are all subject to anchoring and, once anchored, as the name implies, it is very difficult to shift.

Dr MacDonald sees an elderly female patient who is complaining of a worsening indigestion and of burning throat pain that has not been relieved by recent omeprazole script. Dr MacDonald instantly equates burning pain in the throat with reflux oesophagitis. He finds it difficult to move away from this first thought when the patient also discloses increasing shortness of breath on exertion. Dr MacDonald increases the patient's omeprazole. Three hours later the patient dies and post-mortem examination reveals she had suffered a myocardial infarct.

Dr MacDonald later admitted that he remained fixated on the diagnosis of gastro-oesophagal reflux disease (GORD) despite several clues that this was an atypical presentation of acute coronary syndrome.

In several scientific studies Kahneman demonstrated that anchoring can be simulated easily to any audience and can skew their subsequent judgement. Even if information that seems obviously erroneous is presented it is still likely to skew the thoughts of the recipient in that direction. Clinically, we are all prone to become anchored on the first thing that a patient says to us. If a patient who is having a heart attack presents saying 'I have chest pain' we are much more likely to diagnose acute coronary syndrome than we are if the same patient presents saying, 'I have indigestion'. I suppose that, deep down, we all want to believe.

The availability heuristic

If we are not anchored by an opening comment, we are often subject to a phenomenon called availability heuristic or availability bias. The availability heuristic involves giving undue weight or attention to facts that come readily to mind.

Consider a school nurse working in a boarding school. A fifteen-year-old male presented to a school nurse on a Monday morning complaining of testicular pain and swelling that had developed the night before. The boy had vomited once in the night when the pain came on. He had spoken to a house matron and been given paracetamol. The following morning pain was described as mild and the boy did not seem in distress. The nurse immediately thought of testicular torsion but the information that came to mind was that torsion was a condition that caused severe pain and distress. For reasons of discretion she did not examine the boy but arranged for him to see a GP at the end of the school day when the GP did a clinic.

Eight hours later the GP examined the boy and found a testicle swollen to the size of an orange. At surgery an hour later a severe torsion was discovered and the now non-viable testis was removed.

The nurse thought of the right diagnosis but she brought to mind obvious 'available' information about testicular torsion that was all about the dramatic and extremely painful common presentation. Not immediately available to the nurse was information to the effect that some 15 per cent of torsions present 'silently' with very mild levels of pain.

Attention

Attitudinal biases tend to just set us up to fail – they usually do not lead to failure per se. When working under pressure humans are prone to attention bias; that is to say, when under pressure we find it very difficult to pay attention to everything that is going on without feeling overwhelmed. It is far easier to narrow our attention to a specific job in hand or to select a narrow range of focus – usually for something that is familiar to us. This process is a type of attentional bias and in medical practice this can have catastrophic consequences.

Attentional bias – Tunnelling and selectivity

The best-known example of tunnelling bias is the Elaine Bromiley case. Elaine had attended hospital for a routine operation but following induction of anaesthesia the anaesthetist had problems inserting the breathing tube. With rising pressure due to failure to get the tube inserted the anaesthetist became completely focused upon trying to succeed in the task of intubation, failing to realise that his efforts were taking far too long and that he should have abandoned the procedure. The anaesthetist had tunnelled his attention so much upon trying to succeed in one task that he completely overlooked the bigger and more urgent issue that was that the patient was not being oxygenated during his efforts. Sadly, Elaine never recovered from the brain damage that ensued. The NHS is indebted to Elaine's husband Martin who was a British Airways (BA) pilot who had expertise in human factors and incident investigation within the aviation industry. Martin was able to take an active role not just in the investigation of the tragedy of his own wife's death but also in sharing and spreading learning from this terrible episode to health services worldwide.

Tunnelling and selectivity do not affect only surgical procedures; they may also affect any complex multiple-stage task. In 2013 I noted this effect in a number of incidents occurring within the new NHS 111 service. This was epitomised by the case of Chloe.

Chloe – When the going gets tough – tunnel

Chloe is a 13-year-old girl. She has a significant underlying medical condition, adrenal hypoplasia, which requires emergency treatment if she should become unwell.

Chloe arrives home from school and reports to her mother that she is feeling faint and dizzy with blurred vision.

Her mother telephones the NHS 111 service. She does not mention Chloe's underlying medical condition to the health adviser as she assumes that this is 'on her record' and that the 111 service would know this and take it into account at assessment. (While there is a system to alert NHS 111 of potential patients at risk this had not been actioned in this case.) Follow the case through in the outline below and see how attention becomes focused on completion of the task, of adhering to the computerised assessment tool at the expense of noting the bigger picture.

- The HA answers the call – she 'anchors' on the fact that she is dealing with a 13-year-old girl and hence does not anticipate that this will be a difficult or high-risk case.
- The mother mentions vague symptoms – blurred vision and fatigue. The mother does not sound particularly concerned, further anchoring the HA in the notion that this is a routine simple call.
- The HA finds that the first NHS pathways question set chosen is difficult to complete. She consults a clinician and is advised to probe questions further.
- Before she can start again Chloe's mother shouts in alarm, 'Oh my God, what's happened? Someone help me!'
- Chloe briefly collapsed. She recovers quickly and the HA tries to keep the assessment going. Chloe can be heard vomiting in the background.
- The HA decides to continue but to change the question set to one of vomiting. Questions covering a range of conditions that may trigger vomiting are asked of both Chloe and her mother.
- Chloe is spoken to – her voice is deep and she sounds drowsy – not what you may expect from a 13-year-old girl.
- She groans and vomits further during questioning and appears partially disorientated.
- The HA says to Chloe, 'OK, Chloe, I am just going to go through these questions with you as quickly as possible so that we can get you the help that you need.'
- The HA has become 'tunnelled' – she is completely focused upon completing the question set with Chloe as she believes that this is the best way for Chloe to get help.
- 111 health advisers are trained to exit complex medical calls and pass them on to a clinical colleague – the HA was so overwhelmed she failed to do this.
- They carried on and completed an assessment resulting in advice to attend a doctor within two hours.
- Thirty minutes after the call, Chloe collapses. When a paramedic crew arrives they are not able to resuscitate her and she is declared dead at the scene.

Chloe was suffering from an acute adrenal crisis and given the speed of Chloe's collapse it is unlikely that the final outcome would have changed had the HA acted differently, but the case shows vividly how easy it is to become overwhelmed in a process and not notice what is happening to your patient.

It is not necessary for an attitudinal bias to occur first; attention biases may arise at any time, but attention bias is certainly more likely to arise off the back of an attitudinal bias. In this case it was a simple case of anchoring upon the fact that Chloe was a young girl with what appeared to be innocuous symptoms – feeling tired, being dizzy, having blurred vision. The anchoring bias in this case did not just lead to tunnelling. Notice, too, how the HA failed to process the fact that when she spoke to Chloe, she did not sound like a typical 13-year-old but had a deep, masculinised voice. This failure of processing highlights the third member of the triad of factors leading to individual clinical judgement errors – cognitive biases.

Cognitive bias – thinking fast and thinking slow

Our basic attitudinal bias may set us up for attention failure but it may also just be a prelude to poor judgement. Poor judgement does not mean getting something wrong – being right 100 per cent of the time is impossible after all. Poor judgement arises when cognitive biases adversely influence a judgement that, with the benefit of the same information, may have been made differently with more careful thought. Cognitive biases are tendencies to take mental shortcuts to reach a decision and psychological research has shown the presence of many common and consistent biases. Some common biases that particularly affect medical decision making are listed in Table 10.2. There are many others that are easily referenced in psychology texts but it is the principle of recognition of bias that is important for learning rather than academic issues of exactly what type of bias is at play.

Kahneman provides us with a further explanation of the psychology behind such cognitive biases. He posits that humans utilise dual cognitive processes to solve problems – a fast, intuitive, heuristic process that may be called System One, and a slow, logical and methodical process that may be called System Two. Both systems are valid, depending upon the circumstance. Management of clinical emergencies depends heavily upon a semi-structured System One or fast-thinking approach. A complex diagnostic dilemma will clearly require System Two or slow thinking. The problem is that System One or fast thinking is so much easier to do. Particularly when we are busy or tired or just a little bored with the daily grind.

We cannot change the fact that humans find it easier to Think Fast. What we can do is recognise the fact and think about how this affects us in our daily work environment. We can anticipate and plan for cognitive failures and try to embed greater safety in our systems.

WHAT WE DON'T KNOW *CAN* HURT US – DUNNING–KRUGER AND THE RUMSFELD EFFECT

A phenomenon has been noted by researchers from Cornel University in the USA called the Dunning–Kruger effect. This posits that individuals who are unskilled in a given field may overestimate their ability to perform. This phenomenon goes beyond a lack of awareness of limitations. The research identified that 'unskilled' people may not only be unaware of their own 'incompetence' but that they also overestimate their ability within the same field. What is striking about the Dunning–Kruger effect is that we may not know that we do not know something but that we may also be quite confident that we know enough to carry on. We overestimate our ability to cope when our level of ignorance should really make us more cautious.

In a field as broad and rapidly evolving as medicine the potential to lapse into unconscious incompetence is very high. Not knowing that we do not know something may then become very dangerous – if not for us, then certainly for our patients. Remember the Dr Kipling case – Dr Kipling made an error when substituting insulin.

Table 10.2

Cognitive bias	Definition	Example
Confirmation bias	A tendency to look for evidence that confirms or matches the current situation or assessment. Confirmation bias restricts the assimilation of new information needed to accurately update the current situation.	Dr MacDonald thinks that Mrs Agrawal has gastro-oesophageal reflux disease (GORD). He attributes worsening of symptoms when she lies down as evidence of reflux. He minimises the significance of shortness of breath as it does not confirm his original assumption of cause.
Frequency gambling	This involves 'betting' on the condition that occurs most frequently. At moments of diagnostic uncertainty, it is easier to frequency gamble rather than spend the time and effort to work things through more thoroughly.	Dr King is uncertain as to the nature of baby Anna's shaking and has convinced himself that Anna has improved a little while in the waiting room (confirmation bias). He thinks about a paediatric referral but rather than review the history and clinical facts he thinks, 'I can't send every child with a possible fit to paediatrics. It is probably just a viral infection.'
Expectation bias	A tendency to weigh the importance of information based upon its expected value due to its origin rather than upon its own merits.	Nurse Jenks, working for an out-of-hours service, receives a call from a nurse in a nursing home asking for a doctor to visit. A patient has become pale and unresponsive and has a blood pressure of 64/40. Nurse Jenks wonders why an ambulance has not been called but assumes that her colleague in the home must have a good reason for not doing so. On GP arrival the patient is moribund and an ambulance is called.
Outcome bias	A tendency to judge the value of a decision based upon its outcome rather than the decision-making process involved.	Baby Ben sees his GP and is diagnosed with tonsillitis. Parents are reassured that his high fever will settle. Ben dies 30 hours later. At post-mortem no cause is found and the pathologist suspects a genetic heart rhythm abnormality. Despite a thorough exam and plausible diagnosis, the parents of baby Ben remain convinced that something was wrong with the GP consultation and Ben should have been admitted to hospital.

Cognitive bias	Definition	Example
Hindsight bias	A tendency to believe that a certain decision or action was the most obvious to take based upon the evidence of the final outcome rather than based upon the merits of the information available at the time.	Baby Anna died of meningitis. She had an elevated pulse of 170 on assessment. To suggest that Dr King should have known that Anna had significant sepsis because her pulse was elevated is hindsight bias. In this case the pulse was a significant clue indicating that Anna was unwell but we only know this in retrospect. Without knowing the final outcome, the value of an isolated elevated pulse is not that high. Most GPs will not admit a child just because of an elevated pulse so to single out isolated clues and magnify their importance because we know in retrospect that they were important is biased thinking. (Everyone else will do this – try to resist it as an investigator. Notice the clues in retrospect but do not imply that their significance should have been obvious at the time of assessment.)
Attitudinal cognitive biases		
Anchoring	A tendency to fixate upon the first verbal or visual cue and have difficulty mentally moving away from this.	Mrs Agrawal told Dr MacDonald she was having trouble with indigestion. Dr MacDonald became 'anchored' on confirming this initial suggestion.
Availability	A tendency to depend upon information that is readily available or springs easily to mind.	Mr Chen phones his GP practice two days following inguinal hernia repair complaining of lower abdominal pain and diarrhoea. Practice Nurse Hulme has just read a circular advising that there is an outbreak of norovirus locally. Her first reaction to Mr Chen's symptoms is, 'Oh, it's probably norovirus – there is an outbreak locally'. Mr Chen actually has a significant surgical complication.

Attentional cognitive biases		
Tunnelling May also be called: inattention blindness, change blindness and focusing illusion	In a stressful situation, attention narrows and may focus upon the completion of a specific task to the exclusion of processing any other information. It helps prevent us from being overwhelmed with information but it also prevents assimilation of new and often unexpected information. You focus attention on a particular channel of perception, for example, only looking or only listening.	A 111 health adviser trying to complete a computer-aided set of questions despite the patient Chloe clearly deteriorating during the call.
Selectivity	Similar to tunnelling but may have a more psychological element. A clinician may select information to focus upon because of negative or positive psychological associations; for example, selecting to focus upon physical symptoms because of a sense of weakness or hopelessness in being able to assess or manage a coexisting psychological condition or of confronting embarrassing symptoms.	Dr Yates is training to be a GP and is being supervised by Dr Khan, an experienced GP trainer. They see an unkempt young man who has an appointment note saying that he has burning passing urine – possible urinary infection. Dr Yates questions him regarding urinary symptoms and then suggests he provides a urine specimen for testing. Dr Khan interjects, sensing that the overall picture is not right. He asks the man about the obvious wet stain over the crotch of his trousers. 'Have your symptoms made you wet yourself?' The young man replies that he has been dousing himself with water to cool his genitals. His apparent UTI is actually a psychotic delusion that the devil is burning his genitals because of his impure thoughts. An urgent referral to psychiatry ensues. Dr Yates was too timid to ask about the wet stain on the patient's trousers and retreated to the familiarity of physical symptom exploration only.

Dr Kipling was an experienced GP and certainly not a novice. But his knowledge of insulin prescribing had become weak – not because Dr Kipling was lazy or incompetent but simply because of the increasing complexity of modern diabetes management. Pockets of weakness can develop surreptitiously over a period of time. We may be unaware that we have a weakness. We do not like to think of ourselves as unskilled workers overestimating our own abilities but if we do not recognise that this state is very easy to get into then we can be blinded to our own fallibility and think that we are competent to manage a situation when in fact we are not.

Perhaps our biggest area of unconscious incompetence is our lack of awareness of human factors and how they impact our care.

11

Human factors Part 2: Situational awareness and high-pressure environments

Situational awareness is a very useful concept in incident investigation. Its value is that it situates the way that people think and act within the tasks that they are doing at the time. In a sense it combines the procedural and cognitive concepts of Skill, Rule, Knowledge and the cognitive theories of Kahneman et al. and provides an overall model of how humans behave in real-life situations. The concept of situational awareness was adopted into clinical research from the aerospace industry. The National Aeronautical and Space Agency (NASA) in the United States has provided a lot of theoretical research to underpin our understanding of situational awareness. A 'loss of situational awareness' is thought to be fundamental to many types of human error from pilot error in the air and driver error on the ground and, indeed, clinical error in healthcare.

Situational awareness is not dissociated from Skill, Rule, Knowledge or from cognitive and attentional biases; rather, it follows on from them and it is these biases that may lead to a loss of awareness and the subsequent error. The value of this theoretical approach lies in the contextualisation of the error.

Situational awareness is basically defined as 'knowing what is going on around you'. It follows that in any environment, in order to be safe you have to truly understand what is going on. Situational awareness has been defined as having three levels. These correspond to 'Three Whats':

1. What is going on?
2. So what?
3. What next?

At its optimum, situational awareness involves a continuous looping of these three stages.

1. What is going on – this involves the initial assessment of the patient, their history, the examination and so forth
2. So what – this is where you decide what this all means right now – what is the diagnosis? What is the significance of what is going on?
3. What next – what will happen next if nothing changes? What do I need to do to prevent an adverse outcome?

Having decided what is next at level 3, it is vital that one reverts to step 1 and asks again. What is going on? Has anything changed? Is there new information? Is the change what I expected? Do I need to revise what I thought was going on?

Influencing factors such as fatigue, anxiety, distractions, boredom or lack of competence for the task may affect the ability of an individual to maintain situational awareness.
A further significant factor influencing our ability to maintain situational awareness is
the nature of the way we think. We can counter influencing factors by raising awareness
and designing systems of care to minimise external influences, but even the best-designed
system will fail if humans do not attend to biases in the way they think.

USING SITUATIONAL AWARENESS IN INCIDENT ANALYSIS – ADDING A FOURTH LEVEL

Thinking about situational awareness enables us to consider the levels at which different
human factors may impact upon clinical assessment and helps us conceive of what was
actually going on at the time. It is useful – and has been proposed in research and in clinical situations – to add a fourth level to situational awareness: a further 'what' question:
'What may go wrong?'

Table 11.1

Situation awareness level	Human factors	Impact
Level 1 What? What is going on?	Knowledge level factors Unknown unknowns Anchoring bias Availability bias	Either you do not know what is going on or you misunderstand what is going on. All subsequent judgements will be impaired. This is a recognition phase.
Level 2 So what? What is the significance of what you have learnt so far?	Rule-level factors Confirmation bias Expectation bias Tunnelling Selectivity bias	This level is where risk is analysed. Open awareness is essential to ensure that all risk-related evidence that may need to be considered is teased out. This is an analysis phase.
Level 3 What next? What is the risk and how should it be managed?	Skill-level factors Frequency gambling	Putting everything together should result in the right level of risk being recognised and the appropriate action being taken. 'Given this risk I need to do this action.' This is the action phase.
Level 4 What may go wrong? Full awareness should include consideration of potential failings of management plan and what may happen then.	Dunning–Kruger effect Unknown unknowns Skill-level factors Frequency gambling	What safety net can be provided? When should things improve? What may go wrong? When and why should further help be sought?

It is the final safety-net check that should accompany any effective medical-management plan, recognising that we are humans managing complex situations that do not always progress how we thought they would.

The challenge of human-factors analysis is in knowing how deep to dig in the analysis. It can seem that one could find problems with almost any aspect of any examination. Remember that the guiding principle is that we are looking for learning that may lead to improvements in systems of care that will improve patient safety. If this outcome is not apparent you may be either digging too deep or not digging enough.

TESTING YOUR THEORIES

Identifying human factors involves analysis after the event. You may never be certain that what you have identified has actually gone on. Testing your theory with the staff involved is valuable for two reasons. Firstly, if you go back to the staff member involved and sensitively talk them through your findings they will often be able to confirm or modify your thoughts. 'Yes, I can see what you mean . . .' or perhaps, 'I don't think so. That is not how I recall it. It was more like this . . .' Either response is useful. You may reinforce your interpretation, revise it or stick to it in the belief that the staff member lacks insight. Testing the theory is valuable for a second reason and this is that your report may be subject to public scrutiny and it is not fair to colleagues to have an analysis of human failings on their part entered into records without giving them an opportunity to comment, clarify or correct what you have written. They do not have to agree but they should at least be aware of what you think may have gone on.

Further examples of human-factor analysis are available on my website: www.PatientSafetyInvestigations.com

HUMANS WORKING IN GROUPS

'Man is fallible, but maybe men are less so.'

Atul Gawande, *The Checklist Manifesto:*
How to Get Things Right (London: Profile, 2011).

Much of the research about clinical error in healthcare has been undertaken in secondary care settings. This is understandable as the major driver for the introduction of patient-safety initiatives within healthcare in the 1990s was the recognition of the number of potentially avoidable deaths in hospitals that were due to human errors. In secondary care both doctors and nurses and indeed administrators all work as part of a team. There is very little scope for solo practice within a hospital setting. Thus, a key emphasis upon investigation and research has been the exploration of factors associated with team working in secondary care. It has been very interesting to try to apply the principles learnt from secondary care within incident investigations in primary care. The language is the same but it is actually a different world in the community and while the nature of team or group factors remain the same, the way that they impact is different in primary care.

Table 11.2 Factors that influence human performance

Individual human factors	Team or group factors
Hubris – pride	Communication
Fatigue	Authority gradients
Distraction	Different mental models
Overload	Silo mentality
Confidence	Group thinking
Mental models	
Cognitive biases	
Situational awareness	

While the concept of team working has been embraced in community healthcare it is more often the case that commissioners and motivated individuals agree to a collaboration of the willing, rather than there being a true team per se. This may make it very difficult to investigate primary care incidents involving a wider 'team', as community teams usually dissolve into several component individuals who each work for a different organisation with different command-and-control structures and strategies. For example, general practitioners may work with community nurses, palliative care nurses, social workers and mental health workers, perhaps all serving the same individual patient. And yet each worker is working for a separate and independent organisation. Within a hospital one may face interdepartmental politics when investigating a case but at least one can approach a chief executive to assert a common purpose. In the community it may be much more difficult to get cooperation to explore human team factors and it is certainly difficult to effect changes across diverse provider groups. Nonetheless, this should not stop one from trying to explore how team or group factors may have an impact on clinical incidents in primary care. Remember our list of potential human factors (Table 11.2).

What do team or group factors mean in everyday practice? Let us consider the meaning of the terms mentioned above and then look at how these impact in clinical incidents.

COMMUNICATION

In this context, communication problems are those aspects of verbal or written communication that may occur between clinicians or between clinicians and non-clinical members of the team. Consider Table 11.3.

Communication case studies

EXPECTATION BIAS

A registered general nurse (RGN) working in a nursing home calls the local out-of-hours service to request a GP visit for a new resident. She speaks to a telephone advice nurse. A patient recently admitted for a two-week respite has had a bad night. She vomited in the night and appeared sweaty and pale. This morning she was difficult to

Table 11.3

Communication	Questions	Comments
Type	Formal or informal?	Formal communications should have a structure – was this evident? Was it followed?
Mode	1. Verbal or written? 2. Phone or face to face?	Misheard? Tone of voice – may account for 40 per cent of communication Misunderstood? – Accent, volume and so forth Body-language interpretation – may account for 50 per cent of communication
Nature	Patient handover? How many steps in handover? Non-clinical information exchange?	Handovers are high-risk events – accuracy of information degrades with each step as key facts or nuances of meaning get lost.
Language	Native tongue? Technical language?	Language breakdown can occur within teams if some members of team are technical (clinical) and some members are not. Technical language is like a foreign language – consider fluency, context and idiom for both.

rouse and had vomited again and appeared pale. The nurse had taken observations and stated that the patient had a pulse of 94 and a blood pressure of 60/40. The out-of-hours nurse sends an urgent visit request to a visit car. The GP in the car is alarmed at the vital signs recorded and happens to be near the home and attends within 10 minutes of the call. The patient is moribund and an ambulance is called. The patient dies on the way to hospital.

A voice recording is available of the call between the two nurses. On hearing the low blood pressure of 60/40 the out-of-hours nurse gasps but does not otherwise question her colleague's request for a GP visit. At interview the out-of-hours nurse admits that she was alarmed at the history and wondered why her colleague had not called an ambulance but had assumed that as she was an RGN and as she was with the patient she must have a good reason for seeking a GP rather than an ambulance.

This is a communication failing due to expectation bias. Information is assessed and judged based upon the source of the information (the expectation of its value) rather than on its content. Expectation bias is common when communication about patients occurs between peers or between doctors/nurses and paramedical ambulance staff. We are often loath to question our colleagues and invest in them an expectation that they have done the thinking for us. Consider expectation bias when colleague-to-colleague communication is involved in an incident.

TECHNICAL LANGUAGE

An experienced community-based advanced nurse practitioner examines a neonate in a newly opened urgent care centre. She finds the baby floppy and pale with a raised heart and respiratory rate. She contacts the charge nurse at her local hospital emergency department and tells them that she has a baby that they are very worried about. The baby is feeding poorly and seems floppy when handled. The baby also has a raised heart and respiratory rate and looks pale. She is asked to transfer the baby to the children's minors area of the emergency department to await assessment. The nurse practitioner refuses and insists on the baby being seen immediately in the majors department where resuscitation equipment is available.

The baby is seen in majors and is immediately recognised to be very poorly. The baby dies later that day from overwhelming sepsis. This sad death would have appeared even more calamitous to the parents of the baby if the baby had waited for assessment in the minor illness area first.

On review of the incident, emergency department staff cited a lack of familiarity with the level of experience that a community-based advanced nurse practitioner may possess. The charge nurse indicated that where nurses in the hospital escalated concerns about children to them they always did so by using a Paediatric Early Warning score. The narrative description coming from a community nurse suggested to them that the nurse had not fully assessed the child and that the level of urgency was not clear.

Technical language is frequently used, particularly in secondary care settings, to enable simple and unambiguous communication of risk. Unfamiliarity with technical-language protocols may place either the giver or the recipient of information at a disadvantage. Consider technical-language failings when communication occurs across organisations in urgent or emergency settings. Does one organisation use a technical language that is unfamiliar to the other?

HANDOVERS

The wife of a 74-year-old man phones the NHS 111 service. She states that her husband has prostate cancer that has spread to his spine. This has already caused some pressure upon his spinal cord. She has a card from the hospital stating that her husband is at risk of spinal cord compression and to call if he develops new symptoms. She advises that her husband has a worsening of back pain as well as weakness of his legs such that he cannot rise from his seat today.

The health adviser writes notes that the patient has cancer of the prostate and that he has back pain and weakness of the legs and is not able to get up. Because of the wife's concerns they pass the call to a nurse clinical adviser.

The nurse notes that the patient has cancer of the prostate but believes that the main concern is back pain. They question the wife about the back pain and the wife describes significant pain and says that her husband has difficulty rising from sitting. The wife does not mention that the cancer has spread to the spine nor repeat the warning that her husband is at risk of cord compression as she believes that this is already understood. The nurse passes the case to the local out-of-hours GP service. Headline notes indicate 'Low back pain, not able to get up from seat'.

The case is streamed directly to a car for a home visit. The visit GP prioritises other cases ahead of what appears to be a simple mechanical back pain and it is several hours before the patient is assessed and it is discovered that he has significant spinal cord compression.

Handovers are subject to multiple types of communication failure but information decay is a key problem. At each step key elements of history may be omitted from the information transfer with the potential for the end recipient to be significantly misinformed. Always check information exchange and determine what information was passed on whenever there is a handover of care.

AUTHORITY GRADIENTS

Authority gradients refers to the degree of real or perceived power over decision making with regard to the patient or service issues. Essentially it represents the degree to which staff feel able to question more senior members of the team. It may also exist between a clinician and a patient where a patient suspects that something is wrong but feels unable to question the authority of the clinician. Experience in safety-critical team environments and even in high-performing sports teams has shown that a very steep authority gradient is counter-productive – every member of a team needs to be able to speak out if they sense that something is not right. A shallow gradient is ideal but this should not be mistaken for no gradient. A leader must be able to make a decision and run with it – as otherwise there will be chaos – but they should always do so having heard any dissenting voices first.

Authority gradient case study

An experienced GP visits a patient at home at the request of an ambulance crew. The patient is thought to be off their legs due to a urinary tract infection (UTI) and they are put back to bed and commenced on antibiotics. The GP arranges for a nurse from the local enhanced care team to visit later that day to assess care needs and deliver a commode. The nurse arrives an hour later and phones the practice back and speaks to another GP and asks if a doctor could visit to review. She describes that patient as pale and clammy with a raised respiratory rate, a pulse of 130 and a blood pressure of 64/42. The GP suggests that the patient appears to be peri-arrest and that an ambulance should be called. The nurse readily and gratefully agrees. 'I thought that too but I didn't like to just call an ambulance because Dr X had just visited and I didn't want to contradict him.'

In this case it is the authority of Dr X that the nurse did not wish to question, even though she could see that the patient was very unwell. She had hoped that another GP would make the decision for her.

Authority gradients often stop junior or less experienced staff from speaking up even when they can see that something is going wrong. Consider this issue when senior and junior staff are both involved with management of a case and there appears to be incongruous behaviour.

MENTAL MODELS

A phrase or diagnosis will trigger different mental pictures of what is going on in different people. People of different experiences and backgrounds may have markedly different mental images triggered by the same term. Describing a baby as floppy will mean one thing to a mother who may associate the word with a baby who is just tired and 'flopped' in her arms, and quite another thing to a paediatrician who has experience of managing critically ill children. But similar discrepancies can occur between clinical colleagues as well. This is particularly relevant when handover of care occurs. When a paramedic rings a GP surgery and hands over a case, for example, they may describe a patient as being 'off their legs' or 'mentally competent' or 'palliative care'. What the paramedic means by this may be quite different from the mental model that is triggered in a GP by these terms. Potential differences may be compounded by cognitive biases (see below) that may facilitate decisions to trust comments or actions by others that in reality should be challenged or clarified.

Mental models case study

A young man calls an NHS 111 service seeking advice and support for his mother. She developed a severe headache 60 minutes previously and retired to bed and remained there too unwell to rise. Following the NHS Pathways question set regarding headache symptoms the call handler asks a key qualifying question: 'Does your mother feel as though she has been hit on the head with a brick?' The young man relays the question to his mother. 'They are asking if you have been hit on the head with a brick.' The patient groans an answer 'no' in the background. The health adviser chooses the 'no' response to this question. A final outcome of advice to see a GP in 24 hours is obtained. Had the answer to this question been 'yes', then an ambulance would have been triggered. The following day the patient was seen by her GP and was immediately admitted to hospital where a sub-arachnoid haemorrhage was diagnosed.

Clinicians have a very specific mental model of the rupture of a cerebral artery aneurysm that triggers the characteristic explosive headache. The question about being hit on the head with a brick was set by a clinician and intended to evoke the history of the typical onset of a sub-arachnoid haemorrhage. Without the mental model of cerebral haemorrhage, the health adviser was not equipped to appreciate the significance of the son's misunderstanding of the question and did not clarify the key element of the history of the headache – its explosive onset.

Different mental models become significant when staff from teams or groups with significant differences in training or experience work together.

SILO THINKING

Most service industries deliver services via discrete service teams and healthcare is no different. General practice is a silo but so too are individual practices, and so too are individual GPs. Acute hospital services, outpatient clinics, out-of-hours services, 111 services, walk-in centres and pharmacies – all represent a different potential silo. Individual patients pass in and out of different silos either via referral or by self-selection and each silo will have a view on how other silos have managed the patient up until now. In an ideal world the different silos would all recognise that they are but interlocking pieces of a greater system that has the interests of the patient at its heart. Cooperation and support would rule, all in the interests of providing the best service to the patient. Very often this does happen, of course, but at times of pressure there is a tendency to retreat into our silos and batten down the hatches. Referrals from colleagues become a burden and patients who self-refer are simply highlighting the inadequacies of other silos that should have been doing a better job dealing with the patient. Silo thinking does exist in healthcare and it can prejudice anyone when it comes to communicating with colleagues. Consider silo thinking where two different services have communicated or miscommunicated about a patient. Any failings in communication should trigger a consideration of whether prejudices or misperceptions about the function of another service may have been a factor.

Silo thinking case study

The wife of a 42-year-old male calls 111. Her husband developed a flu-like illness 36 hours ago. There is a lot of influenza present in the community. He has become increasingly moribund with a severe headache, neck stiffness, and vomiting. A health adviser completes an NHS Pathways headache assessment and reaches an outcome of an emergency ambulance disposition. NHS Pathways cannot exclude meningitis as a cause of symptoms. At the ambulance-control clinical desk, a decision is made to re-assess the call in view of the patient's age. After a review of symptoms, a decision is made that the man is suffering from influenza. The call is passed from the ambulance service to the local GP out-of-hours service. A busy GP visits six hours later and finds the patient to be moribund and calls an emergency ambulance. The patient dies later that night of meningitis.

Cognitive biases such as expectation bias and confirmation bias were evident in the paramedic assessment of symptoms but at the heart of the case was a silo mentality in which overstretched clinical staff within an ambulance service were encouraged to re-assess any emergency disposition generated by the 111 service because of a lack of faith in the accuracy of 111 dispositions. One silo did not trust the judgement of another.

GROUP THINKING

Groups and teams will develop a culture and ethos either by design or by default. An individual working regularly within a team will tend to take on the culture and thought processes of that team. On the other hand, a group of people meeting together for the first time may rapidly reach a state in which they collectively think and act in a way that is outside the norm for many of the individuals within that group. Individuals may make decisions or act in ways that are contrary to what they would normally think or do because of rationalisations such as 'well that is the way we do it here' or, 'I am not sure, I am just going with the flow'. The 'choice' to act or think may not even be a conscious decision. Encouraging group thinking is an excellent way of building resilience and a culture of excellence into teams but it requires a conscious and sustained effort to maintain it. Group thinking is subject to the phenomenon of regression to the mean and group think can become negative under the influence of dominant personality types within a group. Consider group think whenever a team or group of individuals act together in a way that is negative or contrary to what would be expected.

Group think case study

The mother of an 18-month-old baby speaks to an out-of-hours GP at 6:30 a.m. on a Monday morning. She demands a home visit for her sick child. She says that her baby has been coughing all night and is very short of breath. The doctor tells the mother that the out-of-hours service does not visit children as it is not clinically appropriate. A heated argument ensues – with the mother saying that she has no car and has no money for a taxi and the GP saying it is out-of-hours service policy not to visit children. The call ends acrimoniously. The mother phones for an ambulance. The child is found to have severe respiratory distress and suffers a respiratory arrest on transfer to hospital, fortunately being successfully resuscitated by the paramedic crew. A complaint letter is later received by the out-of-hours service.

The lead for the out-of-hours service is puzzled by the insistence by the GP that the service has a policy of not visiting children as no such policy exists. Discussion with the GP involved as well as other clinical and administrative colleagues reveals a widespread belief that the service has a policy to only visit the very elderly or terminally ill. Guidance that visits are preferably reserved for elderly housebound patients but that a final decision should be based upon clinical merits had morphed into a group view that a policy of not visiting children existed, abrogating any onus upon clinicians to take responsibility for their own decisions.

Once you have fully considered contributory factors, including exploring patient factors and the potential for enhanced learning via human-factors analysis, you need to identify which of the contributory factors had the most impact upon the final outcome. This is the root cause and it is the subject of the next chapter.

12

Root cause

> The root cause of an event is the contributory factor that had the most significant causative impact upon the eventual adverse outcome.

There is a problem with using root cause analysis in healthcare that I have alluded to already. This problem manifests itself most when we come to try to identify the root cause of a clinical incident. In many areas of medicine there is a significant variable factor that makes identification of a root cause difficult. That variable is the patient factor.

Remember that root cause analysis is a tool that was developed to aid problem solving within the motor and the aviation industry; we have just co-opted it into healthcare. RCA works well when the investigation is of an incident in which the expectation is of an essentially faultless process. The assembly of a range of components should produce a functioning vehicle, for example, a plane takes off from London and arrives in New York. Nothing should go wrong and when it does, a process-related fault that has its origin within the support infrastructure, either human or systemic, is likely to be at fault. In healthcare we have processes that have evolved to deal with people who are unwell. Sadly, patients will often suffer harm or even die despite our best efforts. It is the nature of the pathological process. The challenge in identifying a root cause in healthcare incidents then is to be able to separate pathology from process error. It is unlikely that any encounter between a clinician and a patient could be examined without finding some error or deviation (an act or omission – care delivery problem) from policy protocol or guideline of some sort. But did that act or omission and the factors that led to it occurring have any impact upon the final adverse outcome? Was the patient going to die or suffer harm regardless?

When we do believe that an act or omission may have led to harm we have the added difficulty of determining whether the act was wholly or only partially responsible. For a few incidents the answer is obvious – a patient given the wrong medication who dies as a result of the medication, for example, or removal of the wrong leg at surgery or leaving a swab inside the abdomen after surgery. But what about missing a diagnosis of meningitis? Missing a diagnosis of heart disease? It is the disease that kills the patient and who is to say that even if the doctor had made the diagnosis that the final outcome would not have been the same? Significant problems arise when we identify the contributory factors for a care or service delivery problem and assign one of these as the root cause, only to realise that it may be the root cause of the CDP or initial error, but this in and of itself would not have led to the final outcome suffered by the patient.

The issue of whether a CDP was likely to have led to the final adverse patient outcome may be apparent from the outset but in many cases it is not. Giving too much thought to the issue at the beginning of an investigation may skew the analysis so it is right to put the issue to one side until one has completed the investigation and to reconsider it when one has considered the contributory factors to the case, in particular, when one has considered the patient factors.

HOW TO APPROACH THE ROOT CAUSE QUESTION

There are two phases to identifying a root cause. The first phase is to ask the question:
1. On the balance of probability, what was most likely to have caused harm to the patient:
   - The care/service delivery problem(s) identified (what we did wrong); or
   - The patient factor – the patient's underlying condition or their actions?

The second phase is to ask a further question.
2. Of the care/service delivery problems, which is the most significant?

You should remind yourself of what the incident was and, in particular, exactly what the harm suffered was. Be precise – precision matters. Sometimes the harm is obvious but where there is an existing underlying illness the exact nature of harm may not be evident. When there is a missed or delayed diagnosis, for example (see the Lauren case below), the issue may not be the obvious consequence of the illness outcome but that of complications or worsened outcome that may arise because of delayed diagnosis. Once you are satisfied that you have got the 'harm' sorted, you need to decide if this was due to what happened in your service (the CDP/SDP) or whether it was primarily a natural consequence of the illness itself.

CARE DELIVERY PROBLEM OR PATIENT FACTORS? – BARN DOORS AND THE ROOT CAUSE PROBABILITY MATRIX

The primary causative factor for many incidents is obvious. If a huge barn door is in front of you, do not neglect to notice it. Never events are barn-door causative factors – they are obvious factors that you should not miss. If you amputate the wrong leg of a diabetic patient with an ischaemic foot, then you know that the root cause will lie within the factors associated with your service's actions and not be related to the patient's underlying condition. If a patient who is allergic to penicillin is given penicillin and dies following an anaphylactic reaction, then the causative factor will arise from the actions of the clinical team and not be because the patient had an underlying penicillin allergy. These are barn door causative factors where it is obvious that a care delivery problem led to harm. The root cause will then be the contributory factor that had the most impact in terms of leading to the care delivery problem occurring.

In many cases, however, the situation is much less obvious. In such cases the following root cause probability matrix may help. The tool is simply a method of assessing the potential impact of the patient's underlying condition with regard to final outcome. It aims to indicate where patient factors are likely to be very significant as potential root causes as opposed to any care or service delivery problems that may also have occurred. A high score on the matrix suggests that patient factors are highly likely to be the root cause, rather than contributory factors associated with any care or service delivery problems.

Consider use of this tool when the incident involves a missed or inappropriate diagnosis or inappropriate management decisions for specific conditions.

ROOT CAUSE PROBABILITY MATRIX: PATIENT FACTORS

- Step 1: Score the patient's underlying condition for prevalence: 1 = Very common, 5 = Very rare. (Where available use standardised national prevalence data.)
- Step 2: Score the presenting picture based upon how typical the presenting signs and symptoms were. 1 = Very typical, 5 = Very unusual. (Compare case evidence against standardised national reference sources. This is somewhat subjective. Use group wisdom to help decide difficult cases to avoid bias.)

		Prevalence			
	1	2	3	4	5
	2	4	6	8	10
Presentation	3	6	9	12	15
	4	8	12	16	20
	5	10	15	20	25

When considering presenting symptoms, a condition that is reasonably common will often have typical symptoms as well as described atypical variants. Such well-described variant symptoms should not be regarded as very unusual. For example, acute coronary syndrome typically presents with crushing central chest pain referred to the jaw or left arm. A competent clinician would be expected to know, however, that in the elderly and in diabetic patients the presentation may not be typical. A diabetic patient who presented with an episode of sweating and vomiting with only mild chest discomfort should trigger suspicion of ACS. In such a case the presentation score should remain below five even though the presentation is not typical. Guidance on interpretation of scoring is given in Table 12.1.

Table 12.1

Score	Interpretation
1–4	Where the underlying condition is common or the symptoms are typical, even if the condition is rare, it is likely that any unexpected adverse outcome will be the result of care or service delivery problems rather than the underlying condition.
5–12	Where the underlying condition is uncommon or where the presenting signs are not typical, causality may be difficult to determine. Consider 'Cause vs Mechanism' – see below. Consider a joint root cause with patient factors and CDP/SDP with equal causative action.
15–25	Where the underlying condition is very uncommon and the presentation is atypical or very atypical, then the causative factor is likely to be a patient factor – that is to say, the complexity of the underlying condition is likely to be the main root cause for the final adverse outcome.

The root cause probability matrix essentially formalises a process of logic that many investigators would use in assessing the likely cause of a significant incident. It is intended for guidance only and certain elements do require subjective judgement but using the tool may be helpful in demonstrating how you have worked things out. It can promote some consistency in decision making and it will also provide some accountability for decision making.

ROOT CAUSE PROBABILITY MATRIX: TASK/SYSTEM VERSUS HUMAN FACTORS

The matrix may also be used to review incidents in which a care or service delivery problem involves a clinician or administrative staff member making errors with regard to standard procedures, such as medication errors, surgical/anaesthetic errors or protocol-completion errors. The latter include errors arising in the use of computer-assisted clinical-decision aids as used in telephone call centres such as NHS 111 services, ambulance or out-of-hours services. In such circumstances it may be difficult to determine whether human factors or task/system factors are more likely to be the root cause. The same probability matrix may be modified to determine whether the system or task factors identified are likely to be of greater significance than human factors as a final root cause. In this case we assess the novelty of the task or system against its complexity to produce a guidance score.

	Task or system novelty				
	1	2	3	4	5
Task or system complexity	2	4	6	8	10
	3	6	9	12	15
	4	8	12	16	20
	5	10	15	20	25

SCORING

- Step 1: Score the task or system for novelty: 1 = Very frequent use or very well-established tool, 5 = Very rarely used or new tool. (Frequent may be daily or weekly use or performance of the task, tool or system by the individual concerned.)
- Step 2: Score the task or system for complexity – how easy is it to do? 1 = Very easy, 5 = Very complex and difficult. (Has multiple interdependent stages, a high dependency upon 'perfect' performance.)

Task novelty would include use of tools such as NHS Pathways that are relatively new. It may also include use of a newly designed protocol or process.

Distinguish between newly designed tasks and tasks that may be well established but just unfamiliar to a specific clinician. If a clinician tries to do something for which they do not possess sufficient experience, then the question is one of what compelled them to do it. The Dunning–Kruger effect – overestimation of their own ability? Or a service design that compels staff to take risks?

Table 12.2

Score	Interpretation
1–4	Where the underlying task is common, the systems are well designed and the clinician is well trained then, even if the task is relatively complex, it is likely that any unexpected adverse outcome will be the result of human factors rather than the task or system itself.
5–12	Where the underlying task is unfamiliar or new, and where the task is moderately complex, it may be difficult to untangle human factors from task factors.
15–25	Where the underlying task is very novel and it is also complex or difficult to perform accurately, then the key causative factor is likely to be related to the task or system itself, rather than to the individual involved – even if human factors are identified as well. The principle is: don't blame the driver for human errors that are made driving in very difficult circumstances that are beyond their control. These cases should make us consider whether the design of the task or system is optimal. Can we make it safer for the drivers (and ultimately their passengers)?

Some case examples are provided below to illustrate how these tools may be used to help determine probable root causes. Remember that we are interpreting the impact of the contributory factors that we have already identified.

BABY ANNA – DIAGNOSTIC ERROR

Remember that baby Anna sadly died of meningitis. The post-mortem actually revealed that the cause was pneumococcal meningitis. She presented to Dr King with 'shivering' and fever but no specific signs suggestive of meningitis.

- Prevalence – Meningitis presents rarely and pneumococcal meningitis is rarer still than meningococcal meningitis. We would have to score at least 4.
- Presentation – Anna had no specific signs or symptoms to suggest meningitis and presented in what may be called a prodromal phase. Again, a score of 4 or perhaps even 5 would be reasonable.

This gives a probability score of 16–20. This high score would suggest that Anna's underlying condition is very significant and is likely to represent the root cause in this case.

DR MACDONALD – DIAGNOSTIC ERROR

Mrs Agrawal presented to Dr MacDonald with symptoms of acute coronary syndrome. Dr MacDonald diagnosed dyspepsia. Mrs Agrawal died of a cardiac arrest three hours later.

- Prevalence – Acute coronary syndrome is a very prevalent condition in patients of Mrs Agrawal's age. It should have a score of 1 or at most 2.
- Presentation – The presenting symptom was burning throat pain that is atypical for ACS. However, atypical presentations, including burning throat pain, are well documented as occurring in the elderly. A clinician of Dr MacDonald's experience would be expected to know this. A score of 2 or 3 at most would seem reasonable.

This gives a probability score ranging from 2 to 6. This low score would suggest that the root cause is likely to be within the contributory factors that led to Dr MacDonald failing to make the correct diagnosis, and not Mrs Agrawal's underlying condition.

DR KIPLING: TASK FACTOR VERSUS HUMAN FACTORS

Dr Kipling was asked to prescribe insulin for a new patient. He had to substitute one insulin type for another. He made an error of choice and prescribed two incompatible insulin types.

- Task novelty – Insulin prescribing is very common but substituting one insulin type for another is less so, particularly in primary care. A score of 3 or 4 would be reasonable.
- Task complexity – Multiple insulin types, different modes of action and confusing nomenclature with the addition of needing to find a substitute for an insulin not available in the UK make the task quite complex. A score of 4 or 5.

This provides a probability score in the range of 12 to 20. A high score such as this suggests that the root cause is likely to lie in the task or system complexity rather than human factors, even though these may be useful learning points.

CHLOE: TASK FACTOR VERSUS HUMAN FACTORS

Chloe presented to the NHS 111 telephone assessment service. A complex and high-risk underlying condition was not disclosed and the significance of her complex and evolving symptoms was not noted. She died only 30 minutes after the call. Patient factors were the most significant factor in this case but during the call the non-clinical health adviser clearly lost control of the call due to cognitive bias – she over-focused her attention upon completion of the task – answering all the computer-prompted questions. But how much of this was due to human factors and how much was due to the task she was asked to do? Was this simply driver error or was the driver being asked to make too difficult a journey?

- Task novelty – The NHS Pathways tool is a relatively new tool but it has been extensively 'road tested'. Nonetheless, it has only been around a few years. A score of 3 would seem reasonable.
- Task complexity – Pathways requires the driver, the health adviser, to select the right set of questions to ask and also to be able to probe responses and to recognise complexity when it appears. Service operators expect health advisers to be able to complete the majority of cases without escalation to clinical colleagues or ambulances. The complexity of the tool is actually proportional to the case in question – for simple cases the tool is relatively simple to use whereas for complex cases the task becomes much more difficult for health advisers. A score of 4 in this case would be reasonable.

A mid-range score of 12 indicates that both task and human factors are implicated in this case.

(In fact, this case was one of a series of cases that made it clear that the interaction of human and task factors in systems such as NHS 111 has a significant impact upon patient safety. NHS England has accepted a proposal generated from this and other incident investigations to explore this issue in more depth with a formal academic study.)

ALTERNATIVE STRATEGIES

Where the decision remains difficult, it may help to consider the cause and mechanism of harm. This may be a standalone process or it may be done as an additional process to sense-check or consolidate a decision already made.

CARE DELIVERY PROBLEM OR PATIENT FACTORS – CAUSE AND MECHANISM

Where the barn-door approach does not help, or where you feel it is important to consolidate your analysis with further evidence, it can be very helpful to consider both the *cause* and the *mechanism* of death or injury. This may involve interpreting evidence from a post-mortem or from clinical notes. The exact answers may not be present and some 'reading between the lines' may be necessary to infer what may have occurred. This may be beyond the expertise of the investigator and in such cases it is important to seek advice from senior clinical colleagues. This type of analysis does require a forensic type of assessment and not all clinicians are adept at this, so if you do seek help, do not assume that any experienced clinician will do. You may need to gather more information if you have not already established certain facts during the course of the investigation thus far. Following a death, a Medical Certificate of Cause of Death (MCCD) or post-mortem report may be very helpful as this document will list both cause and mechanism of death. You may want to seek access to hospital notes or GP notes, or seek comments from the patient or their representatives.

CAUSE AND MECHANISM

- The cause of death or injury is the illness or injury that led to death or harm
- The mechanism is the physiological derangement that arose that made death or injury occur

For example, meningitis may be a cause of death but the mechanism may be septicaemic shock with multiple organ failure. A myocardial infarct may be the cause of death but the mechanism may be sudden cardiac arrest or congestive cardiac failure.

The reason for noting the mechanism is that this may provide evidence that could either implicate or exonerate a care or service delivery problem as a potential causative factor. Consider the cases of Lauren and baby Ben.

CASE SUMMARIES

Lauren

Lauren was an 11-year-old girl who presented to her GP on a Friday morning with symptoms of lower right-sided abdominal pain and two episodes of loose stool. On exam she was apyrexial and the abdominal examination revealed mild tenderness on deep palpation with no guarding or rebound. A diagnosis of gastroenteritis was made. On Friday evening Lauren's parents took her to see an out-of-hours

GP. Lauren's abdominal pain was worse; she had not had any further diarrhoea but she now had dysuria. On examination she had a temperature of 38.2 and an abdominal examination revealed tenderness in her lower abdomen and right iliac fossa with no guarding or rebound. A urine dip test revealed leucocytes and blood. A diagnosis of urinary tract infection was made and trimethoprim commenced. On Saturday evening her parents returned to the out-of-hours service as Lauren had increasingly severe pain. On examination her temperature was 38.8, her pulse was 120 and she had marked tenderness with guarding in the right iliac fossa. She was referred to the surgeons with a presumptive diagnosis of appendicitis. She was operated on that evening and was found to have a perforated appendix with localised peritonitis. Four months after the incident Lauren had had two further admissions to hospital for abdominal pains thought to be caused by adhesions.

Investigation suggested that to a small extent on the first assessment and to a greater degree in the second assessment, a full exploration of symptoms and signs had not occurred and an opportunity was missed at which a diagnosis of appendicitis may have been considered.

Baby Ben

Two-year-old Ben was brought to see his GP with a 12-hour history of fever and malaise. His parents were anxious that Ben's temperature was more than 40. He was drinking OK but was off his food and lethargic. On examination the temperature was 40.1, pulse was 140, there was no rash or meningism and his tonsils were noted to be enlarged and red. A diagnosis of tonsillitis was made and Ben was prescribed penicillin. The next day Ben seemed a little better in the morning but became lethargic again in the evening. The following morning Ben's father found him dead in bed.

A post-mortem examination could not reveal a cause of death.

An investigation suggested that note keeping and safety-net advice was poor but that overall management was reasonable and that the death could not have been foreseen.

CAUSE VERSUS MECHANISM

In Lauren's case the harm suffered was not appendicitis itself but the complications that occurred due to the fact that the appendix had perforated. While a perforated appendix is noted as the cause, the mechanism is important in this case as we know that both perforation and the complications that ensue are related to the time to diagnosis and the time to surgery. It is not the perforation per se that caused the harm but the time during which a 'leaking' appendix caused damage to surrounding tissue. The mechanism makes it clear that failing to make the correct diagnosis was a significant factor in causation of harm in this case. That is to say, the care delivery problem is most likely to be the source of the root cause in this case, as opposed to the underlying patient condition.

In the baby Ben case the post-mortem was not able to identify a cause of death. There was no evidence of overwhelming sepsis, no evidence of organ failure and no evidence of allergic reaction to antibiotic. A subtle clue was present, however. The pathologist did note very mild pulmonary oedema suggesting that the mechanism of death may have been a sudden cardiac event. The pathologist suspected that Ben had suffered a sudden arrhythmia, probably due to an inherited conduction abnormality such as long QT syndrome. Without further evidence this could not be noted as a cause of death but the PM report did contain evidence to suggest a mechanism, if not the exact cause of the death. This evidence of mechanism indicates that despite the care delivery problems noted in the doctor's assessment these would have not had an impact upon the final outcome. In this case the root cause would be within the patient's underlying physical state.

FINALISING THE ROOT CAUSE

The final judgement as to which contributory factor is the most significant and hence is a single root cause will often be a balanced judgement made by the lead investigator and the team. This is entirely reasonable as we need to recall that a root cause analysis is an investigation with the aim of learning. It is not a judicial enquiry and the standard of evidence and judgement is that of reasonable probability; we are not seeking evidence to make judgements that are beyond reasonable doubt. It is for this reason that I place emphasis upon being able to show how decisions are reached in the investigation.

MIXED CAUSE AND PATIENT FACTORS

Where a single root cause is not identified or where it is felt that the patient's underlying condition remains the primary root cause of the eventual adverse outcome, it is necessary to demonstrate this by providing a narrative to support the view. As usual, this should be a narrative based upon the evidence. Where patient factors appear to be the most significant factor it should be explained why this is the most likely outcome of the investigation. Use of the root cause probability matrix will help in framing the narrative as the analysis you did to arrive at a score on the matrix should provide the basis of your root cause narrative.

The NHS 111 case involving Chloe is an example of a case in which the patient's complex underlying condition is likely to be the root cause, even though there were significant human and task factors involved as well. Within a report this may be expressed by the following narrative:

Can we establish a root cause?

In this case we know that the patient sadly died some 30 minutes or so after contact with the service. Had the case been managed successfully within the 111 service, the best possible outcome would have been an eight-minute ambulance dispatch. However, as the patient was not in an immediate state of collapse it is possible that a 20-minute outcome, ambulance emergency treatment and transfer may have arisen. Assuming an eight-minute response was that outcome, we can estimate that the failures identified above may have delayed the arrival of an ambulance by some 30 to 40 minutes. It is beyond the expertise of the author to establish whether this delay would have been significant in terms of preventing the tragic outcome but the patient was clearly very unwell and may have succumbed to her illness in any case.

On the balance of probability, the authors would conclude that the cause of death was the patient's underlying medical condition – acute severe adrenal crisis presenting rapidly in a patient with underlying congenital adrenal hypoplasia.

ROOT CAUSE

Patient factor: Complexity of underlying condition – acute severe adrenal crisis

This is just an example of how decision making may be framed. Even if one does not agree with the logic, one can at least see how the investigator reached their conclusion and this is important in assuring that the report is open and honest.

A further example of a narrative explaining a case in which patient factors were the final root cause is provided in Chapter 15 where the art of report writing is explored further.

Once you have identified your root cause you will need to consider learning arising from the case. Learning will include whether you think the case continues to meet the threshold for reporting to NHS England or another regulatory authority (assuming you have made an early report that the case represents a Serious Incident Requiring Investigation). These issues are covered in the next chapter.

13

Learning and recommendations

Despite increasing awareness of the importance of the RCA process in investigating clinical incidents in healthcare, it is still the case that being able to identify and implement recommendations that improve the safety of patients remains an elusive goal.

An elegant analysis of contributory factors leading to the undisputed root cause will be of little value if you cannot identify learning and make recommendations that will reduce the likelihood of a further identical or similar incident from occurring. Equally important is the ability to assure that your recommendations have been implemented and that they have had an impact.

In this chapter we will explore:

- How to identify learning from clinical incidents
- How to identify and make recommendations

Identifying learning from RCA investigations is easy.
But many people still get it wrong.

THREE COMMON ERRORS

There are three common errors made with regard to identifying learning.

1. Identifying learning that is not related to the incident
2. Confusing learning with recommendations
3. Stating the obvious

IDENTIFYING LEARNING THAT IS NOT RELATED TO THE INCIDENT

Consider the following examples:

1. A medication error is made by a locum agency doctor who was overly fatigued after working more than 70 hours during the week. The doctor miscalculated the dose of morphine for a palliative care patient leading to a sudden respiratory arrest.
   - Learning: There is a risk in using locum agency doctors.
   - Wrong: The risk is with doctors who are fatigued having to make safety-critical calculations – the fact that the doctor was employed via an agency is irrelevant.

2. A baby dies of respiratory failure associated with pneumonia 24 hours following a GP assessment. The GP had not recorded any vital signs and did not have a pulse oximeter available.
   - Learning: There is a lack of awareness of the signs of pneumonia among clinical staff.
   - Wrong: The risk in this case would appear to lie with the individual clinician whose examination (at the very least their notes) appear suboptimal. There is no evidence that the whole of the service is unaware of pneumonia based upon the actions of one member of staff.

3. A baby suffers brain injury after suffering collapse due to respiratory failure on a bus with its parents on the way in to hospital. The baby was seen by a GP in the morning who had referred the baby to A&E but allowed parents to transfer the baby to hospital without checking how they would get there. The practice nurse was present at the GP consultation and knew the family did not have a car and would have to use the bus but was reluctant to speak up as the GP was the senior partner in the practice. She wishes she had said something.
   - Learning: All babies with respiratory distress should be transferred to hospital by ambulance.
   - Wrong: You cannot extrapolate from this one case to all babies. In this case it is human factors (authority gradient) that prevented the nurse from speaking up. Learning should be about how human factors may affect clinical decisions.

In case 1 investigators conflate two issues – long working hours leading to fatigue and working for an agency. These may or may not be related but the only one that is directly relevant to the incident is fatigue associated with long working hours. This should be the focus of learning.

In case 2 the investigators extrapolate assumptions arising from one case to a whole service. The whole service may well lack awareness of the signs of pneumonia in children but this is not evident from this case. Be wary about leaping from individual actions to those of the whole service unless you can justify it.

In case 3 the learning lacks precision. One case would not be likely to be the justification for a new protocol on transfer of children to hospital – although it may trigger a review of the issue. There appear to be issues with the loss of situational awareness of the GP and also with human communication factors due to authority gradient within the practice – the nurse not wishing to speak up in front of the senior partner. This type of learning may be useful both to the GP and the practice.

CONFUSING LEARNING WITH RECOMMENDATIONS

TOP TIP

Stick to the process – follow the processes outlined and learning and recommendations will not be confused.

Confusing learning with recommendations occurs due to not sticking to process. The process is to think about what you learn and then to think about recommendations. Sticking to process is slow and deliberate work and it is our tendency as humans to leap ahead. As we think of learning we intuitively seek a solution, too. The solution is often ill considered because the learning was not clarified in the first place.

Learning points that contain the words 'should' and 'must' are more likely to be recommendations rather than learning. For example:

- All staff should be aware of the signs of pneumonia.
- Clinical staff must record vital signs when examining children.

Statements such as these are recommendations for action, not learning. See below for advice on how to simplify the process and ensure that learning and recommendations make sense.

STATING THE OBVIOUS

Stating the obvious is akin to simply repeating the care or service delivery problem as a learning point. Learning simply becomes, 'Bad things can happen.' This may be true but it is hardly useful. In case 1 above, an alternative learning point may be:

- Learning: Clinician fatigue may lead to clinical errors.
- This may be true but it is a very weak learning point. We need to try to be more precise. We already know that fatigue leads to errors. In this case we can enhance the value of learning by being more precise about the risk identified.
- Learning: Excessive fatigue creates significant risk by impairing ability to calculate dosage when dealing with high-risk medicines.

The precision is important because in reality a tired clinician may not have an option to rest – they may have to work on. In this case, knowing that fatigue creates a particularly significant risk when having to make calculations about high-risk medication will enable the clinician to modify their practice. They may deliberately seek a double-check of their calculation from a colleague or even defer certain tasks if they are not essential, knowing that they are high risk. Precise learning is important in generating higher impact recommendations.

IDENTIFYING LEARNING FROM CLINICAL INCIDENTS – THE EASY WAY

Identifying learning is simple but is frequently done badly in RCA reports. In order to keep learning and recommendations *smart* it is important that the learning arises directly from the incident in question. To ensure that it does you should try to follow a simple formula: Learning = Contributory factors in reverse.

Consider the logical progress of a root cause analysis investigation in Figure 13.1.

Now consider this in reverse – Figure 13.2.

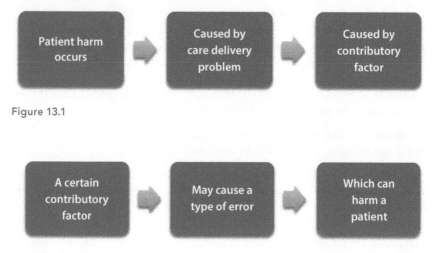

Figure 13.1

Figure 13.2

Remember that the investigatory process is designed to enable learning so the learning is contained within the process itself. You do not need to look or work outside the process to identify your learning. It also follows that the most important learning therefore will be identified by reversing the root cause. Consider a very simple case. Mr Smith attends his GP with a sore throat and is diagnosed with tonsillitis. The GP intends to prescribe penicillin 500mg four times each day (qds), but instead a prescription for penicillamine 500mg qds is produced. Fortunately, the error was identified by a pharmacist and the incident was a 'near miss' with no harm actually occurring. Investigation reveals three key contributory factors including a busy clinic and human factors – a skill level error or mental slip – leading the GP to miss the root cause or main contributory factor which is that on the drop-down menu of the GP computer screen penicillin and penicillamine are listed consecutively. A 'slip' of the mouse easily led to the prescribing error. This type of risk is increasingly recognised in medicine and is due to what are called 'Look Alike Sound Alike' (LASA) medicines. In this case it is the IT system that the GP was using that effectively held a ticking time bomb (latent risk) just waiting for a moment of inattention to allow an error to occur. This type of factor is known as an Equipment factor and it relates to the integrity of the IT system. That is, the degree to which reasonable fail-safe systems are built in. The investigation process would thus yield Figure 13.3.

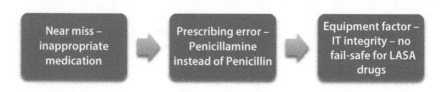

Figure 13.3

Figure 13.4

If we reverse this logic, we will identify the key learning from the incident (Figure 13.4). You can apply this logical process to all of the contributory factors identified within the investigation to ensure that maximal learning is obtained. The difficulty arises when it comes to trying to frame and articulate the learning clearly and succinctly. Let us look at a few more examples.

TURNING CONTRIBUTORY FACTORS INTO LEARNING

Consider some of the cases we have encountered thus far and look at how the contributory factor is simply turned around to identify the learning.

Mr Chen has post-operative complications

Mr Chen has had an open radical prostatectomy and was discharged from the county hospital two days ago. He phones his practice and seeks advice because he has vomited and has now developed watery diarrhoea associated with mild lower abdominal pain. He speaks to the practice nurse who has just that morning read a briefing from the local Health Protection Agency advising that there is a norovirus outbreak at the county hospital. Without further probing, the nurse advises Mr Chen that he probably has a norovirus infection. Mr Chen suffers a further five days of diarrhoea, pain and intermittent vomiting before seeking help again. He is readmitted and a significant post-operative haematoma is evacuated from the pelvis.

Contributory factor – human factors	Rationale
A cognitive bias called Availability bias	Statistically, a post-operative complication is more likely to arise than a hospital-acquired gastroenteritis. And yet the practice nurse jumped (heuristic logic) straight to a diagnosis of norovirus. She admitted that the article she had just read was at the forefront of her mind.

Learning

Availability bias, a type of cognitive bias, can lead to clinical errors where information that has been recently acquired or is easily available to the clinician carries undue weight and skews their judgement.

Human-factors learning is significant in healthcare because it will underpin how we consider and challenge our own patterns of practice and personal behaviour. Understanding human factors and how they influence healthcare interactions is vital if we are to change healthcare culture to create safer environments for our patients.

Dr Kipling and the prescribing error

Mr Havel consults Dr Kipling's practice for management of his type 1 diabetes. When his insulin is repeated Dr Kipling makes an error when substituting one of Mr Havel's insulin types resulting in the prescription of two incompatible types of insulin – both long acting. This error goes unnoticed in 11 subsequent consultations involving five other doctors and is also not picked up by the dispensing pharmacist.

Contributory factor – equipment factor

IT integrity – absence of fail-safe system to prevent prescription of incompatible insulin

Rationale

Insulin substitution is a complex task. While multiple factors played a role, in this case it is noted that some IT providers do have a warning system within their IT systems that alerts a clinician when incompatible prescribing occurs. Had an appropriate alerting system been present on the IT system of both the GP practice and the pharmacy, a potential 24 alerts would have been generated giving a greater chance of preventing the incident.

Learning

Within IT prescribing and dispensing software, failure to provide automatic alerts when incompatible insulin types are prescribed increases the risk of prescribing errors occurring.

When we look at other safety-critical industries, most of the biggest advances in terms of increased safety have arisen either from equipment or system design. Where equipment is involved in an incident, particularly IT systems, it is imperative to consider whether the safety features of the equipment are as robust as they could be. Small improvement steps make a difference. The provision of IT alert warnings is a vexed issue as researchers cite 'alert fatigue' but this is not a reason to dispense with alerts. It simply suggests that the nature of 'fail safe' may need to change from an alert to some other type of action. (IT safety systems are further complicated by the laws around product liability and IT developers are loath to implement changes because of this – but this is another story.)

Dr Simpson and the DVT

Dr Simpson visits an elderly gentleman with a suspected deep vein thrombosis (DVT) in the out-of-hours period. He prescribes low molecular weight heparin and, as per the local protocol for management of DVT in the community, he arranges for a district nurse to visit to give the injection. Dr Simpson fails to leave the correct paperwork for the district nurse and so the injection cannot be given. Delays ensue and there is a gap of 24 hours before the injection is given. The patient dies following a pulmonary embolism 48 hours after Dr Simpson's visit and the family complain that the delay in administering the first dose of heparin was a cause of death. The investigation does not support the claim by the family but in terms of the delay in medication it finds that the protocol for management of DVT in the community had not anticipated differences in care between daytime and out-of-hours practice.

Contributory factor – task factors

Community DVT protocol does not include key guidance on how to enable provision of medication by community nurses in the out-of-hours period.

Rationale

In the out-of-hours period both GPs and community nurses work for separate county-wide services with no link to individual practices. GP instructions to a nurse have to be explicitly written down on a Medicines Authorisation Record that should be left at the patient's home. This fact was overlooked by the clinicians designing the DVT protocol and this left a latent risk within the task of managing a patient with a DVT in the community.

Learning

Clinical protocols that are designed for daytime practice may be inappropriate for out-of-hours or urgent care at times when a full range of support services is not available. Use of such protocols in out-of-hours services may create a latent clinical risk and contribute to clinical incidents.

Once again, learning flows from the contributory factor back toward the occurrence of patient harm or risk. Learning in RCA investigations is simply articulating the findings of the analysis.

Let us finally consider key learning from the baby Anna case.

Baby Anna

Dr King assessed baby Anna and believed that she had a viral illness. He was not sure whether she had had a febrile convulsion but felt that she would not significantly benefit from referral for paediatric review. Baby Anna went on to die of pneumococcal meningitis some 30 hours later.

Contributory factor – patient factor	Rationale
Presentation in the prodromal phase of a meningitis. (A severe and complex illness)	Meningitis is rare and baby Anna presented very early in the illness without any of the typical features of the full-blown disease making it virtually impossible to detect.

Learning

Meningitis may be impossible to detect if it presents in the prodromal phase of the illness.

Secondary learning point

Baby Anna died as a result of the underlying natural pathological process of the disease and therefore the case does not meet the threshold for recognition as a Serious Incident with regard to registration upon STEIS.

TOP TIP

When patient factors are the major contributory factor in an incident, a further learning point may arise with regard to whether the case continues to meet the criteria for a Serious Incident according to a regulatory body.

In the Baby Anna case, the learning identified is quite weak. We are stating something that we already know. Most countries that use RCA as a technique to investigate serious clinical incidents do so because they wish to identify learning that will contribute to improved patient safety. Regulatory reporting systems will therefore be most concerned to identify those cases where the root cause lies within the overall system of care provided for the patient, rather than in cases in which it is discovered that a patient died from the natural pathological processes of their disease. Where you identify that the primary root cause is a patient factor, an additional element of your learning may be that the case does not reach a threshold for recording on national or regional learning databases. In England this is the Strategic Executive Information System (STEIS). If there is learning associated with other contributory factors that is of very great significance, then the threshold may still be met, as the point of recording is to enhance learning after all. What regulatory systems do not need, however, is a lot of 'noise' in the system and recording information that we already know is not likely to be helpful. We already know that children who present in the prodromal phase of meningitis may be missed so this case is not really telling us anything new. For this reason, you may wish to discuss with your commissioners the option of downgrading the case so that it is recorded locally and serves as local learning but is removed from the national regulatory system of recording.

FROM LEARNING TO RECOMMENDATIONS

If you stick to the process, just as learning flows on from the contributory factors (and the root cause is the key contributory factor), so, too, the recommendations flow on from the learning. As with learning, recommendations are really simple in principle, but a lot of people get them wrong.

> Identifying recommendations from RCA investigations is easy.
> But many people still get it wrong!

By now it should be apparent that the value of each stage of the process is dependent upon the step before it. If you get the preceding step wrong, then the next step will surely be wrong as well. If you have got the identification of your learning points right, then you are halfway toward having good recommendations. Poor recommendations may follow from poor learning but they may also follow from failing to follow the RCA process. The acronym SMART (specific, measurable, attainable, relevant and timely) is often used to refer to the attributes of good objectives or project plans. The same applies to recommendations – they should be SmaRt. I have emphasised certain letters in the acronym as RCA recommendations most often fail because they are not *specific* or because they are not *relevant*.

FAILING TO IDENTIFY SUICIDAL INTENT: RECOMMENDATION NOT SPECIFIC

A patient contacted an out-of-hours service late on a Monday evening complaining of low mood and expressing thoughts of self-harm. The patient was able to reassure the telephone triage doctor that they would not act upon their plans and they would consult their GP the next morning. The patient took a fatal overdose on Tuesday afternoon having failed to consult their GP. Voice recordings of the out-of-hours GP telephone call revealed that the patient displayed significant delay in responding to questions, and this was not recorded or noted as significant by the GP. The GP also failed to explore the patient's alcohol history. The following chain of care delivery problem, contributory factor and learning arose (Figure 13.5).

The recommendation arising from the report was: All out-of-hours staff should complete a recognised suicide-awareness course.

Figure 13.5

The RCA only revealed that the GP involved in the incident was lacking in awareness of suicide risk factors. There was no evidence to suggest that every other clinician in the service was equally unaware – hence a recommendation applied to the whole service is too generalised. It may, of course, be true but the evidence does not support this. If the investigator has reason to think that the problem may be one that is shared by a whole service or cohort of clinicians, then what they should do is seek evidence to support this view. This could be done either during the course of the investigation itself or, more sensibly, the lack of awareness and the subsequent gathering of further evidence may in fact become part of the further learning and recommendations of the report. For example, the final learning and recommendations may look like this:

Learning:

- Dr X's lack of training in suicide awareness led to a failure to recognise a patient at risk of self-harm.
- It is not clear whether the identified lack of training in suicide awareness is an isolated problem or affects the service more generally.

Recommendations:

- Dr X should complete further recognised training in suicide risk awareness and should complete a learning reflection summary to be reviewed by the clinical lead for the service.
- The out-of-hours service should complete an appropriate survey of all clinical staff to determine whether a lack of training in suicide awareness is widespread within the service or not.

The question of exactly how the survey is completed is not really the problem for the RCA investigator. As an investigator, you do not have to solve all of the problems that may arise; you simply have to be able to signpost the way forward. Of course, if you are also the service lead you will still have to grapple with the problem but it then becomes a service development issue rather than something you need to complete as part of the investigation itself.

COMMUNICATION FAILURE: RECOMMENDATION NOT RELEVANT

A seven-week-old baby was seen in a GP walk-in clinic attached to an accident and emergency department. The baby was floppy and unresponsive and acute sepsis was suspected. The baby was rapidly transferred to the emergency department resuscitation room where a team of A&E nurses, the GP from the urgent care centre and the hospital paediatric registrar further assessed the baby. The paediatric registrar sought to obtain intravenous access without success. Meanwhile, one of the A&E nurses had placed an intubation trolley and paediatric bag and mask at the head of the bed. After 30 minutes the paediatric registrar placed an intraosseous line and transferred the baby to a paediatric ward. The baby was later intubated and transferred to a specialist paediatric unit but died during the night.

At a case review, a consultant paediatrician questioned whether the baby may have been intubated at an earlier stage. The paediatric registrar admitted being preoccupied with finding intravenous access. The A&E nurse said she had thought of prompting the registrar but he was new to the hospital and she did not know him and she was not confident to speak up. She said she would have done so if it was one of 'our A&E doctors'. The case has strong echoes of the Elaine Bromiley case (see Chapter 10: Human Factors Part 1: The key to enhanced learning) and this was recognised in the case-review meeting. It was pointed out that the authority gradient between nursing staff and medical staff in the department may lead to failure to communicate effectively at safety-critical moments (Figure 13.6).

Recommendation: Nursing staff from A&E to attend human factors training.

In this case the recommendation misses the mark altogether. The problem is not that staff were not aware of human factors such as authority gradients – the problem was the authority gradient itself. Making staff more aware of it will not remove it – although of course it is a start. This is a case in which the recommendation needed to be much more relevant to the identified learning. When British Airways (BA) became aware of the risk of authority gradients and the impact that it may have on communication between different members of the aircraft crew, they did not just implement human-factors training for all staff, they actually created new ways of communicating as well. In this case the RCA identifies the learning that authority gradients may have an impact upon safety-critical

Figure 13.6

communications. The recommendation should be relevant to this issue only. A more relevant recommendation would look like this:

Recommendation: The A&E department should investigate how it may develop communications strategies that overcome authority gradients between staff members during safety-critical activities.

TEASING OUT THE RECOMMENDATION

Notice from the above examples that a recommendation may be a solution to a problem or it may be a suggestion to explore an issue further. As an investigator your expertise will be in the analysis of an incident. You should have some awareness of the types of solutions available to problems but it is not necessary to find a solution to all of the potential problems that you may identify. Some will prove too complex or may even be outside the control of the service involved. In such circumstances the recommendation may simply be about highlighting a problem that needs addressing and using the recommendation of the report as impetus to get this done. In the next chapter we look in more detail at solution design but before you get to that, you need to get the logic of your recommendations right. It helps to follow a process and the following logic algorithms may help. Remember that we have previously identified that contributory factors, and hence our subsequent learning points, will tend to involve patients, people or systems and tasks.

PATIENT-FACTOR LEARNING AND RECOMMENDATIONS

With regard to patient factors in incidents it is not common to learn something new about a condition (Figure 13.7). Incidents will therefore usually be downgraded from a regulatory standpoint and recommendations are likely to involve reminding staff of the risks that are known to be associated with the condition. Case-based learning can be a powerful tool for raising awareness to risks. Even if the learning is already known, you should review local awareness in terms of custom, practice and protocol.

Remember the baby Anna case. We learnt: meningitis may be impossible to detect if it presents in the prodromal phase of the illness.

This is not new learning and thus the scope for recommendations appears to be limited. We might remind staff of the dangers inherent with assessing poorly children. If, however, we review our local practice against national guidance and recall that we also noted that Dr King used an outmoded technique of giving paracetamol and then reviewing Anna in one hour to gauge the response, we may identify more useful learning. Guidance from the National Institute for Health and Clinical Excellence (NICE) (NICE 160, 2013) discourages the practice of giving test doses of paracetamol and further, guidance from the Scottish Intercollegiate Guidelines Network (SIGN) (SIGN 102, 2008) suggests that in cases in which an intermediate risk of sepsis or invasive meningococcal disease is identified, an interim assessment at four to six hours is recommended. Thus, even where you appear to discover information that is already known, there is potential either to identify further learning about your service or to provide further assurance about your service by checking whether the learning fits with your service's usual practice. If you are not sure then you may consider exploring further with an audit or survey.

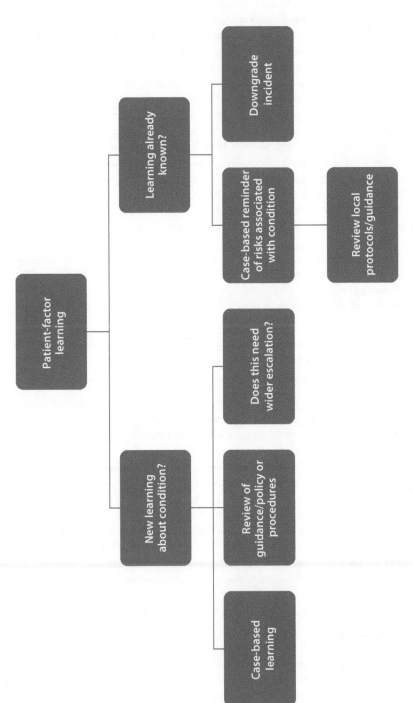

Figure 13.7

If you do identify learning about a condition that was previously unknown, then apart from using case-based learning to raise awareness, you should also initiate a review of any relevant guidance, policy or protocols to ensure that they remain fit for purpose with regard to the condition. Be prepared to escalate learning widely if you have truly identified a new facet of the condition that is currently not known (Figure 13.7).

Human factors remain a big latent risk factor in healthcare. Effective healthcare depends so much upon humans remembering things and doing things properly. In other industries, safety has been improved by removing the human element as much as possible but, for better or worse, that option is very limited in healthcare. This does not mean that the problem is beyond control, however. Over many years, modes and systems of practice have developed that contain risk partly because of a lack of awareness (perhaps a lack of acknowledgement is more appropriate) of human factors but also partly because of a lack of alternative options to counteract the fallibility of the humans at the sharp end of the system. Recommendations that recognise the impact of human factors and seek to promote raised awareness and changes in culture or changes in system or task design are likely to have the biggest impact upon patient safety. Specific solutions are considered further in the next chapter but even if the solution is beyond you, recognising the nature of the problem that needs addressing puts you a long way toward making effective recommendations.

On the basis of the analysis of human factors (Figure 13.8), you may recommend:

- case-based learning – this may be individual or group case-based learning about specific human factors and the impact that these may have on patient safety
- audit-driven change in behaviour – this may be individual or group based
- review of a specific system or task to determine the degree to which it contains latent human-factor risks.

Case-based learning attempts to raise awareness and nudge clinicians toward a more safety-alert culture. It is a relatively weak solution to patient safety risk in itself but it may be strengthened by addition of other changes.

Use of audit to challenge behaviour or culture in an individual or group of clinicians is probably the single most effective method to drive change. It comes with a cost and it requires careful planning and execution (see the next chapter) but it does work. It is a medium-strength solution to patient-safety risks.

The biggest impact in terms of improving patient safety will arise from changes in systems or tasks to eliminate the risk of human error. This is explored further in the next chapter but the essence is to identify where systems or tasks rely too heavily on fallible human judgement to see if an alternative method of managing the issue can be identified.

SYSTEM AND TASK (SAT) FACTOR LEARNING AND RECOMMENDATIONS

Humans can only consistently adapt behaviour to a certain degree (Figure 13.9). The biggest future improvements in healthcare safety are likely to arise through changes in the way we organise health services. This includes looking at how large-scale systems of care are organised but it will also involve looking closely at even the most mundane of tasks

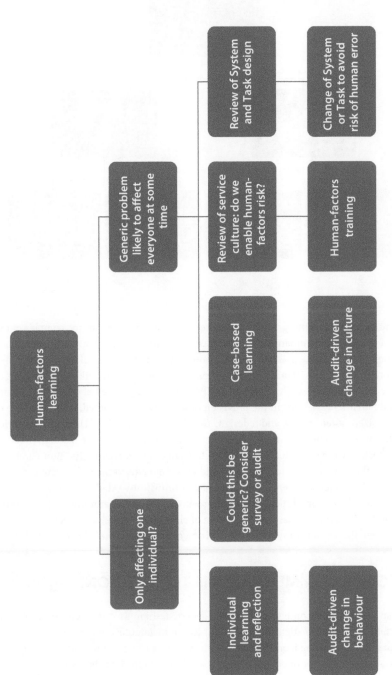

Figure 13.8

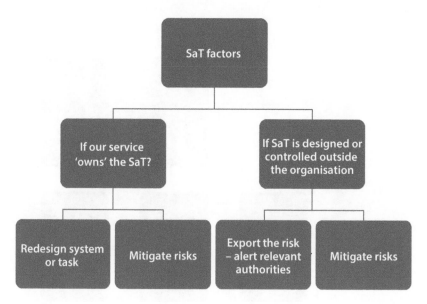

Figure 13.9

that we do and determining if they contain real or latent risk. Are they too complex or too subject to individual human variation in their application to be consistently safe? When we think of wider 'system' issues it is the coordination and delivery of services provided by more than one clinician or more than one practice that is at stake. The creation of service protocols such as the community DVT protocol discussed above, which ensure that all potential variations in the provision of service are considered, is one example of a small-sized system review and redesign. The creation of the NHS 111 telephone service is at the other extreme, one of the biggest examples of systemic service redesign in recent years. Tasks are the individual actions that clinicians and – increasingly – non-clinicians do when they see or speak to a patient. I add non-clinicians to the task inventory as the delivery of healthcare depends as much upon administrative staff dealing with service logistics as well as non-clinical staff dealing with information gathering and risk stratification (NHS 111) as it does with the action of clinicians themselves. When we think of tasks, then, this includes any single action that a member of the healthcare team does.

FROM RECOMMENDATIONS TO SOLUTIONS

We have looked at recommendations in a generic fashion as it is important to get the principles right and to stick to the process. Recommendations flow from learning and learning flows from the identified contributory factors (the most important of which is the root cause). A recommendation may be a solution to the learning issue identified or it may simply be a directive to identify a solution. Solution design is not a prerequisite for an RCA investigation as, clearly, some solutions would be beyond the technical scope or expertise of the investigation team or they may simply take too long to work out. While it is not essential to come up with a solution it is important to understand the nature of solutions design. Having recommended solutions that are specific and relevant, it is also necessary to ensure that solutions are measurable, achievable and time bound. These characteristics complete the SMART acronym, which you should endeavour to apply to all recommendations and solutions. These issues are the subject of the next chapter.

14

Solutions design and changing cultures

'High reliability organisations are not immune to adverse events, but they have learnt the knack of converting these occasional setbacks into enhanced resilience of the system.'

Reason, J, Human error: models and management,
British Medical Journal 2000, 320, p. 770

In Chapter 13 we looked at making recommendations and identified how to make recommendations that were both *specific* and *relevant*. These are two elements of the acronym SMART and it is useful to think of SMART whenever you are trying to make recommendations arising from your investigation. In Chapter 13 we identified that in order to make recommendations specific and relevant, it is helpful to distinguish what type of contributory factors our learning derives from. Generally, it will be possible to classify learning points as one of the following:

- Patient-factor learning – Complex pathology or individual patient bio/psycho/social factors
- People-factor learning – Human-factors learning
- System- and task-factor learning – How services are organised; how individual tasks are performed

At this stage, then, we need to take the learning and broad recommendations further to try to identify solutions that are not just specific and relevant, but also measurable, achievable and time bound. *Measurable* means that you must be able to account for your recommendations – you must be able to show if they have had an impact. *Achievable* relates to whether your recommendation is a realistic solution to the problem – this is all about solutions design. *Time bound* concerns your plan of action for the service to achieve your recommendations. For narrative clarity I will address these issues in the following order.

- Achievable recommendations – Solutions design
- Measurable recommendations – Demonstrating impact
- Time-bound recommendations – Effective action plans

An NPSA review of how other industries have sought to manage safety issues reveals the following principles that underpin safe solution design:

- Simplify
- Standardise
- Minimise the potential for human factors

- Automate
- Fail-safe
- Build in redundancy

The British psychologist Professor James Reason has been highly influential in the field of patient safety. Reason has been particularly influential with regard to recognition of how controls or 'barriers' to harm may improve safety and –conversely – how gaps in controls or barriers allow harm to occur. Reason developed the well-known 'Swiss Cheese' model to explain how the confluence of a series of gaps in different barriers may lead to harm. Combining the principles of safe solution design with an understanding of barrier mechanisms is vital to achieving effective patient safety outcomes. (See Reason J. *Human error*. New York: Cambridge University Press, 1990.)

BARRIERS AGAINST HARM

Barriers or control mechanisms represent effective potential solutions to counter identified risks. Four types of barrier are recognised:

- Human-actions barriers – Training, customs and practice
- Administrative barriers – Protocols and procedures
- Natural barriers – Time and distance
- Physical barriers – Shields, masks, gloves and enclosures

The application of principles of solution design and the understanding of barriers or control mechanisms facilitate the design of appropriate solutions. Even so, there is a recognised hierarchy in terms of solution strength. Some types of solution are simply better than others because they are likely to have a much bigger impact (Table 14.1).

Unfortunately, as with much else in incident investigation, understanding the principles is a good start but when it comes to applying this to real cases, things become

Table 14.1

Solution hierarchy		
Weak solutions	New policies or guidance, retraining of staff	Solutions that rely primarily upon human judgement. They are prone to all of the various weaknesses that arise because of human fallibility
Moderate-strength solutions	Checklist implementation, new protocol or procedure, reducing distractions, reducing look-alike, sound-alike medicines	Solutions that compel people to act in a safer way or reduce known risk factors such as distractions, fatigue or use of known high-risk medicines or procedures
Strong solutions	Change in individual or service culture. Change in system or task design	Solutions that change attitudes and behaviour. Solutions that change whole systems or tasks to eliminate latent risks

complicated. What do all of these principles mean in practice? Achievable solutions will be those that identify appropriate controls or barriers to reduce the likely occurrence or impact of any identified risks to patient harm. Once the principles are understood we can move on to a technique called barrier analysis to help us identify achievable solutions.

USING BARRIER ANALYSIS TO IDENTIFY ACHIEVABLE SOLUTIONS

A number of barrier-analysis tools already exist. The tool below is my adaptation of existing models. If we start with the risks identified from learning from our RCA, then the solutions *may* emerge from consideration of improvements for existing barriers or from the creation of new barriers. I stress that solutions *may* arise as there may be occasions where no new barriers are either evident or realistic. We are looking for achievable within the service in question. A potential barrier that involves work or investment beyond the scope or expertise of the investigation team may be 'exported' or referred to other appropriate authorities.

BARRIER ANALYSIS TOOL

Table 14.2 Risk identified from learning

Specific risks	Existing barriers	Strength	Barrier improvement	New barriers
Recommendation 1				
Recommendation 2				

Let us look at this in practice with some worked examples. Remember the case in which Mr Chen phoned with post-operative complications?

Table 14.3 Risk identified from learning: People factor

Specific risks	Existing barriers	Strength	Barrier improvement	New barriers
Availability bias, a type of cognitive bias, can lead to clinical errors where information that has been recently acquired or is easily available to the clinician carries undue weight and skews the judgement of the clinician.				
Newly acquired or easily retrieved information may skew judgement when taking a medical history	Individual attention and judgement. Training to use a formalised assessment process	Weak – relies only upon individual human factors	Standardise approach to taking and recording medical history	Use of clinical assessment templates
Recommendation 1	Clinicians should ensure that they standardise their approach to taking and recording medical history.			
Recommendation 2	Use of standardised assessment templates			

The risk has been made specific by limiting it to the completion of a medical history because this is the extent of the evidence available within the case. You may reasonably extend this to say that the risk exists throughout the clinical encounter and includes diagnostic decision making and management as well, although if you did, you should document that you are extending your interpretation of the impact of the learning. Barriers against people or human-factor-type risks are generally weak as they rely upon the basic training of the clinician and their ability to maintain attention and focus.

Note that the issue of *how* is not there yet. By separating the *what* of a recommendation from the *how* you avoid potential blocks to solutions where a belief that the *how* may not be possible stops you from focusing on an obvious solution. In this case, if you believe that use of a standardised approach to taking a history may have prevented the nurse from making a cognitive error then you have identified a barrier. If at the same time you think, 'but I will never be able to get our staff to do this', then you risk dismissing the recommendation before you have thought it through. Looking at the principles of solution design one can see that the main issue here was a nurse 'short-cutting' the history and jumping to a conclusion. We are trained to take a formal history that encompasses a full 'history of the presenting complaint' to prevent just this type of error so a very simple solution is to remind the nurse and all other staff of the importance of taking a history in the proper, already standardised format. There are a number of ways that this can be done:

- Messages to staff – such as memos, notices and posters
- Case-based learning – case history with explanation plus memos, notices and posters
- Training course – online, face-to-face / generic or bespoke / attendance only or pass/fail

The first two options are relatively easy to achieve but they do rely on a large degree of self-motivated learning on the part of the recipient. They are good for a well-engaged and well-governed workforce or for less significant learning points. A more formalised training course offers scope for greater impact, although it is clearly a much more onerous recommendation to make. You must be pragmatic when making recommendations and consider the potential financial impact of your proposed solutions.

The weakness of recommendation 1 may be overcome by recommendation 2. You may recommend implementation of the use of a formal assessment template that ensures that clinicians have to ask a full set of assessment questions. By doing this you remove a number of 'human' factors related to jumping to conclusions or taking shortcuts. Templates have their own problems and face resistance from many clinicians, but much like the World Health Organization (WHO) Surgical Checklists, if they are well designed (and subject to revision and improvement) they are almost certainly safer than relying upon basic training and human attention to the task to ensure a safe and thorough history.

Your final recommendations may look like this, including the 'what' and the 'how' (Table 14.4).

Learning derived from risks identified within systems and tasks generally have more specific solutions and may be easier to resolve. New procedures and protocols are relatively easy to create and implement within a small service. For larger services the logistics of implementation become more difficult but are certainly not insurmountable (Table 14.5).

Table 14.4

Recommendation 1	Clinicians should ensure that they standardise their approach to taking and recording medical history. Case-based learning derived from this case and highlighting how this approach may reduce clinical errors will be shared with all clinicians within the service.
Recommendation 2	The use of standardised assessment templates is a potentially stronger solution. The clinical lead will investigate the feasibility of introducing standardised templates within the service.

Table 14.5 Risk identified from learning: System and task learning

Clinical protocols that are designed for daytime practice may be inappropriate for out-of-hours or urgent care at times when a full range of support services is not available and use of such protocols in out-of-hours services may contribute to clinical incidents.

Specific risks	Existing barriers	Strength	Barrier improvement	New barriers
DVT protocol lacks a process to enable district nurses to give injections of low molecular weight heparin in the out-of-hours period	Personal knowledge of individual clinicians. Custom and practice within out-of-hours service	Weak – relies on personal knowledge or recognition of a knowledge gap. New clinicians may miss this	Revise protocol to include specific guidance and creation of relevant forms to enable district nurse actions	Clinical Commissioning Group to introduce a formal requirement to consider out-of-hours requirements whenever new community treatment protocols are created
Recommendation 1	Community DVT protocol to be revised by out-of-hours clinical lead to include specific guidance and the creation of relevant forms to enable district nurses to administer low molecular weight heparin at direction of out-of-hours clinician			
Recommendation 2	All other community treatment protocols to be reviewed by out-of-hours clinical lead to ensure that they are fit for purpose in out-of-hours period			
Recommendation 3	The clinical lead shares learning with the Clinical Commissioning Group and to seek agreement that the CCG will introduce a formal requirement to consider out-of-hours requirements whenever new community treatment protocols are created			

Table 14.6 Risk identified from learning: System and task learning

Within IT prescribing and dispensing software, failure to provide automatic alerts when incompatible insulin types are prescribed increases the risk of prescribing errors occurring.				
Specific risks	**Existing barriers**	**Strength**	**Barrier improvement**	**New barriers**
Prescribing software lacks automated alerts when two incompatible insulin types are co-prescribed	Clinician training and awareness	Weak – human factor prone to variation, decay of knowledge or lack of awareness	Raise levels of awareness of risk	Development of automated alerts in prescribing software
Recommendation 1	Raise awareness of prescribing risk by sharing case-based learning derived from this case			
Recommendation 2	Request IT provider to develop alerting process within prescribing module			

In this case the solution to the problem is relatively straightforward – you have to fix the hole in the protocol. Recommendations two and three would follow on from recommendation one as a common-sense manoeuvre. An issue in which one policy or protocol fails to recognise a particular risk is bound to raise the question about whether other policies and protocols are similarly flawed, and if you don't think of this then someone else will – so try to think laterally when you come across these types of issue.

Sometimes learning may lead to a solution that is outside the scope of the service involved (Table 14.6).

The first recommendation is weak, as even if awareness is raised this is likely to decay with time. The second recommendation is potentially much stronger but it is outside the control of the service. The service may recommend action but it cannot compel manufacturers to act. In this case, in fact, the issue of IT prescribing alerts is a vexed one, as there is evidence that prescribers suffer from 'alert fatigue' and there is an understandable reluctance to add alerts that will not actually serve their purpose. Exactly how alerts should be developed and produced is beyond the technical expertise of investigators and so both the risk of and the responsibility for finding an effective solution need to be exported. That is to say, it needs to be brought to the attention of the relevant controlling body.

MEASURABLE RECOMMENDATIONS – DEMONSTRATING IMPACT

Perhaps the biggest failing of most serious incident investigations is not the quality of the analysis or even the recommended solutions. It is the failure to measure the outcomes and to be able to demonstrate that they have had an impact. When external agencies such as commissioners or regulators visit a service or practice and enquire about serious incident investigations, all that they usually wish to see is evidence that a recommendation has been enacted and, better yet, that it has had an impact. So there are two facets to measurement – one is a measure to demonstrate that a recommended solution has been implemented. The second, much harder, is to demonstrate that this solution has had a positive impact. Within your incident file create a folder to contain evidence of implementation and impact.

MEASURING IMPLEMENTATION OF RECOMMENDATIONS

Actions following information sharing aimed at raising awareness, new guidance or re-training:

- Individual self-reflection: Ask individuals directly involved to produce a written personal reflection acknowledging learning. Self-reflection should demonstrate awareness of the key learning points but also an explanation of how learning will positively influence future practice. Keep the self-reflective piece as evidence of implementation of recommendation.
- Group acknowledgement: Information may be shared with groups within a practice or a larger service by a variety of means: simple emailed messages or memos containing revised guidance, newsletters, face-to-face feedback or formal training.
- Keep a copy of the email including recipient groups.
- For an improved evidence chain, consider also keeping a log of read receipts or acknowledgements. Better yet, create a bespoke acknowledgement that includes acknowledgement not just of reading the message but of the key learning points therein and the potential for impact upon future practice.
- Learning solutions that involve completion of formal training modules may benefit from being able to obtain completion certificates and, ideally, pass/fail scores.

The latter options all take time and resources to both organise and collate. Emailing out an update or guidance document is very easy to do but it is very difficult to prove that anyone has read it, let alone has reflected on it or is likely to amend their actions.

Process or system change is somewhat easier to evidence as there will generally always be a new policy or process map along with a training plan that underpins its introduction. Remember to include copies of these in your evidence file. It can be difficult to find documents that link an incident to a change in practice one or two years after the event and when a new process is already in place.

IMPACT OF RECOMMENDATIONS – CHANGING CULTURE

The gold standard for demonstrating impact is audit. The audit cycle is simple:

Identify a problem – Establish the scale – Implement a solution – See if the solution has worked.

Not only can this cycle demonstrate impact but it is also one of the best ways of driving change within a service, even to the point of changing cultures within a service.

In order to change a service culture you need a combination of a goal, oversight and feedback. Creation or use of a clinical audit cycle provides a very effective tool to do just this. Services such as out-of-hours and NHS 111 services are already committed to regular clinical audit and such audits are easy to adapt to drive change following a clinical incident. Few other practices perform clinical audit, but with a will it could easily be introduced and it would pay dividends in terms of creating a mechanism for driving change in culture.

The process is simple:

- Identify a clinical goal (improved safety-net advice).
- Benchmark current practice.
- Set a new standard.
- Audit and provide feedback.
- Audit and provide feedback.
- Audit and provide feedback.

This process is simple and it works. It does require some effort and commitment on the part of the service leads but knowledge that clinical work is audited and receipt of feedback will change attitudes and, eventually, the culture of practice within a service. It also provides excellent evidence of the impact of your recommendations.

Using this technique I have achieved significant and sustained changes in behaviour in out-of-hours services that I have led with a positive impact upon the incidence of patient-safety incidents. For example, when I took over the service we had a series of incidents in which failure to record medication history, in particularly allergy or sensitivity was a factor. Some GPs typed the information into the clinical notes but did not use the medicines template to record the information because it was an extra step and took a little longer. Unfortunately, this meant that information was not automatically available at future consultations. I changed our audit criteria so as to fail a GP on an audit unless they completed the medicine tab on the computer. I received protests both from GPs whose former good audit scores dropped and also from our auditors who had extra work to do. But over a six-month period, with sustained prodding, behaviour changed for the better. Data got entered properly and the few incidents that we had arising every few months began to diminish. The initial drop in audit scores reversed and returned to pre-change levels but with our GPs now working to a higher standard of care and accepting this as the new culture in the service. We have used the technique on a number of other facets of the clinical encounter as a result of incident investigation, with the same positive result.

TOP TIP

Changing culture is hard work but it is possible.

When you have finalised your recommendations and established how they will be achieved and how they will be measured, you need to ensure that they get done in a timely fashion. Pulling all of your learning and recommendations together is best achieved via an Action Plan. After all of your hard work, it is the action plan that will be the culmination of your work and be the vehicle for the delivery of your objectives.

TIME-BOUND RECOMMENDATIONS: EFFECTIVE ACTION PLANS

An action plan is exactly what it says it is. The key elements to get right are the learning points and recommendations – this should be easy if you have followed the process outlined in the past few chapters. The other area where people sometimes struggle is the timeline for actions. Your action plan can be as detailed or as simple as you wish. Two examples are given below and further advice upon time frames follows. What you will note is that both plans include an assurance process. It is important that a designated individual is responsible for assuring that an action plan has been completed. The designated individual should be a senior member within the governance team of the service or practice – a governance or service manager, practice manager or clinical lead. The extent to which action plan assurance occurs is a key marker of the culture of governance and patient safety within an organisation.

Remember that learning from incidents may include advice that incidents are downgraded on STEIS or other regulatory data bases and may also include guidance regarding application of Duty of Candour. This learning should ideally be incorporated into an action plan as well.

SIMPLE ACTION PLAN

A simple plan is suitable for simple incidents. If there is a single learning point with a relatively straightforward action then you may choose to keep the action plan simple (Table 14.7).

COMPREHENSIVE ACTION PLAN

A comprehensive plan is preferred, particularly by external commissioners and regulators. This will allow them to review an incident investigation by turning straight to the action plan to see what happened and what remedial actions are planned (Table 14.8).

Copies of action plans are available free from my website: www.PatientSafety Investigations.com

ACTION COMPLETION TIMES

The time allowed to complete an action needs to be realistic but also reasonable. Exact time scales may lapse and this is acceptable if there is a good reason but be sure to note this and keep a record in your evidence file. The following is a guide for reasonable time scales for common actions. Clearly, the larger your organisation, the longer it will take to implement large-scale change. Bear in mind that for large organisations it may take time to free someone up from existing work or for them to gather the necessary support team to enable them to complete actions – this may add a month to a recommendation but it should also prompt the need to be explicit about timing to ensure that actions do not drag unnecessarily (Table 14.9).

The time scales in Table 14.9 may seem overly long but implementing change is harder than you may think and there is no point in setting yourself up to fail. Better to overestimate time and deliver early rather than to underestimate and fail in your plans. You should factor in an interim assessment of progress by the governance assurance lead at

Table 14.7 Serious incident action plan

Recommendation	Responsible person	To be completed by:
Recommended action is noted here	Name of person who will complete or be responsible for action	Date by which action should be completed
Does Duty of Candour apply?	Yes	No
Comments: Briefly explain whether DoC applies or not. This will depend on whether the investigation demonstrates that actions within the service were more likely than not to have caused harm to the patient – rather than harm being due to the natural underlying pathology of the illness or condition that the patient was suffering from. If in doubt you may state that Duty is not clear but in the interests of openness you will fully disclose findings of the investigation to the patient or their representatives.		
SIRI status confirmed?	Yes	No
Comments: Briefly comment on whether the incident reaches a threshold for national reporting. If the root cause is clearly a patient factor with other contributory factors having little impact upon the final adverse outcome, then the case may be downgraded (assuming it was recorded on STEIS at the outset).		
Assurance	Completed by:	Date:
Were recommendations completed?	Yes	No
Comments: Ideally explain when actions were completed and briefly explain what evidence exists to confirm implementation and how impact will be monitored. If actions have not been completed, explain why not and what is being done. Sometimes the failure to complete an action can itself serve as useful ongoing learning. Commissioners and regulators will value honesty – particularly so if failure to implement a plan leads to learning about the organisation and a 'plan B'.		

regular intervals or via regular governance meetings where the plan may be a standing item on the agenda until it is completed.

Completing the action plan is the final active process in your investigation. Now all you have to do is write up what you have done. Writing clear and compelling reports is the subject of the next chapter.

Table 14.8

Incident	What we learned	Recommendations	Responsible person	Time by which completed	How we will determine implementation/Impact
Brief description of incident	Learning point 1	Recommended action 1			Newsletters, read checklists, training log
	Learning point 2	Recommended action 2			Service level audit, etc.
Does Duty of Candour apply? Yes No Comments:					
SIRI Status confirmed? Yes No Comments:					
Assurance:		Completed by:		Date:	
Recommendation 1		Action achieved?	Yes No	Comments:	Comment if further control action is needed
Recommendation 2		Action achieved?	Yes No	Comments:	
Recommendation 3		Action achieved?	Yes No	Comments:	

Table 14.9 Action time scales – indicative only

Action	Service size	Time scale
Develop a proposal for action where solutions not immediately evident	Small: < 20 staff	1 month
	Medium: 20–100 staff	1–2 months
	Large: > 100 staff	3 months
Undertake a service review or survey prior to finalising a recommendation or action	Small: < 20 staff	1 month
	Medium: 20–100 staff	2–3 months
	Large: > 100 staff	4 months
Implement a service change – raising awareness, new procedure not needing formal training	Small: < 20 staff	2 months
	Medium: 20–100 staff	4 months
	Large: >100 staff	6–8 months
Implement a service change that requires formal staff training	Small: < 20 staff	3–4 months
	Medium: 20–100 staff	4–6 months
	Large: > 100 staff	8–12 months
Drive service improvement or culture change via targeted audit or bespoke training	Small: < 20 staff	6 months
	Medium: 20–100 staff	12 months
	Large: > 100 staff	18–24 months

15

Writing reports

Writing up the report of a serious incident investigation should be an easy process – after all, it is just a matter of collecting all the evidence and conclusions and presenting them in a coherent way. The process is even facilitated by the presence of report templates that break down the report into neat sections that follow the investigatory process. And yet . . .

Errors commonly occur:

- Key terms are mis-identified.
- Key elements of the report are missed out.
- Care delivery problems and contributory factors are confused.
- Root causes are not clearly linked to the events described.
- The point of the report is hard to grasp.
- Reports are 'clunky' to read.
- Reports do not make sense.

The first few errors listed above are generally due to failing to understand the principles of RCA and pushing on with an investigation and report in spite of this. Training will reduce the tendency to get terms wrong and following the process as outlined in this book and other resources should result in better analysis with clearly identified root causes, learning and recommendations. But even if the investigation has been performed very well and the conclusions are accurate, it can still be difficult to produce a readable report – one that will readily make sense to its readers. This is particularly the case for readers who have little familiarity with the RCA model – and this includes most people, including many medical colleagues but especially patients and their representatives.

The National Patient Safety Agency (NPSA) provide excellent resources for RCA investigators including report templates and RCA guidance. This can be found at www. nrls.npsa.nhs.uk. A suite of report templates is available that will enable you to structure your findings and it is important to follow the main principles of the NPSA format as this is what is expected of healthcare reports. These templates are very useful but I would recommend that you do not simply cut and paste a template and add your organisational logo. A few variations and additions will help to make the report much more readable, especially for those with little awareness of what an RCA investigation is all about. As a simple example of this, the fact that an RCA is an investigation to discover learning and not 'blame' is so well enshrined within clinical governance ethos that it goes without saying. Literally. This fact is not actually stipulated in standard report templates. Unfortunately, many people who read the RCA, particularly patients or their families, are not fully conversant with modern clinical governance ethos. They will often read a report expecting that it will tell them who is to blame for the death or injury to a loved one. And I use the term 'blame' in its commonly understood context of meaning to censure or criticise harshly. The RCA report may thus appear to be a whitewash to many readers.

This can be the case even after you have sat with a relative and explained that you will be investigating to find learning and not blame. Explaining the principles of RCA within the report will not necessarily stop someone reading it from thinking that it is a whitewash but it will certainly help, especially when the report is read by more sophisticated readers.

This chapter will look at the following aspects of RCA report writing:

- Eight simple rules – report-writing basics
- Report formats – must-have and should-have formats
- Narrative style – making it flow, making sense

EIGHT SIMPLE RULES – REPORT-WRITING BASICS

1. Write in the third person.
2. Write for an audience of average lay people.
3. Avoid technical jargon and explain all abbreviations.
4. Keep all staff and the patient anonymous.
5. Avoid negative descriptors.
6. Use evidence and refer to this in your analysis.
7. You may make judgements or speculate based upon the balance of probability.
8. Show your working out.

Writing in the third person is a classical technique for telling a story of what happened from the point of view of someone who was not directly involved. 'On a particular day, a patient presented at a clinic and was seen by a doctor. The following events occurred . . .'

A somewhat old-fashioned dictum is that the writing style of reports is one that should be understood by 'The man on the Clapham Omnibus'. I am not sure what the modern equivalent to the man on the Clapham Omnibus is but try to keep sentences short and avoid multiple clauses or sub-clauses. If you must use technical terms or refer to complex procedures, be aware that it can break up your report if you explain them in full within the body of the report. Consider including a glossary, footnote or appendix to explain technical issues.

Abbreviations may be used but they need to be explained the first time that you use them. This includes medical abbreviations including BP, JVP and 02Sat. This can make a copy of verbatim notes from an examination difficult to read – again consider footnotes or refer to a glossary. If you do include technical information about examination findings you will need to qualify it – that is to say, you will need to explain whether examination findings represent normal or abnormal states.

You may ask a patient or family of a patient how they wish to be referred to in the report. All other staff and third parties should be anonymised. Usually staff are assigned letters of the alphabet. Remember to keep a log of who is who. Do not use staff initials as it is easy to guess identity from initials and where possible avoid gender-specific pronouns for the same reason. It is preferable to say, 'Dr A took a blood sample and then they took it to the receptionist for dispatch . . .' rather than, 'Dr A took a blood sample and then he took it to the receptionist.'

The report must be seen to be fair and open and should not prejudice patient or staff. If someone has done something that is abnormal and that you think represents poor practice or behaviour, do not express your opinion by using terms such as 'poor' and 'substandard'. Instead refer to what was done in comparison with what should or may have been expected to have been done. (Remember to avoid hindsight bias here.) For example, if the notes recorded following a consultation with a child seem poor because they do not include a full range of clinical findings, you may express it thus: 'It is noted that the clinical notes do not record the respiratory rate, capillary refill or temperature. Nor do they reference whether signs of meningism or rash were present. It would generally be regarded as best practice to include these findings in the clinical record.'

Where possible use evidence to validate any comment or opinion. If a patient has a particular condition then review the presentation and management of this against relevant guidelines from NICE or SIGN if available and via standard medical reference texts or online resources (meaning the *Oxford Textbook of . . .* or *GP Notebook*, as examples, rather than Google).

When it comes to analysis of what happened, you will need to interpret evidence. Sometimes you find evidence that conflicts, or testimony that requires a judgement about whether to accept it or not. It is reasonable to form what is called a balanced judgement based upon evidence available to you. If you think that something is more likely than not, you may make a judgement on the balance of probability. It is important to be aware when you are doing this as balanced judgements or speculative judgements are potential weak points in an analysis. Judgements about human factors such as cognitive bias arising during an assessment are usually speculative judgements. A balanced judgement occurs when one has to weigh up evidence without fact. For example, in the baby Anna case, Dr King did not record a number of key findings in the notes. At interview, however, he said that he had examined Anna for rash and signs of meningism and had checked capillary refill but he had simply neglected to record it as he was pushed for time. One could either believe Dr King or not, or one may decide that there was insufficient evidence to decide. In practice, I examined the rest of Dr King's examination and noted that he had recorded a number of vital signs on Anna and the parents had confirmed that an examination had taken place. On balance it seemed reasonable to believe that if Dr King had checked the temperature, pulse and respiratory rate he had also observed other key signs such as the absence of a rash or meningism.

The key point here is that in my report I explained that I was taking a balanced judgement and also explained why I was minded to believe Dr King on this issue. That is to say, I showed my working out. Someone may disagree with my judgement but because they can see how I came to my conclusion, my report is demonstrating openness and honesty and cannot reasonably be accused of covering things up.

REPORT FORMATS: MUST-HAVE AND SHOULD-HAVE FORMATS

The NPSA recommend the report format in Table 15.1.

This format is excellent in that it replicates the process of the RCA investigation and covers all of the issues that should have been addressed. The problem is that it is a very technical format. If we remember the origins of RCA, as a problem-solving tool developed primarily by industrial manufacturers and the aerospace industry, we may imagine a small cohort of managers and technical experts nodding wisely as they digest the findings. RCA reports in industry are not intended for public consumption and the fact that the format is not easy to follow and that the terms are completely unfamiliar to a lay reader is irrelevant. This is not the case in healthcare, however; reports will be viewed not only by the governance team of the service involved but potentially also by a whole raft of other people, most of whom will not have had training in the principles of RCA. They will not be familiar with the terminology and the format will appear alien unless they

Table 15.1

| **Title page** |
| Executive summary |
| **Main report** |
| Incident description and consequences |
| Pre-investigation risk assessment |
| Background and context |
| Terms of reference |
| Level of investigation |
| Involvement and support of patient and relatives |
| Involvement and support for staff involved |
| Information and evidence gathered |
| **Findings** |
| Chronology of events |
| Detection of incident |
| Notable practice |
| Care and service delivery problems |
| Contributory factors |
| Root cause |
| Lessons learned |
| Post-investigation risk assessment |
| **Conclusions** |
| Recommendations |
| Arrangements for shared learning |
| Distribution list |
| Appendices |
| Action plan |

regularly review technical or legal investigation reports. Furthermore, as stated above, the principle of 'learning and not blame' underpins the report but is not stated and therefore many lay readers may struggle with the findings of a report as they are expecting to find someone culpable for death or harm caused to a loved one. Root causes based in systems failures or understandable human factors are not what they are expecting. It is not that the format is wrong, it is just that it could do with a bit of contextualisation for it to make sense. It has become my practice to add contextual comments to reports to try to ensure that all readers at least have the opportunity to understand the principles behind the aims and objectives of the report.

Exactly how this is done is a matter of personal preference and style. I would suggest adding an 'Introduction' as page one, ahead of the executive summary. In other high-level reports, an executive summary is a narrative that contains both an outline of the background and the context of the report as well as a summary of findings. The RCA executive summary is just a summary list of the findings. As such, it may represent a rather abrupt start to a report, particularly for those unfamiliar with this format. The introduction can soften this and give greater clarity to the reader. The following is simply an example of the type of preamble that may be usefully added to a report.

INTRODUCTION

This report is a root cause analysis report and has been conducted following the principles established by the National Patient Safety Agency (NPSA) and NHS England.

RCA INVESTIGATION PURPOSE

NHS England have stressed the importance of recognising that the purpose of a serious incident investigation is to identify learning opportunities for individuals or an organisation that may prevent recurrence of the incident. The 2015 revised guidance emphasises the need to 'focus attention on the identification and implementation of improvements that will prevent recurrence of serious incidents, rather than simply the completion of a series of tasks'.

NHS England, Patient Safety Domain, *NHS England Serious Incident Framework: Supporting learning to prevent recurrent*, March 2015.

An RCA investigation is not a disciplinary investigation and is not intended to censure or criticise individuals involved in the care of a patient. Conduct or behaviour that breaches acceptable professional or service levels will be reported and addressed via appropriate channels external to this report.

An RCA may identify care or service delivery problems during the course of a patient contact with a service that may be valuable from a learning perspective but these may not be causally related to the final outcome of the incident. This is particularly the case where the patient's underlying condition is complex or severe.

ESTABLISHMENT OF CERTAIN PRINCIPLES

In order to ensure clarity with regard to investigatory and reporting principles, the following points are made:

Elimination of bias

A key principle of serious incident investigation is the elimination of investigator bias. The NPSA establish guidance for investigators that stresses the importance of eliminating, as far as possible, two common biases – outcome bias and hindsight bias.

Outcome bias means that knowing that a patient has suffered unexpected significant harm will tend to bias an investigator to believe that errors must have occurred during treatment and this can prejudice judgements against those involved in patient care.

Hindsight bias means that knowing that a harmful outcome occurred as a result of a missed or incorrect diagnosis may lead an investigator to believe that evidence that may have provided a clue to the clinician involved would have had obvious and clear meaning at the time of the incident, whereas in reality this is rarely the case.

In this investigation every attempt has been made to view the evidence available as objectively as possible and to apply the principle of foresight and not hindsight. That is to say, given the information available at the time, could one clearly foresee or predict the final outcome or could one predict that significant harm may ensue?

ANONYMITY

It is usual practice to maintain anonymity of staff and patient in serious incident reports as they may be shared widely within a health community.

TECHNICAL TERMS

The report follows a standard process used in root cause analysis investigations. Where appropriate all technical terms and abbreviations are clarified.

Certain technical terms to describe findings warrant explanation:

Care/Service delivery problems – these are things that happened that may have had an impact on the outcome. They are things that were done that should not have been done or they are things that should have been done that were not done.

Contributory factors – these are the underlying things that may have led to the acts or omissions identified as care or service delivery problems.

Patient factors – this is a type of contributory factor. It represents a consideration of the extent to which the patient's underlying medical condition may have affected the final outcome.

Root cause – this is the contributory factor that is thought to be the most significant as far as the final outcome is concerned.

NARRATIVE STYLE – MAKING IT FLOW, MAKING SENSE

A good RCA report needs to tell a story. Simply listing what happened and your final conclusions does not tell a very clear story. As mentioned above, it is helpful to show how your analysis was conducted and how conclusions were reached. This does require some literary skill and even when you feel you have mastered the technique it is still strongly advisable to ask a 'critical friend' to read your report to 'sense-check' it and proofread it.

A common error in narrative is to combine a description of what happened with a commentary or analysis explaining why it happened. This is particularly the case when the incident is being described. Keep incident descriptions as lean as possible with just a narrative of factual events. The extract below is an example of what *not* to do.

> At 4:30 p.m. Dr A left a prescription for enoxaparin in the home, telling the family that he would leave a message for the district nurses to visit. Dr A should have left an authorisation sheet for the district nurses to enable them to give the injection but they were new to the service and did not know that they should do this. Dr A had had an induction with the clinical lead the previous month and this issue was covered and was signed off by Dr A. Dr A phoned the coordinator at 4:40 p.m. from the visit car to ask for a district nurse to visit. The district nurse arrived at 6:45 p.m. but because there was no authorisation form they could not give the injection.

In this example the inclusion of what Dr A should have done and details of their induction clutter the account of what happened. Where possible limit descriptions of what happened to a purely factual account. Do not embellish with commentary or analysis – this comes later in the report.

The investigation should follow a logical process with one phase of the investigation naturally leading on to the next. The same is true for the report. Sections of the report should appear to flow but if there is a lot of explanation or narrative then one section may seem to appear abruptly and jar the reader. This effect can be minimised by inclusion of linking sentences or paragraphs explaining the purpose of key sections of the report and how they link to preceding sections.

The inclusion of a section titled 'Notable Practice' is a challenge and I often omit it as it has the potential to cause offence to patients and relatives. When a loved one has died, reading that the investigators chose to regard it as 'notable practice' that the patient was seen within 10 minutes of their appointment time may seem insulting. If there is notable practice, ensure, first, that it is indeed notable and, second, that you explain it in a way that is sensitive and constructive. Get someone to sense-check this section to ensure that you are not simply praising a service for doing its job. Seeing a patient on time may seem notable to someone working in busy unscheduled care clinics but it will not seem notable when viewed in the cold light of day.

REVEALING THE ANALYSIS

A large part of the 'work' of an RCA is in doing an analysis to determine care delivery problems, contributory factors and root causes. In the section titled 'Findings', these elements are listed and often a report will simply provide a bullet-point list of findings with little or no explanation of how conclusions were reached. It is helpful to include a section in the report explaining exactly how conclusions were reached. These may be broken up in the relevant sections of the report, may form a separate section or may be added as an appendix or series of appendices depending upon the complexity of the process involved. Revealing the analysis not only enables you to provide a 'story' of the investigation that will allow the report to read and flow better, it also ensures that your report is open and honest and that the reader can see how you have reached your conclusions. It is a more challenging approach but it generally pays off.

SAMPLE REPORT – DEALING WITH CDP, CF AND ROOT CAUSE

Below is an example of how one may deal with reporting the key elements of the RCA, the care delivery problems, the contributory factors and the root cause. The sample is not intended as a definitive model but it is an example of the depth of analysis that one may undertake and an example of the narrative style that one may use.

Main report

The baby Anna case has been previously described – Dr King assessed baby Anna and diagnosed a viral illness. Anna later died of meningitis.

FINDINGS

CARE AND SERVICE DELIVERY PROBLEMS

The NPSA acknowledge and recommend use of a tool called a 'Change Analysis' to help identify care delivery problems. This tool has been utilised in a modified form to assess the performance of Dr A in conducting the clinical assessment of baby A.

Change analysis involves breaking a task down into its constituent parts and then determining whether each element of the task was completed in the incident in question. Where an element of a task was not completed as expected, the relevance of this omission to the final outcome is further assessed.

We wished to review the clinical assessment that Dr A had made of baby A. We know that the National Institute of Clinical Excellence has produced a guidance document for all UK clinicians on the assessment of children under the age of five years who present with a fever. This document identifies a number of key parameters of importance in the assessment of children with a fever and it is expected that an assessment of a child with a fever should include all parameters covered within the NICE guidance. Therefore, the NICE guidance parameters form an effective template against which an assessment of any 'change' from practice can be determined.

NICE GUIDANCE ON ASSESSMENT OF FEVER AS CHANGE ANALYSIS TOOL

Table 15.2 compares the clinical assessment against NICE guidance 2013 on the management of feverish illness in children under five. NICE guidance is in blue.

CHANGE ANALYSIS

Change analysis indicates that all aspects of NICE guidance were adhered to in the assessment of baby A. The identification of red features on clinical assessment would generally warrant paediatric referral. Where amber features are identified, home treatment may be considered if the clinician has identified a probable cause for the fever. In this case Dr A believed that they had identified a cause of fever in the form of a viral infection.

There were omissions within the note keeping with regard to recording the colour of baby A and also with regard to recording details of activity levels. Further, although it is clear that Dr A assessed the level of hydration of the child and recorded key parameters such as pulse rate and temperature, a full range of observations including capillary refill time and appearance of the mucous membranes was not recorded. Dr A had indicated that they did assess capillary refill as part of their assessment but had failed to record it in the notes.

Failure to record a full range of observations as suggested by NICE can be regarded as an omission that constitutes a care delivery problem. Evidence from the rest of the clinical notes and the statements produced by Dr A, however, indicate that they had fully considered the clinical condition of baby A and had formulated a management plan based upon reliable and objective evidence in line with overall NICE guidance. Even if Dr A had not recorded all of the observations made, it seems clear that they had observed the appearance and activity level of baby A and had considered her state of hydration and that the omission of failing to record all of the information that is regarded as current best practice did not have any effect upon their final decision making on the evening.

FAILURE TO REFER FOR A PAEDIATRIC OPINION

While the overall assessment of baby A appears to have been appropriate by Dr A there remains a question of the management. The parents indicate that a suggestion was made to potentially refer for a paediatric opinion, which was then superseded by the agreed plan to give paracetamol and monitor in the clinic. It is also noted that Dr A made an initial diagnosis of febrile convulsion and noted this in the clinical notes and mentioned it to the parents. Dr A advises that they reflected upon this and doubted that this was actually the diagnosis but no definitive decision on this matter appears to have been made.

Current national guidance from NICE does include guidance on management of febrile convulsions and the recommendation is that a child presenting with a first episode of febrile convulsion should be referred to a paediatric unit.

Table 15.2

NICE guidance	Actual events at time of incident	Did change occur? Y/N	What was CPD that contributed to incident?	Comment
1.2.1 Life-threatening features of illness in children				
1.2.1.1 First, healthcare professionals should identify any immediately life-threatening features, including compromise of the airway, breathing or circulation, and decreased level of consciousness. [2007]	Dr A noted that the child was crying and also asked about skin appearance – ruling out the presence of mottling that may have been suggestive of circulatory collapse. No evidence was presented to suggest impaired consciousness, serious respiratory compromise nor circulatory collapse.	N		An immediate life-threatening illness is identified by assessment of breathing, circulation and consciousness. In this case, both the 111 and the GP's medical records confirm that the child was awake and responsive.

Below are the five key criteria that NICE promote as essential for assessment of poorly children. The guidance is referred to as 'Traffic light' guidance as symptom severity is ranked Green, Amber and Red and further action depends upon the colour of key symptom descriptors.

Symptom	Green	Amber	Red	Actual events at time of incident	Did change occur? Y/N	What was CPD that contributed to incident?	Comments
Colour (of skin, lips or tongue)	Normal colour	Pallor reported by parent/carer	Pale/Mottled/Ashen/Blue	The 111 notes state that the patient was not jaundiced. Dr A has commented that they did assess A's colour and that it was better after review of effect of paracetamol dose.	Y		Evidence suggests that Dr A had assessed the colour of A and that no Red features were present. Clinical notes do not include mention of colour of skin, which is an omission.
Activity	Responds normally to social cues Content/smiles Stays awake or awakens quickly	Not responding normally to social cues No smile Wakes only with prolonged stimulation	No response to social cues Appears ill to a healthcare professional Does not wake or if roused does not stay awake	The 111 notes state that the patient was not limp, floppy and/or unresponsive and there was no difficulty in rousing the patient. Dr A has indicated that they had observed A to be reacting normally at examination.			There is evidence indicative of activity levels within Green or perhaps Amber range.

Symptom	Green	Amber	Red	Actual events at time of incident	Did change occur? Y/N	What was CPD that contributed to incident?	Comments
Activity (cont.)	Strong normal cry/not crying	Decreased activity	Weak, high-pitched or continuous cry	Parents did report A as being tired and comment that Dr A said it was difficult to assess A's responsiveness as it was late at night.	Y		Clinical notes by Dr A do not record activity levels, which is a deviation from best practice and is an omission.
Respiratory		Nasal flaring tachypnoea: respiratory rate > 50 breaths/minute, age 6–12 months; > 40 breaths/minute, age > 12 months Oxygen saturation ≤ 95 per cent in air Crackles in the chest	Grunting tachypnoea: respiratory rate > 60 breaths/minute Moderate or severe chest indrawing	The 111 notes state that the patient was breathing at the time of the assessment and was not fighting for her breath. Dr A's records reflect that the patient had a respiratory rate of 40/minute with no recessions or nasal flaring and a clear chest on examination. Dr A indicates that breathing was improved on further assessment.	N		The symptoms and signs do not suggest any significant respiratory distress. Breathing rate identified is within normal limits for age.

Symptom	Green	Amber	Red	Actual events at time of incident	Did change occur? Y/N	What was CPD that contributed to incident?	Comments
Circulation and hydration	Normal skin and eyes Moist mucous membranes	Tachycardia: > 160 beats/minute, age < 12 months > 150 beats/ minute, age 12–24 months >140 beats/ minute, age 2–5 years Capillary refill time ≥3 seconds Dry mucous membranes Poor feeding in infants Reduced urine output	Reduced skin turgor	Dr A considered the patient's hydration by documenting that she had a wet nappy. The patient had a heart rate of 170, which could be accounted for by her initial temperature of 38.7. Dr A advised that they did check the capillary refill time although did not record it.	Y		Clinical notes indicate that an assessment of circulation was made. A raised pulse is noted that is Amber on the traffic-light scale. Best practice is to include further evidence including capillary refill time and appearance of mucous membranes. Dr A states that they observed this but did not document it. This is an omission.

Symptom	Green	Amber	Red	Actual events at time of incident	Did change occur? Y/N	What was CPD that contributed to incident?	Comments
Other	None of the Amber or Red symptoms or signs	Age 3-6 months, temperature ≥ 39°C; Fever for ≥ 5 days; Rigors; Swelling of a limb or joint; Non-weight bearing limb/not using an extremity	Age <3 months, temperature ≥ 38°C; Non-blanching rash; Bulging fontanel; Neck stiffness; Status epilepticus; Focal neurological signs; Focal seizures	In this case the patient's temperature was 38.7 and this improved to 38.3°C after paracetamol. There was no suggestion of neck stiffness or a rash on the 111 encounter and Dr A indicated that there was no meningism although this was not recorded.	N		Temperature is within normal acceptable limits for age. Although not recorded by Dr A, the notes from 111 indicated that no evidence of meningism was present at first presentation.

The author has confirmed that there is not a locally agreed alternative to this guidance and that paediatricians would accept referrals for children with a febrile convulsion.

It is noted that the parents were offered the option of a referral to a paediatric unit but that this was presented as one of three potential options for management.

The failure to refer to paediatricians appears to be a 'care delivery problem' – that is, it is an omission or deviation from best practice.

It must be made clear that a referral to a paediatrician for a child with a fever who may have had a febrile convulsion would not result in an automatic admission. It is usual practice for paediatricians to assess a child and then monitor it for a number of hours. If a source of infection is identified and if the child is stable, he or she is likely to be sent home.

In this case it is not possible to know what would have happened to baby A had she been referred to the paediatricians on call. She did not appear to have any other significant 'red flag' signs on examination. Given that baby A appears to have been in a relatively early stage of her illness when seen without clear signs of meningitis or severe sepsis, it is difficult to predict whether she may have improved in hospital and been sent home or whether she may have caused sufficient concern so as to be kept in hospital and thus for her grave condition to have been noted earlier. It is noted that baby A was seen by her own GP the following morning and remained at home following this assessment as well (see further commentary below). Nonetheless, the failure to refer to the paediatricians must be regarded as a care delivery problem.

CDP SUMMARY

In summary, two care delivery problems are identified:

- Sub-optimal note keeping
- Failure to refer to paediatric services following diagnosis of potential febrile convulsion

The first CDP, while a useful learning point for Dr A, is not regarded as being significant as it is unlikely that it would have had an impact on the final outcome.

CARE AND SERVICE DELIVERY PROBLEMS

- Medical record keeping by Dr A is below recommended standard.
- There was failure to refer for a paediatric opinion.

CONTRIBUTORY FACTORS

The NPSA provides a classification framework for contributory factors that lists different categories of potential contributory factors that may explain the origin of care delivery problems or directly relate to the adverse outcome.

An additional factor that must be considered is what the NPSA calls 'Patient factors'. This includes a consideration of the nature and complexity of the underlying condition that the patient presented with – in this case meningitis.

In 2014, The Meningitis Research Foundation published guidance notes for diagnosis and treatment in general practice. In the introduction to the guidance is the following comment: '*However, if a patient is seen during the early, prodromal phase of meningitis or septicaemia it may be impossible to distinguish them from someone with a milder self-limiting illness.*' (Meningococcal Meningitis and Septicaemia Guidance Notes: Diagnosis and Treatment in General Practice, 2014, p. 2 www.meningitis.org, accessed 1 Aug 2016.) The prodromal phase is associated with symptoms of fever, nausea and vomiting, malaise and lethargy.

The author has considered whether other features of a more progressive stage of illness were present at assessment. It is noted that baby A had a raised heart rate (170 versus a normal upper limit of 150–160) and respiratory rate at the upper limit of normal (40 versus a normal upper limit of 30–40). It is noted that the mother has recalled that baby A had cold feet and was very limp; however, this is not confirmed by the recollection of Dr A.

It is further noted that Dr A recalls reviewing baby A following providing a dose of paracetamol and noting that the temperature had reduced slightly and also that the respiratory rate and heart rate had reduced, although they did not record this.

Given the absence of any other factors to indicate meningitis and the absence of any red flag signs of sepsis and given also the improvement in clinical signs noted by Dr A, the author concludes that baby A would indeed have been likely to be in a prodromal phase of her illness when assessed by Dr A. Dr A had reasonable grounds for believing that baby A had a non-specific, probably viral illness at the time of assessment and it is the belief of the author that neither Dr A nor any other GP would have been likely to have been able to diagnose meningitis or septicaemia at the time of assessment. The presence of a possible convulsion in this context would have been grounds for a paediatric referral as discussed above but it would not in itself suggest the presence of meningitis or septicaemia.

Thus the very nature of the illness of meningitis/septicaemia, and the extreme difficulty of forming a clear diagnosis when the condition presents insidiously and is assessed in a prodromal phase, are themselves significant contributory factors in this incident.

FAILURE TO REFER TO PAEDIATRIC SERVICES: HUMAN-FACTOR ANALYSIS

It has been noted that in this case Dr A had thought at one stage that baby A may have had a febrile convulsion. After further review it was felt that this was unlikely as there was no clear description identified suggestive of true convulsions and that the shivering noted by the parents may have been rigors associated with fever. It is not possible to tell whether baby A had had a convulsion or not, but what is clear is that the issue was not fully resolved by Dr A. We have already established that the failure to resolve this issue and refer to the paediatricians constituted a contributory factor in this case. Can we learn anything further from this aspect of the incident?

A deeper analysis of the actions of Dr A involves considering the actions from the point of 'Human-factor' analysis. The NPSA and other patient-safety organisations have recognised a number of different theoretical frameworks with which to view human clinical decision making. In this case, the authors have considered the case using concepts of 'situational awareness' and 'cognitive bias'. We believe that use of these concepts enables us to identify certain important human factors associated with key decision making from which all clinicians may be able to learn.

Situational awareness involves three levels of knowledge:

1. Knowing what is going on
2. Knowing what this means now
3. Knowing what this means going forward

A loss of awareness can occur at any level. Let us look at the case with this in mind (Table 15.3).

We can see that Dr A had a good level of situational awareness at levels 1 and 2. At level 3, however, they appear to have lost full awareness of the significance of what baby A's symptoms may have meant going forward.

With the benefit of hindsight, we now know that the raised pulse and respiratory rate and the drowsiness noted by the parents may have been early signs of the development of septic shock. The shivering and shaking described by the parents may have been convulsions. With the benefit of hindsight, we now know that the apparent improvement in baby A's condition when reviewed one hour after initial assessment by Dr A was misleading and provided false reassurance that baby A was not significantly unwell.

Table 15.3

Level of situational awareness	Events	Comments
Knowing what is going on	A thorough history and examination occurred A diagnosis was formed	Dr A knew that baby A had an infection, had some abnormal vital signs and had 'shivers' that may or may not have been a convulsion
Knowing what this means now	Baby A was given medicine for fever and monitored for a further hour in the clinic	Dr A knew that the abnormal signs and potential convulsion indicated an infection that was more significant than usual
Knowing what this means going forward	Parents were given option of going home following review at clinic or paediatric review off site Safety-net advice was given to seek review if concerned	Dr A knew that the findings on examination may have been due to a more severe infection but believed that their assessment and management plan had reduced the risk of severe infection being missed to an acceptable level

Human-factors psychology tells us that we tend to lose situational awareness due to inherent weaknesses in the way that we process information – what are technically called cognitive biases. There are a variety of cognitive biases that may affect clinicians when faced with complex or difficult decisions. Two cognitive biases may have been operational in this case – confirmation bias and frequency gambling.

Clinicians tend to form diagnoses by recognising patterns of symptoms and signs. Training and years of experience enable clinicians to very rapidly make assessments and indeed in cases of emergency we rely on clinicians making rapid assessments and decisions. Where clinical cases become more complex it becomes harder to make rapid assessments of patterns of symptoms because in more complex cases there is a much greater overlap of symptoms and signs between different conditions. In this case, there is a great overlap of common and relatively mild symptoms that are present in many mild infections with a few moderate symptoms that are common to both mild and more serious infections.

The condition of confirmation bias is a tendency to form an assessment of a case based upon the majority of the evidence and then to seek to confirm this initial assessment by overvaluing evidence that would confirm the initial assessment and by undervaluing evidence that would contradict the initial assessment.

Thus, confirmation bias may cause a clinician to overvalue a belief that a raised heart rate may be due to the presence of a fever rather than being due to incipient septic shock.

Confirmation bias may also cause a clinician to be falsely reassured by a minor improvement in a temperature reading or pulse rate, as this would confirm the belief that the infection is a mild infection rather than a more severe one. Dr A was noted to comment that it was difficult to assess baby A's level of alertness because of the late hour. This may also represent a bias – minimising evidence that may negate the notion of a mild illness.

The tendency toward confirmation bias is enhanced by another cognitive bias called 'Frequency gambling'. This is the tendency to be falsely influenced by the fact that, for example, the vast majority of children who present with fever will have a minor illness unless they have significant 'red flag' signs indicating severe infection. While this is true in general terms, it is a false reassurance in any individual case as it does not rule out the individual case being the exception to the rule.

In this case, the author believes that Dr A did their best to assess baby A and maintained near full situational awareness but, when viewed with hindsight, they can be seen to lose a key element of situational awareness with regard to the potential consequences of baby A's condition. This led to them not pushing the parents to accept a referral for paediatric review early in the illness. This loss of awareness can be ascribed to a human psychological factor called cognitive bias – specifically confirmation bias and frequency gambling.

The author would not criticise Dr A for this lapse but rather believes that these lapses are the very human elements that account for conditions such as severe sepsis and meningitis being notoriously difficult to diagnose in clinical practice.

By raising awareness of these elements the author believes that other clinicians may learn to try to improve their level of situational awareness by being more aware of the type of human thinking biases that may lead them to making clinical errors.

CONTRIBUTORY FACTORS

- Individual human factors: Loss of situation awareness and cognitive bias by Dr A
- Patient factors: Presentation in the prodromal phase of meningitis

ROOT CAUSE

We have identified two significant contributory factors in this case:

1. Individual clinician factor: Cognitive bias
2. Patient factor: Meningitis/septicaemia presenting in a prodromal phase

It is clear that in this case an opportunity arose for Dr A to refer baby A to paediatric services. Plausible reasons have been described for them to feel that this was not clinically necessary at the time. In hindsight we know that this decision was an error of judgement but hindsight is not foresight and the author believes that, given the same circumstances, a significant number of GPs may have formed the same opinions and managed the case in much the same way.

It is not possible to know what may have occurred had Dr A referred baby A to the paediatricians. Given that baby A's symptoms and signs were those of a prodromal illness that appears to have been slowly progressive at that time, baby A may have been sent home after a period of observation. It is noted, although not within the scope of this investigation, that baby A was seen by her GP the following day. Clearly, however, she may also have deteriorated further while under observation in hospital and timely treatment may have been able to be started that may have altered the final tragic outcome.

On balance, it seems to the author that the most significant factor in this case is that baby A had developed a relatively slowly progressive form of meningitis/septicaemia and that at the time of assessment she was in a prodromal phase. Given the very high numbers of infants with fever who are assessed by urgent-care GPs every day, it is not possible to distinguish a child in a prodromal phase of meningitis from one with a feverish illness due to other viral or bacterial infections.

It is our final conclusion that the root cause of this very sad and tragic incident is the nature of the underlying condition that baby A presented with – that is, the fact that baby A presented in a prodromal phase of a severe illness wherein there were insufficient signs or symptoms present to identify or predict the true underlying diagnosis.

ROOT CAUSE

- Patient factors: Presentation in the prodromal phase of meningitis

SUMMARY

You will develop your own personal style for producing reports but try to bear in mind the common pitfalls and tips provided. The degree of depth of explanation will be proportional to the nature of the incident. Some cases warrant a greater deal of explanation in the report and good liaison with the family and commissioners will give you a clue as to how to proceed. Reports need to be comprehensive but not formulaic – so do not be afraid to amend or adjust the report content or format if it seems sensible to do so.

As indicated throughout the book, further examples of cases, RCA tools and sample reports may be found at my website: www.PatientSafetyInvestigations.com

Glossary

Act Something that was done that should not have been done – an error or deviation from best practice

Belief revision bias Tendency to revise beliefs insufficiently when presented with new evidence – linked to confirmation bias

Bias blind spot Tendency to see oneself as less biased than others and to notice bias in others

Care delivery problem Errors or deviations from best practice or protocol (acts or omissions) occurring during the clinical consultation or delivery of clinical care

Cognitive bias Tendencies to form decisions that are based upon faulty logic resulting in errors of judgement

Compassion fatigue Tendency to lose empathy or compassion due to repeated exposure to human suffering

Confirmation bias Tendency to confirm an existing decision by overvaluing information that supports it and undervaluing information that contradicts it

Congruence bias Tendency to check hypotheses/diagnoses exclusively through direct testing rather than considering alternative hypotheses/diagnoses

Doctor–patient dissonance A new 'red flag' proposed by author based upon incident investigations. A sense that the patient is not convinced or reassured by the diagnosis or formulation made by the clinician. This should be a clue that an error may have occurred and should prompt a revision of your diagnosis or management plan. You may not have it wrong but it is wise to check

Dr Pepper approach A safety-net approach advocated by the author. Following assessment and formulation of a management plan ask yourself the Dr Pepper question – 'What's the worst that could happen?' This creates level 4 Situational awareness (see Chapter 11). Plan safety-net advice based upon anticipating the worst-case scenarios including missed or alternative diagnoses

Dunning–Kruger effect Tendency for unskilled workers to over-estimate their skill level/ability. Experts may under-estimate their ability. In the fast-moving world of modern medicine, it is easy to become unskilled in certain areas without realising it and to soldier on thinking we know what we are doing

Expectation bias Tendency to judge the value of information based on its source rather than on its intrinsic value

Framing effect Tendency to draw different conclusions from the same information depending on how it is framed. For example, we may miss severe symptoms in a child if the parent describes them in a calm or matter-of-fact way

Frequency gambling Tendency to form a judgement of risk based upon frequency of other similar cases that had a positive outcome, rather than relying on the evidence relating to the specific case in question

Hindsight bias Tendency to believe that an outcome was predictable

NPSA National Patient Safety Agency – a quasi-autonomous governmental body, abolished in 2012. Their role is now encompassed within the NHS patient-safety domain

Omission Something that was not done that should have been done – an error or deviation from best practice

Outcome bias Tendency to judge an action based upon its outcome rather than on the merits of the action itself

Patient factors Contributory factors that may account in part or in whole for an adverse clinical outcome that are attributable to the patient's underlying pathology or their behaviour

RASCI A model for cooperation between multiple agencies that may be involved in a serious incident. Organisations are deemed as falling into one of the following categories: Responsible, Accountable, Supportive, Consulted or Informed (RASCI)

Root cause The contributory factor that is most significant in terms of the final adverse outcome. Ensure you understand what the final adverse outcome is

Scope The range of circumstances considered by the report. This may be limited to patient contact with a single service. It may exclude certain factors relating to a case if these are not deemed relevant or accessible

Service delivery problem Errors or deviations from best practice or protocol (acts or omissions) occurring within the delivery of logistical support to a clinical service (administrative errors)

Situation awareness A model to describe awareness of the significance of events occurring now and how these may progress in the immediate future

Skill, Rule, Knowledge (SRK) A model proposed by Rasmussen and modified by Reason to describe the way that humans learn new tasks and in turn how humans may make errors

STEIS The Strategic Executive Information System (STEIS) – a national reporting database for serious clinical incidents

Terms of reference A description of the type of investigation to be undertaken, its purpose, time frame and general objectives. For an RCA it is generally a description of the process itself and hence is often omitted from reports. In RCAs the scope is more significant than the terms of reference

Index